D0615592

This Is Shakespeare

EMMA SMITH

This Is
Shakespeare

PANTHEON BOOKS
NEW YORK

All rights reserved. Published in the United States by Pantheon Books,
a division of Penguin Random House LLC, New York. Originally published
in hardcover in Great Britain by Pelican Books, an imprint of Penguin
Books, a division of Penguin Random House Ltd., London, in 2019.

Pantheon Books and colophon are registered trademarks of
Penguin Random House LLC.

Library of Congress Cataloging-in-Publication Data

Name: Smith, Emma (Emma Josephine), author.
Title: This is Shakespeare / Emma Smith.
Description: First United States edition. New York : Pantheon Books,
2020. Includes bibliographical references and index.
Identifiers: LCCN 2019028316 (print). LCCN 2019028317 (ebook).
ISBN 9781524748548 (hardcover). ISBN 9781524748555 (ebook).
Subjects: LCSH: Shakespeare, William, 1564–1616—Criticism and
interpretation. English drama—Early modern and Elizabethan,
1500–1600—History and criticism. English drama—17th century—History
and criticism.
Classification: LCC PR2976 .S495 2020 (print) | LCC PR2976 (ebook) |
DDC 822.3/3—dc23
LC record available at lccn.loc.gov/2019028316
LC ebook record available at lccn.loc.gov/2019028317

www.pantheonbooks.com

Jacket images: *William Shakespeare*. Private Collection/Bridgeman Images;
(collar detail) British Library, London, UK/Bridgeman Images
Jacket design by Linda Huang
Book design by Matthew Young

Printed in the United States of America
First United States Edition
9 8 7 6 5 4 3 2 1

For Elizabeth Macfarlane

Contents

This Is Shakespeare

Introduction

Why should you read a book about Shakespeare?

Because he is a literary genius and prophet whose works speak to – more, they encapsulate – the human condition. Because he presents timeless values of tolerance and humanity. Because his writing is technically brilliant and endlessly verbally inventive. Because he put it all so much better than anyone else.

Nope.

That's not why; not at all. Sure, that's what we always say about Shakespeare, but it doesn't really get to the truth about the value of these works for the twenty-first century. The Shakespeare in this book is more questioning and ambiguous, more specific to the historical circumstances of his own time, more unexpectedly relevant to ours. Lots of what we trot out about Shakespeare and iambic pentameter and the divine right of kings and 'Merrie England' and his enormous vocabulary blah blah blah is just not true, and just not important. They are the critical equivalent of 'dead-catting' in a meeting or negotiation (placing a dead cat on the table to divert attention from more tricky or substantive issues). They deflect us from investigating the artistic and ideological implications of Shakespeare's silences, inconsistencies and, above all, the sheer and permissive gappiness of his drama.

That gappy quality is so crucial to my approach that I want to outline it here. Shakespeare's plays are incomplete, woven of what's said and what's unsaid, with holes in between. This is true at the most mundane level: what do Hamlet, or Viola, or Brutus look like? A novelist would probably tell us; Shakespeare the dramatist does not. That means that the clues to personality that we might expect from a novel, or from a film, are not there. If *The Taming of the Shrew*'s Katherine looks vulnerable, or ballsy, or beautiful, that makes a difference to our interpretation of this most ambiguous of plays, and if her imposed husband Petruchio is attractive, or boorish, or nervous, that too has an impact. Fantasy casting – where you imagine a particular modern actor in a role – is a very interesting game to play with Shakespeare's plays: if you cast action-guy Mel Gibson as Hamlet (as Franco Zeffirelli did in 1990), you immediately produce a particular take on the play, which is quite different from casting Michelle Terry (at Shakespeare's Globe in London in 2018), or Benedict Cumberbatch (directed by Lyndsey Turner, 2015). That we don't know what characters look like is one symptom of the absence of larger narration and commentary in a play. No authorial or narrative voice tells us more than the speeches of the characters themselves. Stage directions are relatively sparse and almost never tell us how a given action was performed: does Richard II give over his crown, orb and sceptre in Act 4 of his play to Bolingbroke sadly, gleefully, manically, or in fact not at all? The play's choreography is not spelled out for us, leaving this scene typically open to directorial and readerly imaginations.

Shakespeare's construction of his plays tends to imply rather than state; he often shows, rather than tells; most characters and encounters are susceptible to multiple interpretations. It's because we have to fill in the gaps that Shakespeare is so vital.

And there are larger conceptual and ethical gaps too: the intellectual climate of the late sixteenth century made some things newly thinkable (that religion is 'but a childish toy', as Shakespeare's contemporary Christopher Marlowe had one of his characters claim), and overlaid old certainties with new doubts. Shakespeare lived and wrote in a world that was on the move, and in which new technologies transformed perceptions of that world. The microscope, for example, made a new tiny world visible, as Robert Hooke uncovered in his book *Micrographia* (1665), illustrated with hugely detailed pictures including fleas as big as cats. The telescope, in the work of Galileo and other astronomers, brought the ineffably distant into the span of human comprehension, and theatre tried to process the cultural implications of these changes. Sometimes, Shakespeare's plays register the gap between older visions of a world run by divine fiat, and more contemporary ideas about the centrality of human agency to causality, or they propose adjacent worldviews that are fundamentally incompatible. These gaps are conceptual or ethical, and they open up space to think differently about the world and experience it from another point of view.

Gappiness is Shakespeare's dominant and defining characteristic. And ambiguity is the oxygen of these works, making them alive in unpredictable and changing ways. It's we, and our varied engagement, that make Shakespeare: it's not for nothing that the first collected edition of his plays in the seventeenth century addressed itself 'to the great variety of readers'.

His works hold our attention because they are fundamentally incomplete and unstable: they need us, in all our idiosyncratic diversity and with the perspective of our post-Shakespearean world, to make sense. 'Shakespeare' is here less an inert noun than an active verb: 'to Shakespeare' might be defined as the activity of posing questions, unsettling certainties, challenging orthodoxies, opening out endings. I wanted to write a book about Shakespeare for grown-ups who don't want textbook or schoolroom platitudes. Not a biography (there's nothing more to say about the facts of Shakespeare's own life, and vitality is a property of the works, not their long-dead author); not an exam crib (Shakespeare's works ask, rather than answer, questions, making them wonderfully unsuited to the exam system); not a Shakespeare-made-simple (Shakespeare is complex, like living, not technically and crackably difficult, like crosswords or changing the time on the cooker): I wanted to write something for readers, theatregoers, students and all those who feel they missed out on Shakespeare at some earlier point and are willing to have another pop at these extraordinary works.

We all know Shakespeare occupies a paradoxical place in contemporary culture. On the one hand his work is revered: quoted, performed, graded, subsidized, parodied. Shakespeare! On the other hand – cue yawns and eye rolls, or fear of personal intellectual failure – Shakespeare can be an obligation, a set text, inducing a terrible and particular weariness that can strike us sitting in the theatre at around 9.30 p.m., when we are becalmed in Act 4 and there's still an hour to go (admit it – we've all been there). Shakespeare is a cultural gatekeeper, politely honoured rather than robustly challenged. Does anyone actually like reading this stuff?

Yes: and I hope this book will give some indications how. It is not an attempt to cut Shakespeare down to size, but I do hope that it might open out to you a less dogmatic, less complete, more enjoyable Shakespeare. This is a Shakespeare you could have a drink and a good conversation with, rather than one you have to bow before. I don't have a grand theory of Shakespeare to inculcate, still less do I think I have access to what Shakespeare meant. (Confession: I don't really care what he might have meant, and nor should you.) I want to explore the ways in which Shakespeare's plays are spacious texts to think with – about agency, celebrity, economics, friendship, sex, politics, privacy, laughter, suffering, about a tonne of topics, including art itself. Each chapter in the book, on a specific play, takes a different approach. I've picked plays I like and find stimulating. Some of these are famous, so you'd be annoyed to buy a book on Shakespeare that didn't mention them; some are more marginal, but I wanted to say something about how interesting they are (*The Comedy of Errors*, anyone?). I've tried to give a sense of Shakespeare's range across his career, and the plays are discussed in chronological order so that you can see how his writing moves across genres and concerns. But I've also tried to keep the individual chapters self-contained, so that you could read one before going to the theatre, for example, or start at the end if that's where your interest lies.

Together, the chapters cover aspects of performance,

contemporary and original. They sometimes think about historical context and sometimes ignore it completely. They look sometimes at Shakespeare's sources or the influences from his culture, and sometimes at the reception his works have generated in later worlds including our own. They present a Shakespeare who is an Elizabethan and Jacobean writer concerned both with classical literature and the problems of political succession, as well as with more modern themes of identity and scepticism. This Shakespeare knows about intersectionality as much as about Ovid. He is fluent in our contemporary concerns, but he is not simply a mirror for our own solipsistic age. Above all, these plays prompt questions rather than answers. This is what gives them their edge and provocation; this is what forever implicates us in their meanings; and this is why they need your attention. I've called the book *This Is Shakespeare* not to convey a monolith – quite the opposite. Shakespeare takes shape through our interpretations. It's here, in our engagement with the works, that they take flight. This – reading, thinking, questioning, interpreting, animating – this really is Shakespeare.

The Taming of the Shrew

The Taming of the Shrew is one of Shakespeare's earliest plays, and one of his most controversial. Everything, from the name of its heroine to its ideology of gender relations, is contested, to the extent that it's impossible even to begin with a neutral synopsis of the play. Here's why it's impossible.

The Taming of the Shrew centres on the courtships of the two daughters of the Paduan merchant Baptista: Katherine and Bianca. The elder, Katherine, is apparently the shrew of the title, a woman who, depending on how you look at it, is feisty and independent, lonely and misunderstood, or strident and antisocial. Her father – who, depending on how you look at it, is either a worried widower or a patriarchal tyrant – has decreed that Bianca – who, depending on how you look at it, is either beautiful, gentle and agreeable, or exactly the kind of annoyingly insipid, simpering arm candy who you, like her sister, would want to slap – cannot marry until her older sister gets hitched. The stage is set for the entrance of Petruchio, who, depending on how you look at it, is a quirky and unorthodox guy who knows his own mind and wants a woman who knows hers, or a psychopathic bounty hunter with sadistic and misogynistic tendencies. So Katherine and Petruchio are paired off against Katherine's will in a relationship which, depending on how you look at it, is crackling with mutual sexual tension along with a touch of shared S&M domination fantasy, or is cynical, loveless and enforced by a violently patriarchal society. He treats her in a way which – depending on how you look at it – uses distinctly unfunny torture techniques including sleep deprivation, brainwashing and starvation to bend her to his will, or is a zany courtship showing their mutual determination not to yield as an underlying equality beneath their revolutionary union. So, at the end of the play, Katherine is, depending on how you look at it, broken-spirited, parroting patriarchal ideology and utterly submissive, offering to put her hand under her husband's foot, or ironically and unabashedly vocal, preaching the interdependence of husband and wife to earn herself half of a fat wager placed by her husband.

What's more, this whole story is placed as a play within a play, so that a prefatory induction scene sets up this Petruchio and Katherine plot as a play performed for a drunken tinker, Christopher Sly. Sly is being tricked into believing he is a lord, and that a page dressed up as a woman is his wife, by some Bullingdon Club types who are having their bit of cruel fun. So, depending how you look at it, the whole story is framed so as to be obviously implausible and fictional, with even the women as men in amateurish disguise, or as a play which radically aligns the lower classes and women as joint victims of a self-serving male establishment. And yes, the names are contentious as well. We used to call the play's female lead Kate until feminist editors pointed out that this is not neutral either. When Petruchio meets for the first time the woman he has determined to marry, he greets her: 'Good morrow, Kate, for that's your name, I hear' (2.1.182). Her reply is clear: 'Well have you heard, but something hard of hearing. They call me Katherine that do talk of me' (2.1.183–4). Calling her Kate against her will is one of Petruchio's (depending how you look at it) lovable gestures of proprietorial intimacy or a misogynistic microaggression. So, depending how you look at it, the title *The Taming of the Shrew* is a plot synopsis, a how-to guide, a raised eyebrow, or a satirical joke.

Responses to this contradictory play have themselves always been contradictory. Writing at the end of the nineteenth century, the playwright George Bernard Shaw urged men and women to boycott it: 'No man with any decency of feeling can sit it out in the company of a woman without being extremely ashamed of the lord-of-creation moral implied in the wager and the speech put into the woman's own mouth.' But perhaps unexpectedly, Germaine Greer praised the play in her feminist classic *The Female Eunuch*, suggesting that Katherine has 'the uncommon good fortune to find [a husband] who is man enough to know what he wants and how to get it' and further, that 'the submission of a woman like Kate is genuine and exciting because she has something to lay down, her virgin pride and individuality.' Perhaps Greer had been watching Franco Zeffirelli's film version of 1967 which shares this interpretation. Zeffirelli drew on the well-publicized and tempestuous off-screen relationship of lovers Elizabeth Taylor and Richard Burton as Katherine and Petruchio to imply that this was a passionate relationship in which pots and pans, but also underwear, would fly.

But however much theatrical production and critical interpretation strive to settle the play's ambiguities, I want to stress something different here. *The Taming of the Shrew prompts* questions rather than answers them. The question of how to interpret the play is hard-wired into its very structure and amplified in its ongoing reception. Shakespeare's talent for interrogation and scepticism is on display here in this early play, and its history has exemplified one of our most persistent and inevitable recourses when reading Shakespeare. We make his work mean what we want it to mean. Whether Katherine is indeed tamed by the end of the play thus becomes a sharper interpretative parable: how to read Shakespeare?

Crucial to Katherine's contested role in the play is an extended speech she gives at its conclusion. It's long, but I want to quote it in full, not least because its length is part of the point. She addresses her fellow women on stage, admonishing them for being disagreeable to their menfolk:

Fie, fie, unknit that threat'ning, unkind brow,
And dart not scornful glances from those eyes
To wound thy lord, thy king, thy governor.
It blots thy beauty as frosts do bite the meads,
Confounds thy fame as whirlwinds shake fair buds,
And in no sense is meet or amiable.
A woman moved is like a fountain troubled,
Muddy, ill-seeming, thick, bereft of beauty,
And while it is so, none so dry or thirsty
Will deign to sip or touch one drop of it.
Thy husband is thy lord, thy life, thy keeper,
Thy head, thy sovereign, one that cares for thee,

And for thy maintenance commits his body
To painful labour both by sea and land,
To watch the night in storms, the day in cold,
Whilst thou liest warm at home, secure and safe,
And craves no other tribute at thy hands
But love, fair looks, and true obedience,
Too little payment for so great a debt.
Such duty as the subject owes the prince,
Even such a woman oweth to her husband,
And when she is froward, peevish, sullen, sour,
And not obedient to his honest will,
What is she but a foul contending rebel,
And graceless traitor to her loving lord?
I am ashamed that women are so simple
To offer war where they should kneel for peace,
Or seek for rule, supremacy, and sway
When they are bound to serve, love, and obey.
Why are our bodies soft, and weak, and smooth,
Unapt to toil and trouble in the world,
But that our soft conditions and our hearts
Should well agree with our external parts?
Come, come, you froward and unable worms,
My mind hath been as big as one of yours,
My heart as great, my reason haply more,
To bandy word for word and frown for frown;
But now I see our lances are but straws,
Our strength as weak, our weakness past compare,
That seeming to be most which we indeed least are.
Then vail your stomachs, for it is no boot,
And place your hands below your husband's foot,

In token of which duty, if he please,
My hand is ready, may it do him ease.

(5.2.141–84)

The tone of this is wonderfully ambiguous. Is she cowed, brought low, reduced, broken-spirited? In some ways the language of 'our weakness past compare' suggests so, but on the other hand, the very fact of holding forth on stage for an uninterrupted forty-four lines, the longest speech of anyone in the play by far, counteracts this. Is she sarcastically rehearsing a prepared patriarchal conduct piece? Do the increasing rhymes of the speech – sway/obey, hearts/parts, yours/ more, boot/foot, please/ease – suggest the harmony of a settled view, or the singsong of a speech learned off pat? Her condemnation of her sex is so long that perhaps it becomes satirical or sarcastic through repetition, undermining its ostensible meaning. And surely calling women 'worms' is deliberately excessive? Could this be a plot with Petruchio to win the wager? We have not seen them together in the play for several scenes, so it is impossible to know how, or whether, this set-piece might have been set up in advance. Is Katherine brought to proper wifely conduct and educated away from the anti-social behaviour of her earlier life? She seems to say so in this long account of women's obligations to their husbands. Or has she had her spirit crushed?

These large-scale interpretations are made up of the details of particular points in performance. What do the rest of the cast do on stage during this long speech? Are they attentive, amused, uncomfortable? What about Petruchio? When Katherine states that her hand is ready to be placed under her husband's foot, it's a quite different declaration with a quite different meaning if, for example, she is kneeling down in front of him with her hand on the floor, or if she is standing up, arms folded, daring him to request it of her. Clearly the questions don't stop here. Petruchio's response is a single line: 'Why, there's a wench! Come on, and kiss me, Kate' (5.2.185) (he still hasn't got her name). As is quite usual in the early texts of Shakespeare (it is printed for the first time in 1623, as part of the posthumous collected dramatic works known as the First Folio), there is no explanatory stage direction at this point. Shakespeare's plays are very short on stage directions explaining what is happening, and descriptive directions that say *how* action is conducted – angrily, happily, quickly – are virtually non-existent: the action of the plays is thus up for grabs by actors, directors and readers too. Sometimes modern editors usurp this freedom, inserting their own stage directions to clarify what they think is happening. Here, at the end of *The Taming of the Shrew*, the most common interpolated stage direction is the obliging, mutual and perhaps rose-tinted instruction 'they kiss'. Editors assume, that's to say, that Katherine accepts Petruchio's abrupt invitation or that she obeys his brusque command. But there are other staging possibilities here: an unreciprocated or unwelcome kiss, an awkward silence and no kiss at all, a chasm between the couple, or a mistrustful standoff between the sexes.

Sometimes we assume that what seem to us ambiguities in Shakespeare's plays – whether Henry V is a good king, or *Othello* a racist play, for example – are the result of different ethical frameworks then and now. So, this argument goes, scenarios which were quite unproblematic to early modern audiences have gained moral complexity because our attitudes to race, or military expediency, or, in the case of *The Taming of the Shrew*, the relationship between the sexes, have changed since Shakespeare's time. But actually it seems that *The Taming of the Shrew* was always ambiguous, right from the start – and two contemporaneous and related plays help make that visible.

In around 1610, almost two decades after *The Taming of the Shrew*, John Fletcher wrote a sequel called *The Tamer Tamed*. Fletcher was a playwright with the King's Men who would go on to collaborate with Shakespeare on *The Two Noble Kinsmen* and *Henry VIII*, and his riposte to Shakespeare's early comedy might be seen as a more distant kind of collaboration, or perhaps as a professional calling card. That Fletcher's play is written as a self-conscious riposte to *The Taming of the Shrew* is clear. Shakespeare's Petruchio, now a widower, returns as Fletcher's major protagonist. The play begins with wedding guests discussing his second marriage and reminding the audience of his first. Tranio reveals that Petruchio is still haunted by Katherine: 'yet the bare remembrance of his first wife [. . .] Will make him start in 's sleep, and very often / Cry out for Cudgels, Cowl-staves, any thing; / Hiding his Breeches, out of fear her Ghost / Should walk, and wear 'em yet'. This time around, Petruchio's friends assert, he will be in sole charge of breeches-wearing, as his new wife, Maria, already knows her place: 'She must do nothing of herself; not eat, / Drink, say "sir how do ye", make her ready, unready, / Unless he bid her.' The opening scene establishes a patriarchal second marriage with a forceful husband and submissive wife.

But this Petruchio is in for a shock. Fletcher reveals that his seemingly compliant bride has her own hidden agenda on behalf of all downtrodden wives, vowing to bend her new husband to her own will. To this end, she locks Petruchio out of her chamber on their wedding night and fortifies it against his invasion. She thus literalizes a common metaphor in male poetry of the period by turning her own virginity into a martial siege, in which she holds the position of strength. Parleying with her husband from her 'barricaded' bedroom, Maria reminds him of his patriarchal reputation: 'You have been famous for a woman tamer, / And bear the feared name of a brave wife-breaker: / A woman now shall take those honours off, / And tame you.' As Bianca (a woke reboot of Shakespeare's ditsy kid sister) admiringly puts it: 'All the several wrongs / Done by imperious husbands to their wives / These thousand years and upwards, strengthen thee: / Thou hast a brave cause.'

Fletcher's witty, girls-on-top comeback to *The Taming of the Shrew* speaks to Shakespeare's intrinsic ambiguities. Fletcher's Petruchio and his friends recall, with horror, Katherine's untamed wildness, suggesting that she was never really submissive to him at the celebration scene which ends Shakespeare's play. But Maria and her friends also know Petruchio as an exemplary chauvinist who needs to be taught a lesson. Maybe it's significant that the men in the second play experience Katherine's unrepentant fury, whereas the women see her as a victim of a tyrannical husband. Fletcher's interpretation of the gender politics of Shakespeare's conclusion seems equivocal, and this contemporary response suggests that the questions the play has prompted for later audiences were always present. Fletcher hedges the issue about whether

Katherine really is tamed into submission to her husband by the end of the play, thus identifying this uncertainty as a thoroughly contemporary view. His interpretation of that final speech shows that Petruchio both has, and hasn't, tamed his shrew, and the existence of his sequel suggests that *The Taming of the Shrew* is itself not quite complete, not quite stitched up: from the start it prompts and participates in arguments about gender relations, rather than adjudicating or settling them. As we'll see repeatedly in this book, Shakespeare's plays are questions rather than answers.

To add to the ambiguities, let's throw in another version of the play. Shakespeare's *The Taming of the Shrew* was first printed in 1623. But there is another text, with the title *The Taming of a Shrew*, published, without authorial attribution, in 1594. *A Shrew* is a text whose relation to *The Shrew* is very difficult to ascertain. It has a similar plot, and a central character called Kate, who is a scold, and who is to be married to Ferando in order to help the suitors of her two, more popular, sisters. The play proceeds pretty much as the Shakespeare version we are more familiar with, with scenes of taming involving food and sleep deprivation, but two points of comparison help us sharpen our appreciation of the more familiar Shakespearean text. The first is that problematic final speech. The Kate of *A Shrew* (in this play there doesn't seem to be any tension over abbreviating her name) gives quite different reasons why women should submit to their husbands' authority. In Kate's oration, women's intrinsic inferiority is biblically sanctioned from the get-go. In the Book of Genesis, she reports, from Adam 'A rib was taken, of which the Lord did make, / The woe of man so termed by Adam then, / Woman for that, by her came sin to us, / And for her sin was Adam doomed to die.' It's a hoary old story amplified by a false etymology beloved of early modern misogynists. The prefix 'wo' in 'woman' actually comes from 'wife', a word that came into Old English from Germanic, but it was a popular 'joke' to link it with 'woe', an expression of pity or grief. So Eve was 'woeman' – the notion of woman and of bringing sorrow to man were handily combined.

Seeing blatant anti-women sentiments in the final speech of *A Shrew* helps us to look again at the particular arguments Shakespeare gives his Katherine. She argues that men have particular obligations to women, and so women have reciprocal responsibilities in turn. This is the rhetoric of mutual obligation, something that has a distinct role in sixteenth-century debates about Protestant 'companionate marriage'. Marriage, while not a union of equals, nevertheless carried mutual responsibilities, in which each partner endured limits on their individual freedom within a bond of reciprocity. As the wife had responsibilities to the husband, so too he had responsibilities to her; the wife's subservient conduct is secured by the husband's generous protection of her. Katherine's speech draws on this understanding of marital reciprocity, arguing that the husband is 'one that cares for thee, / And for thy maintenance commits his body / To painful labour both by sea and land' (5.2.152–4). If we set aside the obvious objection – is Petruchio ever likely to commit *his* body to painful labour by anything, given that his whole aim was to 'wive it wealthily' (1.2.74)? – we can see that Katherine's speech implies a different marital relationship from the Garden of Eden scenario invoked by Kate, where the woman is an afterthought made of spare male matter, who then brings sin and death into the world. And that speech in *A Shrew* ends with the stage direction 'she lays her hand under her husband's feet', thus providing the accompanying gesture of subordination that is not stated in Shakespeare's text, where the gestural gap allows for an alternative choreography.

So maybe *A Shrew* is clearer about its Kate's taming, as it incorporates her into outdated ideas of marriage that have been replaced by a more mutual ideology promulgated by Protestant advice books on companionate marriage, and by Katherine at the end of *The Shrew*. Perhaps. But here too there are questions. The second point of comparison between these sister plays is their treatment of the wider framing narrative. Shakespeare's play begins with a tavern landlady kicking out the drunken Christopher Sly, whereon he falls asleep. A hunting party of lords with dogs finds him and decides to enjoy 'a pastime passing excellent' (Induction 1.65): to take up Sly, wash him and dress him in fine clothes and pretend that he is a nobleman who has been 'lunatic' (Induction 1.61). Sly is persuaded by, or goes along with, this jest, accepting Bartholomew the page as his wife, and proclaiming 'I am a lord indeed' (Induction 2.71). The trick segues into a play, performed ostensibly as part of the 'lord's' recuperation: a 'pleasant comedy' will 'frame your mind to mirth and merriment' (Induction 2.131). That inset play, set in Padua, is our story of the suitors to the daughters of Baptista. The suggestion is that Sly and Bartholomew watch the entire play from the sidelines, although if that's the case, Shakespeare doesn't make much use of them: they have a moment of dialogue after the first scene, with Sly proclaiming this 'a very excellent piece of work' (1.1.251), and then no more. In reading the play, perhaps we don't notice this too much, but the structure is awkward on the stage.

Many modern productions have taken advantage of *A Shrew* because it supplies a more extensive, mock-chorus role for Sly as a commentator on the unfolding plot, and in particular because it has a final sequence that closes the parenthesis that the opening scenes established. *A Shrew* ends with Sly returning to the stage in his own clothes; he is woken by the tavern-keeper. Befuddled with drink and sleep, Sly grumbles: 'gi's some more wine. What, 's all the players gone? Am not I a lord?', and then announces 'I have had / The bravest dream tonight that ever thou / Heardest in all thy life.' 'You had best get you home,' is the unimpressed reply, 'For your wife will curse you for dreaming here tonight.' Sly is unabashed: 'Will she? I know now how to tame a shrew . . . I'll to my / Wife presently and tame her too, / An if she anger me.' So, *A Shrew* closes with Sly suggesting the play *he* has seen is a handbook to wife-taming that he will implement in his own household. Not only is the play about taming a shrew, but it is a manifesto and instruction guide for others to do the same. There's a similar moment in Shakespeare's play when Petruchio, alone on stage after he has sent the travel-wearied Katherine hungry to bed, declares: 'Thus have I politicly begun my reign' and tells the audience, 'He that knows better how to tame a shrew, / Now let him speak.' Tis charity to show' (4.1.174, 196–7).

Should we take Sly's promise seriously as an assessment of the play? Or does a plot summary from a drunken tinker immediately mark itself as preposterous and deluded? Is

Sly a figure for the audience, or a pitiful patsy who doesn't understand the first thing about theatre, or wives, for that matter? Does bringing back the frame device re-establish the Kate/Ferando plot as a self-conscious fiction, something that could happen only within these quotation marks that signal make-believe? And in any case, can this tell us anything about *The Shrew*, which only introduces but does not bring back Christopher Sly and in which this ending of the frame doesn't exist? Does the Katherine and Petruchio plot in Shakespeare's version retain those introductory elements of self-conscious fiction or does that fade away? Are we supposed to take this comedy seriously at all?

Answers to these questions can be only partial or contingent. What's more important is to acknowledge, from the first chapter of this book, how Shakespeare's works prompt questions rather than answering them. The ambiguity over whether Katherine is tamed at the end of *The Taming of the Shrew* is intrinsic to the play – it isn't a problem that arises because we do not now accept the kind of gender ideology that the Elizabethan audience would have supported, so it's not the problem of history. Rather, the early modern evidence of the *Taming of a Shrew*, that quarto version of the play from 1594, and of *The Tamer Tamed*, the Fletcher play in the Jacobean period – as well as the play's own structure and ambiguities – mean that the question was always present. Shakespeare's plays hold our attention because they offer narratives through which we can shape our own contemporary concerns. A flick through the modern production history of *The Taming of the Shrew* is exemplary: the suffragettes, the post-war reiteration of gender conservatism, and second-wave feminism have all found the play hospitable and relevant to their concerns. If the twenty-first-century iteration of the problems between the sexes looks different from its late-sixteenth-century counterpart, the questions still remain.

CHAPTER 2

Richard III

Richard III's opening lines are also their most familiar: 'Now is the winter of our discontent / Made glorious summer by this son of York' (1.1.1–2). Their recognizability may obscure just how unusual they are. Richard is the only one of Shakespeare's major characters to begin his own play. You may recall – perhaps you've experienced this in the theatre – the bewilderingly oblique way Shakespeare tends to begin his plays, via marginal characters whom we struggle to place as they recount or anticipate some major narrative event in a conversation that begins in the middle, leaving us flailing (beginning Shakespeare's plays at their beginning is not always the easiest place to start). Not so in *Richard III*. The opening stage direction in the first printed edition is 'Enter Richard, Duke of Gloucester, *solus*' – meaning alone – making it absolutely clear that not only does he open the play, he does so, uniquely, in soliloquy. He begins, that's to say, by addressing the audience. From the outset, we are his creatures.

Richard III is described as a 'tragedy' in its first publication, but the story of Richard's path to the throne, and of his eventual defeat in battle reads more like a modern criminal biopic. The details of the plot are less important than its overall shape of rise and fall. In large part Richard's success is due to his capacity for ruthless violence. The synopsis of the play that serves as a lurid blurb to potential buyers of the first print edition stresses this aspect: 'Containing his treacherous plots against his brother Clarence, the pitiful murder of his most innocent nephews, his tyrannical usurpation, with the whole course of his detested life and most deserved death'. It's a compelling prospectus, but actually rather misleading: Richard's primary tactic in the play is seduction rather than elimination. And among Richard's many conquests during the play, from Lady Anne to Buckingham, from the Lord Mayor to his deluded brother King Edward, we – the audience – are the first, reeled in hook, line and sinker by this confiding, charismatic, funny opening speech. Richard strategically lays bare his own vulnerabilities, describing himself as 'not shaped for sportive tricks' (14), 'rudely stamped' (16) and unable to 'prove a lover' (28). He confesses, with some pride, that he is 'subtle false and treacherous' (37) and that he plans to set his brothers Clarence and Edward in 'deadly hate' (35). At that moment Clarence enters, and we are sworn to silence: 'Dive, thoughts, down to my soul' (41).

This apparent candour is utterly beguiling. Even though – perhaps because – we are in no doubt about his ruthless self-interest, Richard establishes an immediate alliance from the outset. This intimacy with the audience will be carefully managed through a stream of asides and sardonic remarks, where only we know his true meaning, keeping us from forming any real attachment to any other character. The very title of the play seems to have succumbed to his charms and to endorse his ambitions. Richard, Duke of Gloucester, doesn't actually become King Richard III until Act 4, but his play has no doubt he will get there: from the opening he is the king-in-waiting. And the very rhythm of that first soliloquy enacts the dominance he is going to exert over his play. I'm not a huge fan of that classroom staple of Shakespeare studies we identify triumphantly as iambic pentameter. It's not always clear to me what we actually know when we say that somehow Shakespeare's lines go 'de-dum de-dum de-dum de-dum de-dum', other than that they don't therefore sound very interesting. But what *is* interesting about Shakespeare's use of rhythm is when it changes or surprises us, as here. 'Now is the winter of our discontent' begins decisively with an inverted rhythm – the stress is on 'Now', the first syllable, not, as regular iambic pentameter would have it, on the second. It calls us to order; it tells us who is boss.

Shakespeare writes *Richard III* as a final part of a historical story, written after a series of plays on the reign of Henry VI, the king whose corpse 'bleed[s] afresh' (1.2.56) as his murderer Richard comes to woo his daughter-in-law Lady Anne. We'll return to the notion of *Richard III* as a play in a series below, noting for now that Richard's dramatic dominance registers a new political and theatrical order. The contrast between the turbulent maelstrom of competing interests in the *Henry VI* plays is striking. Those previous historical dramas on the Wars of the Roses dramatize the absence of any authoritative leader by distributing the roles widely across the theatrical company, the Lord Chamberlain's Men, originally formed in 1594 by a group of eight shareholders, including Shakespeare. The plays' historical politics and their dramaturgical politics are aligned: no single character is any more important than any other. By contrast, Richard registers his own ambition, seizing his own play by the scruff of the neck right from the start, and he doesn't let go: his hold on the politics of his country is matched by Shakespeare's fascist dramaturgy which is designed explicitly to showcase his charismatic authority.

Richard's role is huge. He speaks around a third of the play's lines, a proportion not far off that of Hamlet in his play. He is on stage for two-thirds of the play, around two-and-a-quarter demanding hours of stage time. The part is sometimes identified as Shakespeare's first major collaboration with the leading actor and fellow Chamberlain's Men shareholder, Richard Burbage; his first play that is a star vehicle rather than an ensemble piece. This is the partnership that will bring us Othello and Lear and Macbeth and Prospero over the next two decades, and here, at its inception, it irresistibly elides the charisma of both Richards. Richard (III) is himself a consummate actor, so much so that we wonder if there is anything underneath. He performs his own role self-consciously: his cues to his loyal sidekick Buckingham in his appearance before the Lord Mayor and citizens, when he appears as a devout hermit between two bishops, are good examples of his actorly delight (he's the opposite, in a way, of the theatre-phobic Coriolanus, discussed in Chapter 18). The long history of the performances of this play, from Colley Cibber to David Garrick, and from Laurence Olivier to Antony Sher, demonstrates that it is almost impossible for Richard to overact: the histrionic quality of his deformed and manic self-presentation is intrinsic to the hammy part. Subtlety is not part of Richard's armoury; hyperbole and self-conscious excess are the keynotes from that first long opening soliloquy.

There's so much to dislike about Richard, and yet – or so – he is beguiling, seductive, ravishing, within the play and outside it. It's almost as if the play's popularity itself testifies to a kind of audience masochism. And within the drama, there is little chance of resistance to Richard's will, as we see in the early scene with Lady Anne. As the most extreme, circumstantially unsympathetic person with regard to Richard – he has, as he cheerfully acknowledges, 'butcherèd' (1.2.67) her husband and father-in-law – Anne plays the role of the sceptical audience deciding whether to take up Richard or turn against him. Inevitably, the scene gets us signing on the dotted line after being softened up by that opening speech: like her, we choose him. Richard's rhetoric works to make Lady Anne feel she is complicit in, or culpable for, his behaviour: 'I did kill King Henry; / But 'twas thy beauty that provokèd me.' ' 'Twas I that stabbed young Edward; / But 'twas thy heavenly face that set me on' (1.2.167–8, 169–70). And as we laugh at his callous epigram 'I'll have her, but I will not keep her long' (1.2.217), we too have entered into a masochistic compact with this alluring protagonist. Part of the audience's role in relation to Richard is encapsulated in this feminized, enchanted revulsion. Perhaps it's not surprising, therefore, that one of the only anecdotes we have about Shakespeare actually tells us more about the desirability of Richard Burbage as Richard III. A joke in the diary of the law student John Manningham at the beginning of the seventeenth century reports that: 'Upon a time when Burbage played Richard III there was a citizen grew so far in liking with him, that before she went from the play she appointed him to come that night unto her by the name of Richard III. Shakespeare, overhearing their conclusion, went before, was entertained, and at his game ere Burbage came. Then message being brought that Richard III was at the door, Shakespeare caused return to be made that William the Conqueror was before Richard III.' This jest mobilizes Richard's sexual magnetism for his audience. Like Lady Anne, we (both men and women) are violently, masochistically smitten with this ruthless celebrity actor.

But there's a structural problem in making Richard so alluring. In the chapter on 1 *Henry IV*, I suggest that in his fat, roguish anti-hero Falstaff, Shakespeare created a moral monster. For the prodigal son plot of that play to work out, the young prince needs to reject the baleful influence of Falstaff and distance himself from his former drinking companion. But the audience can't get enough of this funny, disreputable figure: they want more Falstaff. The morality of the story and the pleasure of the performance are at odds. By the time he came to write 1 *Henry IV*, Shakespeare had already experienced a similar impasse in *Richard III*. Because the end of Richard's story can't really be the jubilant accession to the throne he has so long plotted to possess. No: in *Richard III* Shakespeare's pragmatic end goal is actually the defeat of Richard by Henry, Earl of Richmond, better known to history as Henry VII and more familiar to his own audiences as the grandfather of the Tudor dynasty and of Queen Elizabeth I.

Richmond thus has a vital historical role. He is Richard's nemesis, the end of his megalomaniac progress to the English throne. But he also symbolizes and enacts the end of the Wars of the Roses, that long historical fallout from the deposition of Richard II that scarred the second half of the fifteenth century and animates Shakespeare's history plays. Richmond enters Shakespeare's play in the last act. On the eve of battle, Richard is cursed in a dream by the ghosts of his victims, who then go to Richmond to bless his enterprise. Richmond marries the daughter of Edward, Elizabeth of York – Richard's niece. At Bosworth Field, Richard is defeated by Richmond in single combat; Richmond is crowned and announces that 'We will unite the white rose and the red' – the houses of York and Lancaster – and bring an end to conflict: 'Now civil wounds are stopped; peace lives again' (5.8.19, 40).

Mid-twentieth-century approaches to Shakespeare were very clear that in Richmond Shakespeare presented the idealized solution to all that dynastic and political turmoil he had previously dramatized. The standard critic on this is E. M. W. Tillyard, who argued that Shakespeare's history plays were broadly propagandistic, a means of consolidating Elizabeth's power by providing a genealogical and historical sanction for Tudor rule. Richmond's victory at Bosworth Field at the end of *Richard III* marks the establishment of the Tudor dynasty, and the play suggests that the Tudors have thus delivered England from tyranny: 'The bloody dog', Richmond proclaims, 'is dead' (5.8.2). Following Tillyard, in an influential argument that still pertains in some critical and theatrical quarters now, the 'Tudor myth' that was Shakespeare's subject in his history plays reaches its culmination in the presentation of Richmond: the providentialist arc of the history play sequence is completed in this act of reparation and restitution. After a sequence of illegitimate kings following the deposition of Richard II, and a period of violent and turbulent civil expiation for this political and ethical crime, according to Tillyard, Richmond comes to reinstate the tarnished monarchy in the blessed form of the Tudors. In this play, writes Tillyard, Shakespeare 'accepted the prevalent belief that God had guided England into her haven of Tudor prosperity'.

It's slightly unpalatable to think of Shakespeare as an early recipient of the toadying prize *Private Eye* awards as the OBN (Order of the Brown Nose), and indeed, there are lots of ways to challenge this vision of Elizabethan politics in general and *Richard III* in particular. Not least, it's good to remember that Tillyard was writing in the war-weary England of 1944, when co-opting Shakespeare to a buoyant vision of eventual delivery from hostilities and suffering was all too important: we tend to find the meanings we need to in Shakespeare's plays (which also explains why more comfortable times have felt more able to excavate the violent and unresolved politics of his histories). For another thing, the establishment of the Tudors by Henry VII was by no means the end of the dynastic problems: we might recall those six wives and the struggle for an heir to Henry VIII, for example. More immediately, presenting the Tudors as the only sanctified antidote to civil war would have been a backhanded compliment in the early 1590s, when even the most optimistic and gallant politicians had given up on the idea of the fifty-year-old queen marrying and having an heir. By the time Shakespeare had begun his career as a playwright, the Tudors were – although it wasn't advisable to say it out loud – toast, a dynasty that had run out of heirs and steam.

Many more recent critics, trying to assess how Shakespeare's history plays might intervene in contemporary political debates, have suggested that their role is rather to rehearse repressed anxieties about the Elizabethan succession. This argument goes that history plays try out different versions of monarchies in decline, different versions of power changing hands, so they are documents of political uncertainty rather than of historical triumph. The turn to history in the culture of the late sixteenth century can itself be seen as a sign of cultural anxiety – a turn to the past rather than a step forward into the future. The political future, for the Elizabethans, was decidedly uncertain, so they looked instead to the lessons of the past. Finally, perhaps Richmond's underdeveloped characterization in the play allows for a different interpretation. A disturbing conclusion to Michael Boyd's 2007 Royal Shakespeare Company production had Richmond delivering his pious and platitudinous final speech as his flak-jacketed troops watched the audience through the sights of their machine guns. Is it peace that Richmond brings, or military dictatorship? History is full of examples of tyrants who looked like liberators. Does his victory really register as the triumphant conclusion to the politics of conflict, or does it appear rather as another contingent version of the theatre's appetite for parables of regime change?

Is Richmond, then, the play's hero? Perhaps we could phrase the question another way. Imagine you are an ambitious actor going to a casting call for *Richard III*. What's the part you're hoping for? Right. Shakespeare has done as much as he possibly can, I think, to minimize and to downplay Richmond's role. We know that Shakespeare cannot, in writing history plays, change historical fact, although he does lots of work to shape the baggy narratives of the chronicles into drama. Winners and losers, kings and challengers, appear in his plays as they do in the historical record, even as events, battles and motives are collapsed or manipulated. Henry, Earl of Richmond, won the Battle of Bosworth Field on 22 August 1485, killing King Richard III to take the throne. The play acknowledges this historical fact. But it does so quite grudgingly, quite minimally, without any real attempt to characterize Richmond, to integrate him as Richard's antagonist, to make him attractive, or to counter whispered suggestions that his own claim to the throne is questionable. He is in three scenes only, perhaps about fifteen minutes of stage time. He doesn't even exist until Act 4, where he is first mentioned, and doesn't appear on stage until Act 5, scene 2. In the play in performance he is the necessary but personally uninteresting sap who will speak the dead protagonist's eulogy, whose presence calls time on the whole play. He has to appear, but in silencing the interesting, charismatic, dramatic Richard, he is almost an anti-theatrical figure. Once Richard has gone, the play is over. This is a play resolutely about Richard, not Richmond.

So the structure of the play reinforces those audience sympathies with which it begins. Richmond's role is as nemesis, but it is also as the figure known to classical drama as the *deus ex machina* – a person, sometimes divine, sometimes human – who comes in unexpectedly at the end of the play to sort things out. The phrase was originally used by Horace as a negative: playwrights, he instructed, should not resort to this lame mechanical trick, a classical version of 'and then I woke up and it was all a dream'. In Shakespeare's hands it seems that the inadequacies of the device are being consciously deployed for bathetic effect: Richard's personal charisma, his will to power, his dramatic vitality, can be defeated only by the inevitability of historical fact, not by any dramatic rival. Richmond is no match for him. Only the clunkily unlikely *deus ex machina* device can manufacture Richard's downfall. Richard Loncraine's 1995 film set in 1930s fascist London, with Ian McKellen as Richard, ends with his refusal to be captured, jumping from an impossible height into the inferno of the battle, set against Al Jolson's disconcertingly jaunty 'I'm Sitting on Top of the World'. It's a discordant ending but one that emphasizes Richard's irrepressible will as an invincible victory over his duller enemies. Richmond has only that most equivocal of triumphs, that of being alive at the end of a Shakespearean tragedy. This is the hallmark of the nonentity (the Prince in *Romeo and Juliet*, Fortinbras in *Hamlet*, Malcolm in *Macbeth*: who cares?).

Richmond's minor presence in the play disrupts the historical *telos* – from the Greek, meaning the end or purpose, from which we get 'teleology', the movement towards that end or purpose. The play's position in a wider sequence of Shakespearean history plays also complicates that *telos*. Shakespeare writes his histories rather as George Lucas makes his *Star Wars* films; that's to say, he writes towards an 'end of history' moment. For Lucas this is Luke Skywalker becoming a fully fledged Jedi and destroying the Empire; for Shakespeare it is the victory of Richmond at Bosworth Field. So the end of *Richard III* takes the historical story to a point where there is no possibility of pursuing it any further. 'Abate the edge of traitors, gracious Lord' (5.8.35), prays the godly Richmond, as he predicts that his descendants will 'Enrich the time to come with smooth-faced peace, / With smiling plenty, and fair prosperous days' (5.8.33–4). But while this may be a worthy political aspiration, it is not a very dramatic one. Who'd want to go to a play about 'smiling plenty and fair prosperous days'? And a play about the Tudor monarchs might be a political minefield: it's not until much later, in the relative monarchical safety of the Stuart King James, that Shakespeare writes his collaborative play about Henry VIII. So, what both Shakespeare and George Lucas do is to pursue their popular and audience-tested themes by reverting to an earlier, prequel part of the story. After the end, that's to say, we go back to the beginning. The next plays, on Richard II and Henry IV, return us to an earlier chronological point in the story, just as they return us anew to a world of conflict and embattled sovereignty. Only if we order the plays in the order of their historical reigns do we get Richmond's victory as the final instalment: as audiences experienced these plays in the Elizabethan theatre, Richmond's victory was only provisional, temporary – rather like the victory at Shrewsbury at the end of 1 *Henry IV*, or the Battle of Agincourt in *Henry V*. It concluded only an episode, a single afternoon at the theatre, not the whole story. Next time they came to the playhouse it was all swords and conspiracies and jostling for the crown again.

Since the twentieth century, it's been fashionable to perform complete sequences of Shakespeare's history plays so that audiences can trace the entire arc from the historically earliest, *Richard II*, to the latest, *Richard III*. There is no evidence from the Shakespearean period that these history plays were seen as serial or episodic in their own time, or ever performed in this way back then: rather they were complete and self-standing dramatic entertainments. The habit of reading them as a sequence has been cued by their arrangement in the first collected edition of Shakespeare's plays of 1623. The First Folio collection was compiled after Shakespeare's death, and therefore we cannot attribute its organization and presentation to the author. This volume is divided into comedies, histories and tragedies, and although there's no obvious order of the plays in the other two categories, the histories genre has been carefully organized, and in some cases the plays have been retitled, to make historical chronology the organizing principle. They are presented here as a serial epic rather than a set of individual plays – what the theatre director Trevor Nunn called the 'first box set'. It is in print in the First Folio that *Richard III* takes on its conclusive position, and it is this arrangement of the history plays that gives rise to Tillyard's providentialist *telos*. It's not surprising that the Folio misses out all the description of Richard's crimes that animated the solo publication of the play, and instead gives us this extended title: 'The Tragedy of Richard the Third: with the landing of Earl Richmond, and the Battle at Bosworth Field'. The First Folio arrangement of the history plays thus makes Richmond's climactic entry into *Richard III* overdetermined as the ending not only of this play, but of a sequence, and a larger morally structured historical narrative of crime, violent expiation and restitution.

It's worth reiterating that this idea of historical and ethical sequence is a later construction, not the experience of the first playgoers to the histories. Nor is it necessarily the experience of *Richard III* itself. To be sure, the play can end only one way, but it also puts off that conclusion as long as it can. Partly because of Richard's personal dominance, and partly because of the play's nostalgic themes, this is a play that keeps resisting forward momentum. And crucial to this anti-teleology are the play's women.

Shakespeare has amplified the role of women in the play, in contrast to his later history plays where he seems to squeeze them out. Here we have Richard's mother, the Duchess of York; the queen, Elizabeth, wife to Edward IV; Lady Anne; and, additionally, Queen Margaret, the widow of Henry VI. Margaret's presence is decidedly ahistorical: the real Queen Margaret died in France, having been taken prisoner after the death of her husband. Shakespeare has resurrected her as a memory of the past, and in particular the past of his own *Henry VI* plays in which she is such a prominent character. As such she is one of the structural features that is constantly dragging the play backwards, away from its teleological resolution in Richmond, reminding Richard that he cannot forget the past casualties of his rise to power. The women are established as mourners for the dead, and their speeches are full of recollection and remembrance. At her first entrance Margaret reminds Richard, and us, of his actions: 'Out, devil! I remember them too well. / Thou killed'st my husband Henry in the Tower, / And Edward, my poor son, at Tewkesbury' (1.3. 118–120). Richard responds in kind: 'In all which time you . . . Were factious for the house of Lancaster; . . . Let me put in your minds, if you forget, / What you have been ere this, and what you are; / Withal, what I have been, and what I am' (1.3. 127–33). In part the struggle between Richard and the chorus of bereaved women in the play is a struggle over the historical past and who has the right to tell it.

This indicative encounter between Richard and Margaret therefore takes on something of a meta-theatrical quality about the play itself as a version of history, and a contested one. Tudor historians since Sir Thomas More, writing in the reign of Richmond's son, Henry VIII, had worked to demonize Richard III – and Shakespeare's Richard embraces this vision enthusiastically: 'I am determinèd to prove a villain,' he declares in his opening soliloquy (1.1.30). The line is double-edged: 'determinèd' has the dual meaning both of human agency, and of some sort of cosmic direction. The question of whether Richard does determine his own fate or has it determined for him echoes through the play. There's a related question about his physical body. Richard begins by describing himself as 'not shaped for sportive tricks', 'Deformed, unfinished' as he 'descant[s] on mine own deformity' (1.1.14–27). The precise nature of this impairment has been variously interpreted on the stage, and so too has its relation to his behaviour. Is Richard deformed because he is wicked, or wicked because he is deformed?

So it is the women who take on the play's own historian roles, recording and lamenting the past as in this exchange in Act 4:

> I had an Edward, till a Richard killed him;
> I had a husband, till a Richard killed him.
> Thou hadst an Edward, till a Richard killed him;
> Thou hadst a Richard, till a Richard killed him.
>
> (4.4.40–43)

Their conversations are anti-teleological at many different levels. First, they usually do nothing to advance the plot, and in fact they often interrupt the action. The scene immediately before this one of lament has brought the exciting news of Richmond's advancing forces, and when Richard enters, his question is apposite: 'Who intercepts me in my expedition?' (4.4.136). In its depiction of female grief the scene also has no historical precedent, so is itself a Shakespearean interpolation into the unfolding of events. And in its language, as the example above illustrates, it privileges circularity, retrospection and repetition over linearity and teleology. Even at this point when the play is hurtling towards its conclusion, that's to say, there is a counter-movement. Associated with women, this undertow pulls away from the future towards the past. For Shakespeare, history is contradictory, with a backward movement to counterbalance forward momentum. Richmond may have won, but who remembers him?

The Richard III Society – 'working since 1924 to secure a more balanced assessment of the king and to support research into his life and times' – has long tried to challenge Shakespeare's distorted portrait of the king. But the question of whether the portrait of Richard is historically accurate or not is less important than the fact that its charismatic power challenges historical narrative itself. Audiences at *Richard III* are drawn to Richard and kept at a distance from Richmond: and, like Shakespeare himself, none of us bothers to stick around to see what happens next. It is Richard, not Richmond, who begins and ends this story.

CHAPTER 3

The Comedy of Errors

Writing in the late eighteenth century, George Steevens observed of *The Comedy of Errors* that 'in this play we find more intricacy of plot than distinction of character.' He didn't mean it as a compliment. Complex, multi-faced characterization has become intrinsic to what we most value about Shakespeare, and at its most extreme, this critical method tends to minimize the plays' plots or, at best, to read them solely as vehicles for the revelation and development of character. Shakespeare's comedy about two sets of identical twins whirling around the ancient coastal city of Ephesus (situated in modern Turkey) certainly seems to prioritize plot over character, even though that plot is fairly simple. Separated at birth, the twins coincide but are ignorant of each other's existence. Basically, whichever twin you think it is on stage at any one time, it's actually the other one. Messages are not sent, goods are not paid for, wives are mistaken. Hilarity ensues – or, as the account of the play's first performance as part of the Christmas revels at Gray's Inn in 1594 put it, 'nothing but confusion and errors; whereupon it was ever afterwards called "The Night of Errors"'. And given that *The Comedy of Errors* comes identifiably early in Shakespeare's career, it has become associated with a youthful or apprentice mode in his writing. The Shakespeare of *Errors*, so this argument goes, has yet to mature into the poet of *King Lear*.

There's certainly some truth to the idea of this play as an immature work. For a start, the source, *Menaechmi* (*c.* 200 BCE), by the ancient Roman playwright Plautus, was virtually a set-text for Elizabethan grammar school boys, and thus, like other of Shakespeare's early plays, including *Titus Andronicus*, *Errors* seems particularly indebted to youthful reading. 'Immature poets imitate; mature poets steal,' wrote T. S. Eliot: here, the young Shakespeare's response to his source is to duplicate. Plautus has only one set of twins – the equivalent of the Antipholuses (Antipholi?). Shakespeare introduces a second set, their servant duo of Dromios. The play is short by Shakespearean standards, has no subplot, and moves to a largely predictable conclusion in which the identity of the twins is revealed. It isn't susceptible to theories of comedy as socially regenerative, or as a festive safety valve as in later plays, nor does it play explicitly with issues of gender and sexuality, as in the popular cross-dressed heroines elsewhere in the comic canon. There are no sociologically interesting outsiders, no homosocial bonding, no parallel cases from social history, although there has been some interest in the master–servant dynamic in the play as it relates to contemporary England. *Errors* has tended to be understood in terms of what is missing, or in the way it anticipates the more sophisticated treatment of its themes in later plays – the reappearance of twins in *Twelfth Night*, for instance, or the unity of time (where the length of the plot and the length of the actual play are aligned) in *The Tempest*.

But on the other hand, Shakespeare had probably written

half a dozen plays before *Errors*, as well as his wildly popular erotic narrative poem *Venus and Adonis* and a darker companion piece, *Lucrece*: he was hardly a newbie. Associations of immaturity rarely attach themselves to his next play, *Richard II*, not because it is distinct in time but because it is often asserted to be distinct in quality. There's often a circularity to arguments about chronology and artistic value in which earliness becomes synonymous with a lack of aesthetic sophistication, and that perceived lack of sophistication is cited as evidence that the play must be early (in the chapter on *The Tempest* we'll see the same argument, with different implications, proposed about the chronological and aesthetic quality of 'lateness').

The Comedy of Errors has been consistently underappreciated, I'd argue, in part because we don't know how to appreciate plot. Contemporary culture, the study and performance of Shakespeare and our own intrinsic narcissism tend to encourage the view that character is destiny. *Errors* challenges this humanistic view of the world by emphasizing, in ways that anticipate the experience of modernity, the alienation of a mechanical universe. Think Charlie Chaplin on the accelerating assembly line in *Modern Times* (1936), and you have something of the comic terror captured in *The Comedy of Errors*.

But before that almost industrialized sense of personal estrangement, first there is that problem of character. I want to suggest that it's not so much that Shakespeare fails to develop character in this play (although I'm not averse to calling Shakespeare out for his failures); rather, that he rejects its causational significance. That's to say, the play's flat characterization is meaningful, not a mistake. It delivers a world in which humans are at the mercy of cosmic forces – and those cosmic forces are represented in this play as plot. The existence of the twins rejects notions of individual autonomy from the start: twins are, and are not, distinctly separate people. They confound ideas about the autonomy of the individual and exist as a visual challenge to our investment in our own uniqueness. The two Antipholuses and the two Dromios are separated situationally, but not in terms of their personalities: they exist as different people in plot terms, rather than psychological ones.

And moments where we feel we may access something more specifically personal often turn out to be frustrating. Take Antipholus of Syracuse in 1.2. Having arrived in Ephesus to look for his long-lost brother, he has a short soliloquy. So far, so good: aren't soliloquies when we meet characters alone and enter a privileged relationship with them and their feelings? But Antipholus of Syracuse's metaphor collapses that singularity even as it asserts it:

> I to the world am like a drop of water
> That in the ocean seeks another drop,
> Who, falling there to find his fellow forth,
> Unseen, inquisitive, confounds himself.

> (1.2.35–8)

His image of the water drop is hardly a propitious one for asserting individuality. It's not simply that he is indistinguishable from his twin brother, which will be the burden of the unfolding plot, but something more existential. It is that he is also indistinguishable from everything else – not just the

one close sibling he looks exactly like, but the whole inde-
terminate wash of humanity. The fact that he has a twin is
simply a cruel amplification of his general unremarkability
in this indistinct tide. The erasure of individualism is complete, and it is enacted through the contorted syntax of his
final phrase,

> So I, to find a mother and a brother,
> In quest of them, unhappy, lose myself.

$$(1.2.39-40)$$

Embedded in these lines is the phrase 'I lose myself', but this
statement of loss is itself dissipated, divided by the intervening inverted clauses. Even when he's alone, Antipholus is
psychically at sea: it's like something Estragon might say in
Beckett's *Waiting for Godot*. And as if to confirm that the language of Antipholus' stunted soliloquy is about commonality
rather than individuality, Shakespeare gives it again to another character. When Adriana encounters – as she thinks –
her husband (it's not, which both comically undermines her
sentiment about their indissoluble bond and tragically enacts
the image of individual blurring intrinsic to her imagery), she
reminds him of the inviolability of two made one through
marriage in a similar image: 'know, my love, as easy mayst
thou fall / A drop of water in the breaking gulf, / And take
unmingled thence that drop again / Without addition or diminishing, / As take from me thyself' (2.2.128-32). Marriage
is here indistinguishable from the watery commingling that
seems to be the recurrent difficulty of individuation.

What *The Comedy of Errors* seems instead to suggest is that
characterization is a property not of the internal but of the

external. Things outside us bolster or secure our identity. In particular, it is in being recognized by others that identity is fixed; it is by operating within a social system that personhood is achieved and secured. The twins get their identity from place – they are 'of Syracuse' or 'of Ephesus': two states separated by 'enmity and discord'. But part, then, of his existential crisis is that when we meet Antipholus of Syracuse he is in, or even (confusingly) of, Ephesus. By giving both sets of twins a shared name, despite Egeon's perplexing statement that, as babies, they were so alike 'As could not be distinguished but by names' (1.1.52), *Errors* indicates that the proper name has lost its function. It is precisely not doing its job of distinguishing one person from another. Names as signals of individual identity break down here, both in the themes of the plot and in the apparatus of the play: reading the play in its first printing in the First Folio – try it! – is almost impossible, not least because the editorial standardization of the Antipholuses and Dromios into 'of Ephesus' and 'of Syracuse', which gives the modern reader a kind of mastery over the confusion, is absent. The experience of reading the play in its first printed edition must, intentionally or not, have mirrored the disconcerting confusions of the play on the stage.

If the play locates identity in exteriors, it also understands selfhood through property. *The Comedy of Errors* is an unusually prop-dependent play for Shakespeare: a gold chain, rope and money all participate in encounters that hopelessly confuse both sets of twins. These objects indicate connection and interaction, metaphorically or literally, but they also stand in for personal identity. When the goldsmith spots

Antipholus wearing his gold chain, he immediately identifies him as the man who has taken delivery of the chain and not paid for it: it's the chain rather than anything more personal about him that (erroneously) fixes his identity. The plot's confusions are confusions less of individuals than of props: it's the fact that the man doesn't know anything about the money he was given that identifies him as a different man from the one who does. Part of the play's insight is thus that character is expressed not through the inner but the outer. It makes no claim for the specific or autonomous individual: rather, its cleverly constructed clockwork plot moves towards the reunion of a family, the restitution of those persons into their rightful social places. As individuals they are insubstantial: within a comic network each is stabilized by interconnections with the others.

In some ways this is a more general point about Shakespearean comedy, where individuals find their true selves in romantic, social and economic ties within communities and the movement of the drama is towards joint celebration (like the banquet that is always the last panel in the *Asterix* stories) rather than – as in tragedies – isolation and death. But it might be possible for us to think about this in a more explicitly psychoanalytical way and thus to link *The Comedy of Errors* with something that Shakespeare explores elsewhere in his work: the idea of a split personality, or a self refracted across several characters. This was a common idea in medieval theatre, known as the psychomachia (literally, spirit battle, or conflict of the soul). In works such as the fifteenth-century morality play *Everyman* about the soul's preparation for a righteous death, actors played not individuals but personified aspects of behaviour. The cast of *Everyman* includes actors embodying Good Deeds, Knowledge, Beauty, Kindred and Discretion. Thus their dramatic interactions are less about the encounters of human beings, and more a series of allegorized behaviours that together make up a single subject: essentially, a psychomachic play takes place inside a human mind. Although Shakespeare is usually credited with the break away from these old-fashioned kinds of characterization and the discovery of a more modern, interior psychology, it might be useful to see *Errors* as a secularized form of the psychomachia. Perhaps the two Antipholuses and the two Dromios are less separate and complete pairs of people and more images of one person divided, seeking not the other but the self. In later comedies, Shakespeare will disguise this quest as a romantic one: it's in the beloved that the self finds completion. But here the psychic solipsism is more naked. These guys are not looking for partners but for themselves. Searching for his family, Antipholus of Syracuse will lose himself: it is less his mother and brother that he is looking for than a sense of his own plenitude.

Often in recent productions the play has been performed with a single actor doubling the role of the twins, particularly in the Dromio scenes. The 1983 BBC television production, for instance, has Michael Kitchen playing both Antipholuses and Roger Daltrey as the two Dromios. This technique has the paradoxical effect of adding a sort of verisimilitude – of course everyone's confused because the twins look so alike – and also of creating an uncanny disjunction. Later in Shakespeare's career this sense of doubling is used in some interesting ways: as the chapter on *A Midsummer Night's*

Dream discusses, it's common to double the earthly rulers Theseus and Hippolyta with their fairy counterparts Oberon and Titania, and in a play so concerned with the sleeping and waking worlds, this equivalence tends to suggest that the forest in that play is the dreamscape of Athens in which repressed or hidden personalities can emerge. This seems a helpful insight into *The Comedy of Errors* too. Antipholus of Syracuse is able to experience all manner of vicarious behaviours without taking responsibility for them. As a traveller in an unfamiliar city, he encounters a friendly courtesan, has another man's wife welcome him into her bedroom and is given expensive consumer goods without payment. What's not to like? Ephesus is, for him, a fantasy world of actions without apparent consequence: adultery without punishment or guilt, gold chains without a bill. Typically the plot of the play works by making one brother take the rap for what the other has done: in the case of the Dromios it's a beating, and for the Antipholus twins an ear-bashing from a disgruntled associate. The play offers a dance of actions and displaced or ducked consequences. The twins seem a kind of wish-fulfilment device, or an id indulgence, where repression is lifted and behaviour liberated. Under the guise of being someone else, even unwittingly, the characters are able to rehearse alternative selves and alternative behaviours.

What the plot reveals is that such liberation can only be temporary. The characters are caught up in accelerating and repeated dreamlike scenarios in which their identities blur and dissolve under pressure of events. 'Am I in earth, in heaven, or in hell?' Antipholus of Syracuse wonders as an unknown woman greets him as her husband: 'Sleeping or waking? Mad or well advised?' (2.2.215–16). 'What, was I married to her in my dream?' (2.2.185). Adriana urges her husband/brother-in-law into the house and bars the door against visitors. When her real husband arrives home, his way is stopped by the servants, because, as they tell him, he is already inside, supping with his wife. It's an allegory of self-alienation, in which the self is dependent on being recognized, or not. It's a funny scene, but part of its humour is compensatory for its terrors. For both Antipholuses this scene is stressful, as if both getting what you want and being prevented from getting what you want have their psychic costs. And these levels of anxiety escalate, as in this Folio stage direction from the end of Act 4: 'exeunt *omnes* [all], as fast as may be, frighted'. The play, that's to say, speeds up like Chaplin's malfunctioning conveyor belt in *Modern Times*: it embodies the breathless, involuntary, panicky momentum of plot over character. Its lexicon of magic and the supernatural is striking – more mentions of witches than in *Macbeth*, more mentions of conjuring and magic than in *A Midsummer Night's Dream*, more references to Satan than in any other Shakespeare play: these all feel like alternative non-human explanations of why things happen (see the chapter on *Macbeth* for more on theories of causation) or putative answers to the question of who controls the plot. Plot, not character, is destiny in *The Comedy of Errors*.

The stage direction 'as fast as may be, frighted' is prompted by events catching up with the bewildered Antipholus and Dromio of Syracuse. Running from the many residents of Ephesus who want something from them, they seek sanctuary with the abbess. Women – the slighted wife Adriana, the unnamed Courtesan who will welcome Antipholus of Ephesus when he is displaced by his unknown brother and banished from his own house, and now Emilia the abbess – are seen as crucial to male identity. Female characters in the play don't enjoy the same self-doubt or self-questioning as the men: the female body becomes the site of male self-assertion. We don't have to be fully paid-up Freudians to see that what happens at the end of the play is that a chaste nun-mum sorts it all out. Emilia is revealed as the ultimate guarantor of the twins' identities, as she promises 'full satisfaction' (5.1.402) to the husband and sons she has not seen since the shipwreck thirty-three years previously.

This screwball stress on plot links the play to a particular kind of comedy: farce. The Romantic poet and critic Coleridge called *The Comedy of Errors* a farce, defined by its 'strange and laughable situations. The story need not be probable, it is enough that it is possible.' More modern iterations of farce suggest its preoccupation with doors, thresholds and access to spaces (back to Adriana's bedchamber and the chaste enclosure of the abbey), or with its characteristic velocity: John Mortimer wrote that 'farce is tragedy at a thousand revolutions per minute', and *The Comedy of Errors* moves frenetically through some of the existential territory that the later tragedies will extend at considerable length. Interviewed by the *New York Times* about his own successful modern farce *Noises Off* (1982), Michael Frayn describes the play in terms that are entirely appropriate to *Errors*: 'It's about an anxiety everyone has, that he may make a fool of himself in public, that he may not be able to maintain his persona, that the chaotic feelings inside may burst out, that the whole structure may break down. I suspect people are seeing the kind of disaster they fear may happen to them, but one that's safely happening to these actors. They're discharging fear and anxiety in a way that doesn't hurt.'

Maybe the designation of the play as farce helps with the question of how to appreciate its priority of plot over character. But it also raises the issue about laughter's relationship to comedy. We may feel that laughter and comedy are twins, birthed at the same moment, but that was not the case in the early modern period. The courtier poet Philip Sidney wrote to distinguish 'delight', the warm enjoyment of comedy which 'hath a joy in it, either permanent or present', from the 'scornful tickling' of laughter, which he identified as a vulgar response to 'things more disproportioned to ourselves and nature'. His examples are revealing about the ways Shakespeare's world is quite different from our own: 'we are ravished with delight to see a fair woman, and yet are far from being moved to laughter. We laugh at deformed creatures, wherein certainly we cannot delight.' That laughter might be a symptom of distance rather than empathy is challenging, but it's something that *The Comedy of Errors* seems to interrogate. The insights of a later theorist of laughter seem helpful: the French philosopher Henri Bergson, whose work *Le Rire* (*Laughter*) was first published in 1900. Bergson argues that laughter always arises from a situation in which the human body behaves like a machine or, more precisely, like an automaton. Comedy, Bergson proposes, 'enables us to see a man as a jointed puppet' and is derived from 'something mechanical encrusted upon the living'. It is not human warmth that gives rise to laughter, but the encounter with something rigid and mechanical: 'we laugh every time a person gives us the impression of being a thing.'

People are things in *The Comedy of Errors*, defined by exterior appearance and by the transfer of props, and as the plot accelerates they become increasingly, frenetically mechanical. And our response, according to Bergson, is decidedly unsentimental. Comedy demands separation and coldness, or, in his memorable phrase, something 'like a momentary anaesthesia of the heart'. Not only, that's to say, are the characters of *Errors* alienated from themselves and each other, but they are alienated from the audience. Privileging plot over character in this play rejects our empathic engagement and refuses, for the most part, to offer us distinct characters in recognizable situations. Rather, *Errors* cultivates the Bergsonian anaesthesia of the heart that is the precondition of laughter. Or, to put it another way, *The Comedy of Errors* is pure comedy because we do not really care about the Antipholuses or the Dromios or which is which: it is cardiac anaesthesia in five acts.

CHAPTER 4

Richard II

Richard II is a play in which one king is deposed and another takes his place. What is remarkable about the depiction of this momentous transfer is that we don't really know whether it was a good thing or not. The great unanswered question of the play is whether it was right – historically, politically, ethically, personally, dramatically – for Bolingbroke to take the throne from his cousin Richard. This question insinuates itself into the play's imagery and choreography, and hangs over its stage history and critical reception – and the following sequence of history plays struggle with its unquiet legacy. Is Richard the rightful martyred king, or is he hopelessly, recklessly, inadequate to the task of government? Does Bolingbroke represent might, right or modernity? What might it mean for a play of the last decade of Elizabeth's long reign to represent the overthrow of a lawful monarch in such equivocal terms, and to dare even to ask the question about which of the men occupying England's throne might be better at the job?

Richard II is a signal example of Shakespeare's simultaneous interest in politics and his avoidance of the partisan. It's this feature of his writing that has enabled the plays to be co-opted for very different ideological agendas (see the chapter on *Julius Caesar* for more on this). It is impossible to derive any stable sense from *Richard II* of Shakespeare's own view on the conflict between Richard and Bolingbroke. On one hand, Richard is the legitimate king, but/and he is solipsistic, selfish and potentially tyrannical. On the other hand, Bolingbroke is a usurper, but/and he is pragmatic, charismatic and widely supported.

What would contemporary audiences have thought? An official Elizabethan sermon inveighed against rebellion, arguing that Lucifer was the 'founder of rebellion', that earthly kings were 'ordained of God' and that even rebellion against a wicked ruler was not to be sanctioned: 'a rebel is worse than the worst prince, and rebellion worse than the worst government of the worst prince that hath hitherto been.' This might suggest that orthodox contemporary sympathies ought to be with Richard (although it's always worth recalling that the messages that an institution most actively promulgates are often, by definition, ones to which not all its members automatically subscribe – otherwise why the need to keep telling them?). But then, Bolingbroke is not presented negatively by the play, which ends with his having achieved the throne without any signal of divine wrath. At one level *Richard II* suggests that the murder of a king has no immediate consequences. And although the subsequent history plays show this isn't true, the experience of this play shows no punishment for Bolingbroke's actions. I don't think Shakespeare writes his plays to convey messages – quite the opposite. In this book I try to suggest how he asks questions rather than answers them, and the reminder of the old Hollywood saying, 'if you want to send a message, use Western Union' is a good one for the early modern theatre. Nevertheless, you might be justified in thinking, as you left the Curtain

Theatre in the late afternoon after a performance of *Richard II*, that you can depose and murder a rightful king and no punishment falls on your head.

The play neither hides nor maximizes Richard's faults, and its apparent impartiality means that neither candidate is idealized. Richard has his favourites, those 'caterpillars of the commonwealth' (2.3.165), but Bushy, Bagot and Green are less effective and less venal than in other narratives of the story. The chronicler Raphael Holinshed, one of Shakespeare's sources, summarizes Richard's downfall as the result of his shortcomings as a ruler: 'by reason he was so given to follow evil counsel, and used such inconvenient ways and means, through insolent misgovernance and youthful outrage'. These sound very dramatic and stage-worthy behaviours, but Shakespeare ignores the cue. The only example of these failings we see is Richard's sequestration of John of Gaunt's assets. And while this act is distinctly, even deliciously, callous – 'Pray God we may make haste', says Richard, hearing of Gaunt's sickness, 'and come too late!' (1.4.63) – it is explicitly undertaken not to bankroll some luxurious monarchical frou-frou, but to fund 'our Irish wars' (1.4.61). Elizabethan Londoners would have recognized both the expense and necessity of such a campaign, for war was still being waged in Ireland in the 1590s when the play was performed. Shakespeare gives Richard a soliloquy in prison in the play's final act that creates sympathy for him; he develops an extended role for Richard's wife, Queen Isabella, who is virtually invisible in the sources, solely for the purpose of humanizing the king; he silences any protest from the common people and their complaints against the social elite in a play so resolutely highbrow that even the gardener speaks blank verse and sophisticated political theory.

In making Richard a weak king Shakespeare is obviously influenced by *Edward II*, a history play by his brilliant contemporary, Christopher Marlowe. Yet where Marlowe depicts a sexual relationship between Edward and Gaveston, homoeroticism in Richard's court is largely underplayed and does not seem to be a factor in the king's apparent inadequacies (although modern performances, such as the 2012 BBC television version of *The Hollow Crown* with Ben Whishaw as Richard, sometimes emphasize it). Gaunt's own rhetorical resistance to Richard's rule is impressive: his famous patriotic lament for 'this sceptred isle' was an immediate hit, included in popular books of quotations from 1600 onwards. Gaunt's charge that Richard is 'Landlord' (2.1.113) of England, not king, is never countered, and his nephew's high-handed behaviour immediately confirms rather than contradicts the allegation. But later in the play, when the Bishop of Carlisle defends the king's divine right, there is again no argument, simply the cleric's imprisonment in the Tower of London. Gaunt's and Carlisle's perorations, one against and one for Richard, are both literally unanswerable: the play shows us different viewpoints without ever adjudicating them. Perhaps this is the residue of humanist education techniques likely to have been part of Shakespeare's experience at school: the skill of arguing *in utramque partem* (Latin, meaning literally 'on both sides'). Schoolboys learned the importance of using rhetoric to construct persuasive and plausible characterizations of opposing arguments. In its depiction of Aumerle, at first fiercely loyal to Richard but ultimately won over to

Bolingbroke's support, the play dramatizes its own process of persuasion. Everyone – even including Richard's horse Roan Barbary – comes to see Bolingbroke's unstoppable claim.

When it was first published, the play was titled *The Tragedy of King Richard the Second* – and a number of early quarto editions which attest to its contemporary popularity carry that title. How might reading it as a tragedy affect the question of how we read Bolingbroke's actions and their dramatic weight? Richard himself lays claim to occupy the central dramatic role, if not the moral pole position, conventionally offered to the titular character in tragedy. As with King Lear, or Coriolanus, or Macbeth, or Romeo and Juliet, it is Richard's death that brings the play to a close. Shakespeare has cut his historical material into this particular shape: obviously, there's lots more of the story still to come, since, unlike tragedy, history does not come to an end. As we saw when thinking about Richmond in *Richard III*, in the final scene of a tragedy there tends to be little investment in what is coming next. When Fortinbras enters at the end of *Hamlet*, or when Edgar (or perhaps it is Albany) tries to say something sententious at the end of *King Lear*, we know that they are just temporizing: the light has gone out from the tragic world and we are not interested in, or convinced that there is, any future beyond the end of the play. But there is another aspect to *Richard II*, which is its engagement with the ongoing processes of history. History continues. The death of one king inevitably means the coronation of another: the king is dead, long live the king. As Richard's reign ends, we hear about Bolingbroke's 'unthrifty son' (5.3.1) for the first time – the figure who will eclipse his father in the *Henry IV* and *Henry V* plays: here, the mention works to announce that his dynasty has a future. Part of the myth of monarchical sanctity – what the medieval historian Ernst Kantorowicz memorably dubbed 'the king's two bodies': one physical and subject to mortality like any other person, the other sacred and continuous – is that the death of a king is not the end. The death of the great man, like Richard, is not actually tragic in this schema – it is the necessary and inevitable renewal of the role. Hereditary monarchy, like history itself, is actually opposed to tragedy because it cannot invest in the significance of the individual over the role. When the play was reprinted amid the other plays of the historical sequence in the collected Folio text of 1623, its title was modified to *The Life and Death of Richard II*. Historical sequence cannot have room for individual tragedy.

But try telling that to Richard, who certainly believes he's in a tragedy. Sometimes favourably characterized by critics as a 'poet king', he deploys a range of emotive and figurative language to describe the events of the play from his own perspective. In particular he likens himself to Christ, and his rival to Judas, and his courtiers to those who stood by at this betrayal:

> Did they not sometime cry 'All hail!' to me?
> So Judas did to Christ. But He in twelve
> Found truth in all but one; I, in twelve thousand, none.
>
> (4.1.160–62)

In such moments the figurative language makes it quite clear that Richard himself believes Bolingbroke's actions to be a sinful betrayal against divine order, but, as Mandy Rice-Davies famously said (in a slightly different context), 'he would, wouldn't he?' Richard utters stereotypical laments, preferring to talk than fight. As his enemies advance in the middle of the play, he responds with an ecstasy of self-pity to news of the capture of his allies, then invites his followers to 'sit upon the ground, / And tell sad stories of the death of kings' (3.2.151–2). Richard's commitment to the genre of tragedy makes him passive, whereas Bolingbroke, firmly engaged in the work of history, is active. If Richard tries to write himself into a tragedy through this topos of martyrdom, Shakespeare partly cooperates, giving him a tragic hero soliloquy in which he reveals his own mental anguish: 'Thus play I in one person many people, / And none contented' (5.5.31–2). Bolingbroke, by contrast, has no soliloquy, no intimation of privacy or interiority. His motives are opaque: we never know, for instance, when he decides that his rightful quest to regain his own inheritance shifts into a challenge for the crown itself. His role on stage is a masterclass in what is unspoken. He delivers short, pragmatic speeches in response to Richard's long self-justifications. The scene in which Richard reluctantly hands over the symbols of office is indicative: nine poetic lines to Richard, followed by Bolingbroke's 'I thought you had been willing to resign' (4.1.180); three lines for Richard and then again 'Are you contented to resign the crown?' (190); then speeches by Richard of twenty-two, fifteen, nine and fourteen lines, with hardly a word in edgeways for anyone else. Richard may be losing control of his kingdom in this scene, but he never loses control of the stage. Even once the scene-stealing Richard is imprisoned offstage, Bolingbroke's character remains obscured. Different performances can make his final lines of regret for Richard's death in which he vows a pilgrimage 'to the Holy Land / To wash this blood off from my guilty hand' (5.6.49–50) sound variously stricken, horrified, regretful, contented or coldly pragmatic.

For some analyses of the play, its governing principle has been understood as one of opposition, built on a perceived contrast between the two protagonists. Thus Richard versus Bolingbroke, poetry versus realism, metaphor versus plain-speaking, the feudal king versus the pragmatic politician, divine right versus realpolitik, chivalric jousts versus political murder, the medieval world of absolute monarchy versus the modern world of expediency. All these oppositions make regime change in the play come to stand for a historical watershed. Productions of the play such as Michael Bogdanov's English Shakespeare Company (1986), which clothed Richard in gaudy, foppish, Regency clothes and Bolingbroke in sober Victorian black, or Rupert Goold's 2012 depiction of a shimmering, gold-robed Richard facing the chainmail of his opponent, emphasize that there are two worldviews at stake here, not just a reshuffle of descendants of Edward III (Richard was the son of Edward's eldest son; Bolingbroke the son of his fourth son). On the other hand, we could say that the two are in fact similar rather than distinct. A famous Royal Shakespeare Company production in 1974 directed by John Barton preceded each performance with a dumbshow in which an actor playing Shakespeare crowned, at random, either Richard Pasco or Ian Richardson, marking him as Richard and the other as Bolingbroke for that evening. It's something that's worked in other plays since, flipping the casting of Frankenstein and the 'monster', or Mary Stuart and Elizabeth I, or Dr Faustus and Mephistopheles, and in *Richard II*, too, the technique suggests the similarities rather than the differences between the antagonists, and the randomness of the fall of the dice (in fact box office demands often trump this apparent chance, because punters will book twice if they are guaranteed the opposite casting). Richard's own image of the crown as 'two buckets filling one another, / The emptier ever dancing in the air, / The other down, unseen, and full of water' (4.1.175–7) suggests their interconnectedness in a play that uses the word 'cousin' more than any other except the deeply familial *Much Ado About Nothing*. Deborah Warner's 1995 production with Fiona Shaw as Richard and David Threlfall as her near-twin Bolingbroke stressed the intimacy of their familial relationship and the personal grief that derives from public politics.

And Bolingbroke's behaviour as king emphasizes that perhaps he is a chip off the old Black Prince block, rather than a radical alternative. The clue is in the way he speaks. As in *Romeo and Juliet* and *A Midsummer Night's Dream*, written around the same time in Shakespeare's career, *Richard II* makes extensive use of end rhyme (our usual term for Shakespeare's verse, 'blank', means that it is unrhymed, but like lots of these classroom generalizations, it's not always true). In the early scenes of this play, rhyme is particularly associated with Richard's own quixotic authority, and with the formalized denunciations of his lords:

MOWBRAY: Then, dear my liege, mine honour let me try.
   In that I live, and for that will I die.
RICHARD: Cousin, throw down your gage. Do you begin.
BOLINGBROKE: O God defend my soul from such deep sin!

                       (1.1.184–7)

The theme of the scene here is divisive conflict and unspoken tension, but that's lacquered over with the formal quality of rhyme, which urges towards harmony and connection. If you find it difficult to work out what's actually happening as *Richard II* begins, your fog is absolutely spot-on: this is a scene about obscuring rather than communicating meaning. Basically, what can't be said here, for obvious reasons, is that the king himself may be implicated in the death of the Duke of Gloucester. (It's one of the ways this history play is preoccupied with what can't be truly known about the past.) So rhyme functions in this scene to try to keep the lid on its potentially explosive energies: it's the linguistic embodiment of Richard's regal authority. Relatedly, Bolingbroke tends to prefer unrhymed speech as he makes his way to the throne. But we can see that along with the crown, he also takes up rhyming, with a prominent tendency towards couplets in his final scene. Here it is possible to hear the hint of insincerity that rhyme can sometimes convey to modern ears, a sense that authentic response is subordinated to mere linguistic echo. Somehow the fact that Bolingbroke's expression of sorrow at the murder of Richard is in rhyme makes the sentiment seem sinister and phoney:

> Lords, I protest my soul is full of woe
> That blood should sprinkle me to make me grow.
> Come mourn with me for what I do lament,
> And put on sullen black incontinent.
> I'll make a voyage to the Holy Land
> To wash this blood off from my guilty hand.

> (5.6.45–50)

That the play's new king sounds rather like the old one replaces Shakespeare's even-handedness with something rather bleaker: the impossibility of real political change. As the Polish theatre director Jan Kott put it in his visionary book *Shakespeare Our Contemporary*, 'for Shakespeare history stands still. Every chapter opens and closes at the same point.'

John Barton's introductory casting dumbshow in his 1974 production also brought out the play's own self-consciousness about political theatre and theatrical politics. The image of the king as an actor is a trope that recurs throughout Shakespeare's history plays and throughout the culture that prompted them. Elizabeth I's own much-quoted line, 'We princes, I tell you, are set on stages, in the sight and view of all the world duly observed', acknowledges the theatricality intrinsic to spectacular early modern monarchy in an age in which progresses, entertainments and a spin-doctored public image all drew on the vocabulary of the stage. But here in York's speech about Bolingbroke's entry into London with his defeated rival, the familiar image has an interesting twist:

> As in a theatre the eyes of men,
> After a well-graced actor leaves the stage,
> Are idly bent on him that enters next,
> Thinking his prattle to be tedious,
> Even so, or with much more contempt, men's eyes
> Did scowl on gentle Richard.
>
> (5.2.23–8)

The difference between the old and the new kings or, more pointedly, between the legitimate and the usurping sovereign, is not the difference between the true and the copy, the real monarch and the counterfeit player, as we might expect from the simile. Rather, the contrast is between a good, 'well-graced' actor and the 'tedious' one who follows him. Both kings are likened to actors, both are pretending, and neither, according to the logic of the imagery, can fall back on authenticity to endorse their claim. Rather, Bolingbroke is just a better, more pleasing and convincing, actor.

The logic of the theatre – that the audience prefers the better actor and is restless and contemptuous of a lesser performer – is deeply subversive when attached to the issue of monarchy, because it replaces authenticity with facility: it overlays the question of who is the rightful king with the one of who is the better king. Even to ask whether Bolingbroke's actions in taking the throne might be justified is therefore a politically challenging question, and the play's even-handedness becomes itself a highly charged political intervention. It's a political act specific to the circumstances of the play's composition, when the story of Richard II resonated through late Elizabethan culture.

History plays have their boom in the theatre of the 1590s as exciting and vicarious articulations of concerns and cultural anxieties around the Elizabethan succession. That is to say, they are plays about late-sixteenth-century politics, rather than the politics of their own period. Play after play, by Shakespeare and by others, obsesses on moments of transfer, showing weak or embattled kings challenged by rivals, a vacant throne, civil war, the intrigue of noblemen and advisers; no history play ever depicts the long and relatively settled reign of an established monarch. While Elizabeth had made discussion of her succession a crime punishable by death, plays and other texts on historical subjects enabled the asking of otherwise censored questions about what might happen at the end of her long reign. By the mid-1590s she was into her sixties: everyone was asking, in whispers, who would rule next.

Richard II plays a particular role in this story. For one thing, its publication history suggests that it may have been censored: that unequal scene in Act 4, where Richard hands over the crown, orb and sceptre to Bolingbroke before Parliament, is not present in any of the quarto texts published during Elizabeth's lifetime. Many critics feel this was due to censorship: showing a lawful king being deposed – perhaps particularly through the quasi-legalistic instrument of Parliament – may have been thought too subversive (although on the other hand we could argue that the play is more sympathetic to Richard with the scene included, since it gives him such poignant speeches and allows him to dominate his less histrionic rival).

We also know that the rivalry between Richard and Bolingbroke comes to have a particular connection with the fortunes of the most prominent and controversial of Elizabethan noblemen, Robert Devereux, 2nd Earl of Essex, an intimate of Elizabeth and a champion of more active militaristic engagement in the Protestant cause in Europe. After the failure of his military expedition to Ireland in 1599 (mentioned by Shakespeare in *Henry V*), Essex fell from favour, and he and his supporters mounted a disastrous attempt to persuade Elizabeth to reinstate him which became an ill-fated rebellion in February 1601. Essex was arrested and executed for treason. *Richard II* is on the sidelines of this story. A writer of a prose history on this particular historical period, who dedicated it to Essex as a proto-Bolingbroke, was thrown into the Tower of London for his pains, and the Lord Chamberlain's Men, Shakespeare's company, were paid by Essex's supporters to perform their old play of *Richard II* on the eve of their abortive revolt. Presumably there was some sense that this play would help gather support for Essex's own challenge.

After the failure of Essex's rebellion, the Lord Chamberlain's Men were summoned by the Privy Council to account for their part in the affair. Their spokesman Augustine Phillips claimed they merely took a commission to perform an old play, and since they were back at Elizabeth's court performing within a month, their participation – or perhaps the play itself – cannot have caused too much concern. But the idea of a play being co-opted for political action – however doomed that action might be – has been extremely attractive to recent historians of early modern drama. E. M. W. Tillyard saw the histories as an essentially conservative cycle of crime, expiation, punishment and then deliverance (discussed in the chapter on *Richard III*). By contrast, the Essex rebellion *Richard II* is a radical challenge to political orthodoxy. Advocates of this transgressive reading delight that the usurping actions of Bolingbroke are dangerously endorsed by the play. But my sense of *Richard II* is that it allows for these ideological certainties but does not underwrite them. Readers, critics and performers have tended to find confirmation of their own politics in the play's careful impartiality: again, we make Shakespeare mean what we want him to mean.

CHAPTER 5

Romeo and Juliet

A handful of Shakespeare's plays begin with expository pro-
logues. We're in ancient Troy amid the war of 'ravished Helen'
(Prologue 9), says the Prologue to *Troilus and Cressida*; did
you see Part 1 and can you remember where we left things?
asks the Prologue to *2 Henry IV* ; bear with us as we try to
depict grand battles within the limits of the stage, says the
Prologue to *Henry V*; welcome to olde-worlde storyland, says
the Prologue to *Pericles*. Only in *Romeo and Juliet* does the
Prologue summarize the entire play, deaths and all. Because of
Romeo and Juliet's extraordinary cultural reach, we all already
know something about the play before we read it. But even if
we don't, or even if back in 1595 we didn't, we soon will. 'Two
households', 'Verona', 'ancient grudge', 'star-crossed lovers',
'take their life', 'two-hours' traffic of our stage' (Prologue 1,
2, 3, 6, 12). Yada yada yada. Two minutes in, and there's nothing to play for.

Romeo and Juliet is distinctive in making so immediately
explicit what is coming.

> Two households, both alike in dignity
> In fair Verona, where we lay our scene,
> From ancient grudge break to new mutiny,

Where civil blood makes civil hands unclean.
From forth the fatal loins of these two foes
A pair of star-crossed lovers take their life,
Whose misadventured piteous overthrows
Doth with their death bury their parents' strife.
The fearful passage of their death-marked love
And the continuance of their parents' rage –
Which but their children's end, naught could remove –
Is now the two-hours' traffic of our stage;
The which if you with patient ears attend,
What here shall miss, our toil shall strive to mend.

(Prologue 1–14)

In the language of film reviews, this needs a spoiler alert; in the language of narrative theory, it is an extended prolepsis, or flash-forward. The play is thus strongly teleological, heading inexorably to a conclusion that is already written. The lovers are dead, in terms of our experience of the play, before we even meet them. They are introduced to us only to flesh out a fatalistic plot. Not only does the Chorus tell us the plot outline in a sonnet form – characterized by a fourteen-line structure and predictable rhyme scheme, heading relentlessly towards its closing couplet – it is also full of the language of determinism: the 'fatal loins' of the families has the idea of 'fated' as well as 'fatal' meaning deadly; the lovers are 'star-crossed', so astrologically fated; they are 'misadventured', meaning unlucky. Their love is always already 'death-marked', before it even begins at the Capulets' party. The language, therefore, and the worldview of the Prologue stress the inevitability, the pre-scriptedness, the already-happenedness of the events that are still to unfold in the playhouse. It's a clever trick of the director Baz Luhrmann, in introducing his 1996 film, to have the Prologue delivered by a newscaster: the bland, almost formulaic structure of Shakespeare's verse here fits the reported, after-the-fact, too-late-to-be-different indifference of broadcast news. And the sonnet's rhythmical structure also serves the same purpose. Those alternate end rhymes also produce inevitability in microcosm: once the pattern has been established, we are simply waiting for the completing rhyme. Each positive or relatively neutral term turns bad or is negated by its rhyming completion: dignity becomes mutiny; scene becomes unclean; foes, overthrows; life, strife; love, remove. Both the formal structure and the fatalistic language underline the proleptic or spoiler-like character of the opening Prologue. And this anticipatory quality is itself an anticipation of later elements in the play which turn on premonition or a doomed future, such as Romeo's anxiety: 'I fear too early, for my mind misgives/Some consequence yet hanging in the stars/Shall bitterly begin' (1.4.106–8).

What, then, is the purpose and effect of so completely pre-empting the play's outcome in its opening lines? First, it's worth recalling that early modern audiences and readers were less interested in shock endings or surprise fictions than we are – or think we are. Ideas of originality have a high status in twenty-first-century ideas of art, but that's not the case for the sixteenth century. A humanist education system suspicious of novelty, sometimes judging invention or fiction as morally compromised because untrue, taught generations of playwrights and poets that translating, reworking and rewriting existing texts was the sign of the artist. For readers and audiences, this intellectual method known as *imitatio* also offered the particular in-crowd pleasure of spotting those sources and appreciating the craft and invention worked on them. When the law student John Manningham saw *Twelfth Night* at Middle Temple in 1602, for example, he noted its similarity to *The Comedy of Errors* and to Plautus' *Menaechmi*: not by way of complaint about a tired or hackneyed plot, but rather with the enjoyment of narrative familiarity and pride at his own ability to recognize precedents. Long narratives in the period often had intermediate plot summaries – short precis verses precede the long cantos of Edmund Spenser's epic poem *The Faerie Queene* (1590), for instance. Such examples suggest that the pleasure of reading was not in the surprise and fulfilment of seeing how things turned out in an uncertain plot, but rather in enjoying the variations on an established theme.

Perhaps we are not in fact so far from this in the modern world: watch any movie trailer and it's pretty self-evident what's going to happen. I'm a particular fan of those Internet lists of movie clichés which reveal how much of our mass entertainment is enjoyable precisely because it operates within existing narrative paradigms. You may know the sort of thing. If the movie hero has a sidekick who mentions his family in the first two minutes of the film, the sidekick will surely be killed, especially if he has a photo of them on his desk, and even more especially if that includes a dog, which will also be killed. Our hero will fight one man in the gang at a time while the others dance around menacingly with their fists up, will show no pain even during the most terrific beating, yet will wince prettily when a woman attempts to clean a wound just over his right eyebrow, etc. etc. So *Romeo and Juliet* operates within a cultural world in which originality and surprise are not high entertainment values, but we might wonder whether ours is any different.

A second point about spoilers is more specifically generic. Can tragedy even have a spoiler? If we know the play is called 'The Tragedy of Romeo and Juliet', are we really ever in any doubt about how things will turn out? Some evidence suggests that Renaissance tragedies were performed on a stage draped with black, which would have the same giveaway quality. The French playwright Jean Anouilh, who wrote a version of the Greek tragedy *Antigone* in the mid-twentieth century, introduced into his play a description of the nature of tragedy that has no precedent in Sophocles' original. Anouilh's Chorus argues that tragedy is 'restful' because there is 'no need to do anything. It does itself. Like clockwork set going since the beginning of time.' I am always rapt by watching those unfurling patterns of dominoes set off by a single tap: like these, Anouilh suggests, tragedy just needs the 'flick of a finger'. One related observation that's commonly made about tragedy is that human agency is reduced so as to be non-existent. The critic Susan Snyder had a great take on this, arguing that Shakespeare's tragic world is governed by the inevitability of the conflict between human and cosmic law, the contradictions inherent in the individual or his or her circumstances. There's no turning back, no alternative. Against this inevitability, Snyder offers the useful contrasting principle of 'evitability' as the governing condition of Shakespearean comedy, which rewards opportunism and pragmatism as it twists and turns to avoid obstacles and come to its redemptive or procreative conclusion. Inexorability, therefore, that already-known-ness that is such a significant function of *Romeo and Juliet*'s Prologue, is the hallmark of tragedy itself.

So is tragedy the genre in which the human's capacity to affect his or her situation is most undermined? Questions of agency in tragedy are discussed in more detail in the chapter on *Macbeth*. Maybe the popularity of tragedy as an early modern form reflects this cultural interest. At the time of Shakespeare's writing, philosophies of causation were on the move. They began to shift away from the providential, theocentric views of medieval Christianity – broadly, things happen because God says so – via Machiavelli's unsentimental stress on human ingenuity and significance in *The Prince* (circulated widely in the second half of the sixteenth century), and emerged somewhere about the philosopher Thomas Hobbes's *Leviathan* (printed in 1651), where things happen because humans, individually and collectively, behave in particular self-interested ways. The fatalistic worldview of the *Romeo and Juliet* Prologue may have its own agenda: blaming some cosmic agency also lets humans off the hook, so that the death of the young lovers is less the fault of their pointlessly feuding elders and more some unavoidable and predestined tragedy. The Prince's announcement at the end of the play that 'Some shall be pardoned, and some punishèd' (5.3.307), suggests a judgement that can target responsible human agents. To put it another way, the play moves away from those mysteriously fatal loins and misadventured piteous overthrows to a more explicitly temporal and judicial explanatory framework. But, if it was all always going to be like this, it feels a bit harsh to pin the blame on any particular – and probably minor – character for making it happen. In a story of star-crossed lovers, is it really the apothecary who is at fault for selling Romeo the poison? Isn't he just a cosmic plot device, the emaciated cat's paw of fate?

So *Romeo and Juliet* has already happened, is already written, in some metaphysical sense, because that's the genre of tragedy. And in a more local sense, it's already written because, like pretty much every play he wrote, here the story pre-exists Shakespeare's retelling. There are stories of doomed lovers on opposite sides of some human divide in cultures across the world, and long before the English Renaissance, but the direct source Shakespeare used for *Romeo and Juliet* was a long narrative poem by Arthur Brooke, translated from the Italian under the title of *The Tragicall Historye of Romeus and Juliet*, and first published in 1562. Brooke's poem also starts with a sonnet: perhaps that gave Shakespeare the idea. The comparison of the two is revelatory. Here's Brooke:

> Love hath inflaméd twain by sudden sight,
>> And both do grant the thing that both desire
>> They wed in shrift by counsel of a friar.
> Young Romeus climbs fair Juliet's bower by night.
> Three months he doth enjoy his chief delight.
>> By Tybalt's rage provokéd unto ire,
>> He payeth death to Tybalt for his hire.
> A banished man he 'scapes by secret flight.
> New marriage is offered to his wife.
> She drinks a drink that seems to reave her breath:

They bury her that sleeping yet hath life.
Her husband hears the tidings of her death.
He drinks his bane. And she with Romeus' knife,
When she awakes, herself, alas! she slay'th.

Brooke is absolutely clear that the blame for this is on the couple themselves. There's a moment of seeming to personify the agency of 'Love', but the human decision is clear: 'both do grant the thing that both desire'. Their lustful behaviour leads to their downfall. There's none of that fated or star-crossed language of Shakespeare, and even Brooke's particular version of the sonnet, the kind without a rhyming final couplet, has a less inexorable sense of form than that of his imitator. So Shakespeare changes the motivation or causation for the tragedy quite distinctly. Brooke's prefatory material is all moralistic, and in particular, anti-Catholic. His take-away message is that young people should do what their parents say, or terrible consequences will ensue, and especially they should avoid gossipy old women and dodgy friars (Brooke's poem as a whole is a bit more sympathetic to the lovers than this framework suggests, but it starts in very didactic mode). We can see that Shakespeare – as often – jettisons this moralistic notion. No one reading *Romeo and Juliet* could really generate from it the moral that children should obey their parents, since those parents have forfeited moral authority because of their unexplained and therefore unjustified family feud and so are not presented as sources of moral authority.

On the other hand, it's interesting to see that Shakespeare can change the framework for the tragedy, but he cannot transform it so completely that the lovers can escape their families and live happily ever after in Mantua. The tragedy retains its inexorable shape. The fatal law governing events here is not just one of genre in general, but of the source in particular. The standard line on how Shakespeare uses his sources is that he transforms them from prosaic dross into poetic gold (tweaking 'Romeus' to 'Romeo' – genius?). That may well be true, but it's also the case that he is rarely able to reshape them significantly. The source for Shakespeare seems to trace out a narrative arc that is irresistible. (*King Lear* is an important exception here, as we will see in the chapter on that play.) The play is thus overburdened and overdetermined by many preceding structures, including those of genre and of source. No wonder it needs to blurt out in the Chorus at the beginning the shape of what is to come. It starts to look as if this issue of hobbled or restricted agency is as much a feature of the playwright as the characters: like his Romeo and Juliet, Shakespeare too is playing out a cosmically preordained script, with little of that contingent or playful evitability that Snyder identifies as the roadmap for comedy.

The relation between the Prologue and the play, then, turns out to be something rather like that between Brooke and Shakespeare: in each pair, the first is proleptic or anticipatory, but also pre-emptive, setting out the course the second must follow. The Renaissance theorist George Puttenham defined the rhetorical term for this: a 'manner of disordered speech . . . we call it in English proverb, the cart before the horse, the Greeks call it *Hysteron proteron*'. The English version of this term, putting the cart before the horse, suggests haste – and there is indeed a kind of premature quality to this play that is so shaped by youthful impatience and hurry, with its adolescent protagonists rushing towards their destiny, heedless of Friar Laurence's caution: 'Too swift arrives as tardy as too slow' (2.5.15).

Lots of elements of this play are about coming too soon, and the sexual pun is somehow unavoidable: *Romeo and Juliet* is shaped as the structural equivalent of premature ejaculation. If, as many theorists have conjectured, the pleasure we take in narrative is somehow paced like sexual pleasure – enjoying anticipation, foreplay and climax – then this play needs to learn to take its time. Consummation – sexual, but also narrative – is too quick, wrongly placed: the couple exit with the friar to be married in 'short work' (2.5.35) at the end of Act 2. What should be the end of the play, if it were to end like a comedy – in marriage – is brought into the middle, and so there's nowhere good to go. It's a structural *hysteron proteron*, as those Greeks would have it: it puts the cart before the horse. We might compare this briefly to the contemporaneous play which shares many surprising aspects with *Romeo and Juliet*: *A Midsummer Night's Dream*. At the beginning of the comedy, Duke Theseus is impatient to be married. The whole play operates as a kind of pretext or a time-filler, so that the time until his marriage to Hippolyta and its nocturnal consummation can pass by more quickly. At the end of the play, the fairies bless the marriage bed, bride and groom leave the stage and marital sex happens, presumably, outside the frame of the play.

By contrast, *Romeo and Juliet* is a play that can't wait and has no truck with delayed gratification. The Chorus already spills out the story even before we've settled into our seats, and we learn in the first act that Juliet is not yet fourteen years old. Her father initially tells Paris to wait: 'Let two more summers wither in their pride / Ere we may think her ripe to be a bride' (1.2.10–11). Then he relents: the marriage starts to be a matter of days rather than years away. What day is it? Juliet's father asks Paris. Monday, is the reply. 'Well, Wednesday is too soon' (3.4.19), says Capulet, before setting the marriage day for Thursday. Paris wishes 'Thursday were tomorrow' (29); Capulet's question 'Do you like this haste?' (3.4.22) seems merely rhetorical.

Juliet cannot wait for Romeo to arrive:

> Gallop apace, you fiery-footed steeds,
> Towards Phoebus' lodging. Such a waggoner
> As Phaëton would whip you to the west
> And bring in cloudy night immediately.
>
> (3.2.1–4)

Her rhythms here are impatient, breathless – the opening word 'Gallop' deploys an initial stressed syllable (like Richard III's opening speech, this is technically called trochaic rather than iambic), so that even the language is in too much of a hurry for all that leisurely de-dum de-dum business. And Juliet's own imagery for her impatience understands that it is not just that she is too eager for Romeo's arrival, but that she is too eager for this adult experience:

> So tedious is this day
> As is the night before some festival
> To an impatient child that hath new robes
> And may not wear them.
>
> (3.2.28–31)

Her simile is from childhood experience, and it movingly captures the gap between the present and the hurried future to which she is committing herself.

We used to assume that Shakespeare intended this play to represent a high romantic love because early teenage was a normal time for Elizabethans to be married – an assumption based on some evidence of very young betrothals in noble families, where children were affianced to perpetuate long-term dynastic alliances. But the average age for marriage was probably only slighter lower at the end of the sixteenth century than it is now in Western countries – around the mid-twenties. It's therefore clear that everyone who was watching the play would have thought that Juliet was too young for this, and although we don't know Romeo's age, there's no particular sense of an age gap, so it is likely he was also seen as too immature for marriage. The fact that Juliet's age is so emphasized by the Nurse, in a comic monologue fixing her age to the memory of ' 'Tis since the earthquake now eleven years, / And she was weaned' (1.3.25–6), means that we are supposed to notice it. Only a tiny handful of Shakespearean characters are identified by precise age. To put the point another way, no actor of the actual age of Juliet could now perform this role professionally, as the producers of Baz Luhrmann's iconic film version of the play from 1996 found, when they initially cast the fourteen-year-old Natalie Portman in the title role but realized she was required to act in ways technically illegal because of her age. Leonardo DiCaprio (then aged twenty-two) was cast as a Romeo who is likeably gawky and clumsy, a big, overgrown and uncoordinated teenager. It's a clever cinematic attempt to humanize a character who can seem a bit two-dimensional, but it's also a way to human-ize a helter-skelter plot that is too quick and needs to slow down. As Friar Laurence says, sagely: 'Wisely and slow. They stumble that run fast' (2.2.94). Unfortunately, the friar is so beguiled by the anticipated honour of uniting the feuding families that in his other hand he brandishes the tragedy's starting pistol. Puttenham's inversion, that *hysteron proteron*, is here developmental as well as rhetorical and structural. The Chorus's spoiler serves as a metonym – a rhetorical term for a part substituting for the whole – for a play which is always ahead of itself, precocious, impatient, too much too soon. Even that 'two-hours' traffic of our stage' sets the clock ticking – it's hard to think the play could ever have been over so fast, but somehow it adds to its hectic quality.

So far I've suggested that the play was always already tragic. But there's an alternative reading. Perhaps that tumbling hectic pace overshoots comedy and brings *Romeo and Juliet* to its tragic conclusion. The play misses a comic redemption by a matter of minutes. It's entirely appropriate to the play's characteristic impatience that it ends with Romeo killing himself just that bit too quickly to realize that Juliet is not ac-tually dead. Perhaps this is a play that becomes, rather than is, tragic. A Restoration adaptation performed it on alternate nights with a happy ending. Young people, programmed to-wards romantic love and sexual reproduction, really belong in a comedy. Disapproving parents also have a role as arche-typal blocking figures in comedy, a genre that tends to see the young win out over their elders' blinkered prejudices. *A Midsummer Night's Dream*'s Egeus, for instance, is another father dead set against his daughter's choice in marriage, but his objections are simply overruled as the play comes to its multiply marital comic ending. In *Romeo and Juliet* it's often Mercutio's death – itself a consequence of Romeo's awkward and hasty intervention in the fight with Tybalt – that is seen as a generic tipping point, the moment at which the play stops being a comedy and turns to the sombre choreography of tragedy. The play leaves the busy and social world of the play's opening (Verona is the kind of Italian city in which Shakespeare sets his comedies), and the lovers must set aside their comic companions, the Nurse and Mercutio. The movement of the play is towards the lonely world of tragedy, which ends in the charnel-house claustrophobia of the Capulet tomb.

If, after all, this is a play that could have turned out differently – if only the friar's messenger had not been quarantined by the plague, if only Juliet had woken seconds earlier – then perhaps the presence of the Prologue does something different. If this is a tragedy morphing out of a comic matrix, as Susan Snyder would put it, perhaps the purpose of the Chorus is more pointedly pre-emptive. It might look as if this could all turn out well, but you've already heard that it won't. Don't get your hopes up. These comic-looking elements are actually all foreclosed in a tragic narrative. Even if the play itself looks evitable rather than inevitable, the Prologue makes clear that there's only one way it can end.

One last footnote to this story of tragic inevitability. Like others of Shakespeare's plays, *Romeo and Juliet* exists in a couple of distinct early editions, with textual variations that speak to the life of the play on stage and in development. When it is printed in the First Folio, one other difference has crept in. No Prologue. *Romeo and Juliet* in the Folio edition – the one that its editors bragged presented the 'perfect' copies – begins with the street fight between the Montague and Capulet servants, without any tragic or star-crossed framing. Without that pre-emptive, deterministic Prologue, without the opening *hysteron proteron*, without that perverse relaxation Anouilh attributed to tragic inevitability – it's quite a different play.

CHAPTER 6

A Midsummer Night's Dream

With its fairies, funny ass's head, rhythmic rhymes and magical woodland setting, *A Midsummer Night's Dream* has long been considered to be Shakespeare at his most child-friendly. It's often the play to which younger readers are first introduced in school, and generations of adaptations, from Charles and Mary Lamb's at the beginning of the nineteenth century, to the Walt Disney 'House of Mouse' cartoon at the end of the twentieth, have emphasized its accessibility and suitability for younger audiences. Take the character of Puck: we all know him, right? A sprite-like fellow, a fairy spirit, magical servant to the fairy king Oberon, he flits about the enchanted wood like a male Tinker Bell crossed with the traditions of the green or wild man. He's usually wearing green tights to show off his light-footed quickness and dancer's legs; he may well be youthful, and is usually bare-chested, smiling with a kind of cheeky innocence. He promises whimsically to 'put a girdle round about the earth / In forty minutes' (2.1.175–6) and ends the play with the apologetic Epilogue:

> If we shadows have offended,
> Think but this, and all is mended:
> That you have but slumbered here,

> While these visions did appear;
> And this weak and idle theme,
> No more yielding but a dream . . .

(Epilogue 1–6)

He messes up Oberon's instructions, to be sure, but it was an easy mistake: how was he supposed to know that there were two youths in the wood, both wearing Athenian garments? He's naughty, yes – the dictionary definition for the nineteenth-century adjective 'puckish' sums it up as 'impish, mischievous, capricious' – but never malign. He observes the human world with dispassionate wisdom: 'Lord, what fools these mortals be!' (3.2.115). Puck's short, rhyming lines and playful physical jests place him centre stage in the imagination of a play that, since the Victorian period, has been seen as delightfully innocent and childlike.

In fact, Elizabethan ideas of Puck were far from this cheery, domesticated fairy trickster. Shakespeare actually calls his character Robin Goodfellow, a name that suggested to contemporary culture a frightening hobgoblin with a potentially diabolic lineage. The poet Edmund Spenser listed Puck among the 'evil sprites', and popular folklore was full of his 'mad pranks and merry jests', as a book of 1628 put it. This publication had a title page with a woodcut of Robin Goodfellow as a huge, torch-bearing dancing satyr with shaggy thighs and cloven feet, a man's naked torso and a bearded head bearing horns. Most prominent of all is his huge, erect phallus. This Puck is indeed a 'merry wanderer of the night' (2.1.43), associated with rough sexual energy and fertility, not with the balletic magic tricks of a children's party.

Our schoolroom version of *A Midsummer Night's Dream* has neutered a much darker, sexier play: the 'dream' of the title is more Dr Freud than Dr Seuss, and the vanilla framing device of marriage creates erotic space for a much raunchier and riskier set of options, from bestiality to pederasty, from wife-swapping to sexual masochism. This really isn't a play for children, as a school party discovered at an unexpectedly raunchy Royal Shakespeare Company performance. Shocked staff hurriedly ushered them out when, as their teacher explained to journalists: 'What we saw was not what we were expecting. It was sexually explicit. The production has driven a coach and carriage through our school's religious and sex education policies.' Nor is *A Midsummer Night's Dream* a great hymn to marriage, as critics used to argue, perhaps originally performed at some aristocratic Tudor wedding. Rather, its attitude to marriage is knowingly sardonic. Rediscovering an X-rated *A Midsummer Night's Dream* means engaging with its dark, adult depictions of dangerous desire.

From the outset, *A Midsummer Night's Dream* casts a jaded eye on romantic conventions. Theseus, Duke of Athens, sighs impatiently for the new moon and his 'nuptial hour' (1.1.1), even as he acknowledges to his bride Hippolyta that: 'I wooed thee with my sword, / And won thy love doing thee injuries' (1.1.16–17). There is no reply from his Amazonian consort. Productions often take the hint, bringing the captive queen on stage in chains, or depicting her as a disdainful or unwilling partner in the anticipated marriage: the hints of coercive or sadomasochistic sex are sometimes present. The 2016 BBC television version adapted by Russell T. Davies and directed by David Kerr, for example, had Hippolyta muzzled and straitjacketed. As both prisoner and bride, Hippolyta establishes marriage as bondage (with its simultaneous associations of erotic and domestic servitude), setting the scene for Egeus, who brings for judgement by the duke the case of his disobedient daughter, Hermia. Hermia wishes to marry Lysander; Egeus favours Demetrius as her suitor. Again, marital choice is constrained, and love and imprisonment are aligned. Egeus threatens to kill Hermia 'according to our law' (1.1.44) if she refuses his chosen suitor: Hermia maintains that she will not accept 'the unwishèd yoke' (1.1.81) of marriage to Demetrius. The stakes for her refusal are high, and the silent presence of Hippolyta on stage throughout this trial amplifies the presentation of Athens as a patriarchal world deeply inimical to women's desires. No wonder the wood to which the lovers escape is so associated with powerful women – from the fairy queen herself, Titania, to an apparent allusion to Queen Elizabeth as 'a fair vestal' (2.1.158) or 'imperial vot'ress . . . / In maiden meditation' (2.1.163–4).

But neither are women's desires endorsed and corroborated, as they usually are in Shakespearean comedy, where women typically know what they want and how to get it (think of Rosalind, or Viola, or Helena in *All's Well That Ends Well*). Hermia's childhood friend Helena is also in love with Demetrius (who was previously in love with her but has shifted his attentions to Hermia, earning the scornful designation of 'spotted and inconstant man' from his rival (1.1.110)). With two male and two female lovers, the plot is now set. Various twists and turns ensue, since, as the play archly remarks, the 'course of true love never did run smooth' (1.1.134), but in the end these two couples marry. But whereas later romantic comedies will work hard to characterize and differentiate their lovers, *A Midsummer Night's Dream* gets both of its men from Shakespearean comedy central casting. It's hard to remember, still less to care, who gets off with whom at the end, or to find any means by which to distinguish Demetrius from Lysander. Given that Hermia professes herself ready to become a 'barren sister' in a 'shady cloister' (1.1.71–2) rather than marry herself to Demetrius, it is surely significant that the play gives her vehement preference so little encouragement. To all other eyes, Demetrius and Lysander are virtually interchangeable. The stress throughout the play is not on the lovers' ultimate distinctiveness but on their interchangeability. 'Demetrius is a worthy gentleman', Theseus tells Hermia, trying to persuade her of her father's preference. 'So is Lysander', comes the reply (1.1.52–3). Lysander urges his own claim as equivalence rather than superiority: 'I am, my lord, as well derived as he, / As well possessed' (1.1.99–100).

Elsewhere in Shakespeare, love rivals tend to be characterized as risibly unsuitable: the oafish Cloten who desires Imogen in *Cymbeline*, for instance, or the unfeasible desire of Phoebe for a woman-dressed-as-a-man in *As You Like It*. These plays present as alternatives suitors who are clearly implausible, and they are unsupported both by their love object and by the play plot. By contrast, *A Midsummer Night's Dream* gives us two lovers who are similar rather than different, with equal social and personal claims to love Hermia – and, for that matter, Helena. The plot twist, aided by Puck's bungling application of a love potion, turns the men's joint attention away from Hermia to Helena: again, they are in-distinguishable lockstep. Even Lysander himself can claim only to be as worthy as Demetrius. In place of romantic comedy's usual valorization of its individual couples, *A Midsummer Night's Dream* suggests that any combination is as good as any other (although it's striking that, contrary to the playfulness with sexuality that marks *Twelfth Night*, written five or six years later, here it seems unthinkable to Shakespeare that Puck's mischief might result in – horror! – same-sex desire).

So *A Midsummer Night's Dream* is less a romantic comedy in which boy meets girl than a satire on romantic comedy, in which boys ricochet between girls at random, revealing the shallowness of their impulses. The genre's absurd conventions are thoroughly parodied, especially the trope of love at first sight, roundly satirized in the application of Puck's love potion. The botanical description of this elixir makes the bawdy implications clear: 'a little western flower – / Before, milk-white; now, purple with love's wound – / And maidens call it love-in-idleness' (2.1.166–8). Purple with love's wound, indeed. 'The juice of it on sleeping eyelids laid / Will make or man or woman madly dote / Upon the next live creature that it sees' (170–72). It's a pharmaceutical skit on romantic comedy, for a play in which the eyes are the most prominent erogenous zones, and sight, rather than speech (as in the banter and flirtation of *Much Ado About Nothing*, for example), carries the frisson of sexual contact.

Puck uses his potion to mix up the Athenian lovers, but the play's most savagely gleeful matchmaking comes as Oberon anoints the sleeping Titania. Enraged by Titania's refusal to relinquish a changeling boy in her charge, Oberon seeks to humiliate her with the help of love-in-idleness:

What thou seest when thou dost wake,
Do it for thy true love take;
Love and languish for his sake.

Be it ounce, or cat, or bear,
Pard, or boar with bristled hair,
In thy eye that shall appear
When thou wak'st, it is thy dear.
Wake when some vile thing is near.

(2.2.33–40)

The 'vile thing' that Titania takes for her true love is indeed part animal: it is the brash weaver-cum-actor Nick Bottom, who has been transformed with a magical ass's head. Titania is immediately enamoured of this creature and takes him to her fairy bower.

Victorian illustrated editions of Shakespeare established a whimsical iconography for this scene, in which the queen of the fairies sat decorously in her flowery gazebo, bedecked with greenery, perhaps stroking the ears of a snoozing creature with an ass head garnished with flowers. Sir Edwin Landseer's 1851 painting of the scene, *Titania and Bottom*, is a good example of this nineteenth-century interpretation: Titania, in a gauzy but modest frock, snuggles into her asinine paramour, overlooked by fairies and a disconcertingly alert white rabbit claimed to have inspired another alarming dream work, Lewis Carroll's *Alice's Adventures in Wonderland*. All very decorative and decorous. But surely the effects of the potion are intended to be more carnal than this enchanted whimsy, if they are to have the effect of making Titania relinquish her infant charge? 'Tie up my love's tongue' (3.1.193) (you'd have to silence the garrulous Bottom somehow if you had any other plans for him), Titania instructs her fairies, and 'lead him to my bower' (189). So she can stroke his ears? Come off it! A magically infatuated and passionate fairy queen, a man with a donkey head, an inviting grassy bower: it's not rocket science. The sleeping Bottom probably hasn't conked out because of his exertions preparing the duke's wedding entertainment. This is a scene that toys with unshowable scenes of sex and bestiality and that invites us to unseemly speculations about a lover hung like a donkey (it's a biblical phrase: a lustful woman in the Book of Ezekiel is described in the Geneva bible as 'dot[ing] upon their servants whose members are as the members of asses'). It embodies a transgressive sexual encounter straight out of the pages of Shakespeare's favourite reading, the classical manual of inter-species carnality, Ovid's *Metamorphoses*. The half-ass Bottom is a grotesque, comic version of Ovid's Minotaur, the monstrous combination of bull and man that roamed the Cretan labyrinth and was ultimately killed by Theseus. Shakespeare's comedy has suppressed this dark version of his mythical duke's backstory, but not completely: in the figure of Bottom its dangerous energies are translated into lewd absurdity.

Titania's word for her desires is, of course, 'love': 'how I love thee, how I dote on thee!' (4.1.44). In the sixteenth century, as now, this word encompassed a range of emotions and behaviours, from romantic yearning to passionate sex. Once we see Titania's bower less as a sentimental nursery illustration and more as a site of pleasurable sexual transgression, we can recognize other sexualized meanings in the play.

The issue of the Indian boy so beloved of both Titania and Oberon, and the source of the passionate discord between them, also carries an erotic charge. The repeated adjectives of Puck's account make it clear that the boy, who never appears in the text of the play but is often incorporated in stage productions, is an object of heightened desire:

> For Oberon is passing fell and wroth
> Because that she, as her attendant, hath
> A lovely boy stol'n from an Indian king.
> She never had so sweet a changeling;
> And jealous Oberon would have the child
> Knight of his train, to trace the forests wild.
> But she perforce withholds the lovèd boy,
> Crowns him with flowers, and makes him all her joy.
>
> (2.1.20–27)

The adolescent boy who is a love object for both men and women is something Shakespeare will explore in his depiction of cross-dressing heroines later in his comic career: here, the desirable boy is kept in the margins. But his role seems to be to crystallize versions of impossible desire in the play, and their challenge, as here, to marriage. The fairy quarrel between Oberon and Titania over this child results in their violent estrangement. And their 'dissension' (2.1.116) has a catastrophic impact on the human 'mazèd world' (113): crop failure, extreme weather, climate change. Love here produces 'a progeny of evils' (115): those 'monstrous' births that were understood by the Elizabethans to register the sinfulness of the parents or their transgressive sexual union.

Just as Victorian ideas about childlike fairies have shaped

the play's reception, so too has the often-repeated assertion that the play was written for performance at some aristocratic marriage. Since there is no evidence for this, and no specific wedding has ever been convincingly identified as the occasion for the play, the idea looks like one of those critical myths that are useful largely in telling us what we would like to believe. Making A *Midsummer Night's Dream* all about marriage is an attempt to regularize its depiction of desire, and turn its energies towards a celebration of the socially conservative institution of marriage rather than the transgressive energies of sexual desire. In fact, the play actually explores the disconnect between intense and discomfiting sexual desire on the one hand, and the social, patriarchal pragmatics of marriage on the other. Marriage is structurally necessary, both for Elizabethan society and for romantic comedy, but it is presented here as a conventional and compromised inversion of the powerful, unreciprocated and nightmarish passions the play explores so insistently.

Violent, uncontrollable, animal desire is the real dynamic that A *Midsummer Night's Dream* lets loose – and then proceeds to try to bundle back up within the regulatory structures of marriage. Dreams are one way of indulging this alternative libidinous economy. Hermia's panicky description of her dream of Lysander's faithlessness is unmistakably phallic: 'Methought a serpent ate my heart away, / And you sat smiling at his cruel prey' (2.2.155–6). It follows from their exchange about how to regulate sexual desire in the dangerously unregulated and uncivilized wood: 'Lie further off, in humane modesty. / Such separation as may well be said / Becomes a virtuous bachelor and a maid' (2.2.63–5). Puck, the wood and desire itself conspire to challenge the stability of Hermia's conventional morality, as she comes to see sex and sexual attraction as potentially dangerous and destructive. But Hermia is not the only sleeping, and dreaming, character in the play: Lysander, Helena, Demetrius, Titania and Bottom all also sleep for some part of the drama. This opens up the possibility that what happens to them afterwards is in their dream rather than reality (Dorothy's faint just before she sees her Kansas house whirling away to the Technicolor Oz might be our prototype here). Bottom claims he will write an account of his erotic escapade and call it 'Bottom's Dream'. And right at the end of the play, Robin Goodfellow's epilogue suggests the whole play has been 'no more yielding but a dream' (Epilogue 6). Like modern Hollywood, the early modern theatre is a kind of dream factory, providing theatregoers with an escapist fantasy from which they only reluctantly awake to return to their humdrum lives. But escapism has a darker side too: sometimes it's a relief to wake up.

Thomas Nashe, Shakespeare's contemporary, influence and sometime collaborator, wrote a treatise about dreams that helps us to understand some of the Elizabethan meanings. For Nashe, dreams access a kind of primordial tumult: 'no such figure as the first chaos whereout the world was extraught, as our dreams in the night. In them all states, all sexes, all places, are confounded and meet together.' We might see the play's structural juxtaposition of the different worlds of the court and the wood, the human and the animal, upper and lower class, fairy and mortal, male and female, as corresponding to this pre-creation entropy into which Nashe suggests dreams pitch us anew. Nashe also suggests that dreams parody our waking experience: 'On those images of memory whereon we build in the day comes some superfluous humour of ours, like a jackanapes, in the night, and erects a puppet stage, or some such ridiculous idle childish invention.' A ridiculous idle puppet stage in the night? Surely this must be the mechanicals' laughable play, 'The Most Lamentable Comedy and Most Cruel Death of Pyramus and Thisbe' (1.2.11).

The play of the doomed lovers Pyramus and Thisbe that Peter Quince and his troupe of Athenian artisans have been rehearsing takes up much of the final act of *A Midsummer Night's Dream*. In performance it is often extremely funny, in an over-the-top slapstick style – splicing physical comedy, an emphatically lacklustre script, *Carry On* innuendo and faux-poor technical execution. But in its central story, the playlet again shows us desire as destructive and violent. Like Hermia dreaming of attack by a snake, Thisbe is menaced by a lion. This seems to symbolize her own animal desires, or perhaps those of her lover, who announces that 'lion vile hath here deflowered my dear' (5.1.287) and discovers the tell-tale blood-stained garment that is equivocal evidence for both sex and death. Pyramus' own suicide when he assumes Thisbe is dead underlines the ways in which desire is lethal, replaying the psycho-sexual dynamic of *Romeo and Juliet*. The chronology of Shakespeare's plays is not sufficiently clear for us to be sure whether 'Pyramus and Thisbe' follows and parodies *Romeo and Juliet*, or whether it might pre-empt that tragic play's camp claims to high emotional seriousness. Wherever it fits into Shakespeare's work, part of the problem with 'Pyramus and Thisbe' in the modern theatre is that it can play as just too effortfully funny, even hysterical, in its desperate attempt to overlay the play's anxieties and displace its violently sexual urges into slapstick. The play's real concerns – those desires that tempt us to our own destruction – keep bobbing up to the surface. *A Midsummer Night's Dream* uses comedy not to perpetuate romantic clichés but to look beneath them. It is, writes Jan Kott, 'the most erotic of Shakespeare's plays', adding that in no other play 'except *Troilus and Cressida*, is the eroticism expressed so brutally'.

That desire might be the darker side of marriage is the play's overarching thematic example of the structure of duality that shapes *A Midsummer Night's Dream*. Those doubled lovers are part of a system of doubling and double-vision that extends throughout the play. For a start, *A Midsummer Night's Dream* makes heavy use of rhymed couplets: more than half of its lines are rhymed, and this high proportion is amplified by companion rhetorical devices that repeat phrases and syntax to create linguistic echoes. We are tuned in to this verbal music early in the play (it's not surprising, given its lyrical energy, that this is one of the Shakespeare plays that has had most musical adaptations, from Purcell to Mendelssohn to Britten). In the opening scene we can hear Helena and Hermia's parallel phrases and shared rhymes working to emphasize the mirroring or doubling of the two female characters.

HERMIA: I frown upon him, yet he loves me still.
HELENA: O that your frowns would teach my smiles
 such skill!
HERMIA: I give him curses, yet he gives me love.
HELENA: O that my prayers could such affection move!

HERMIA: The more I hate, the more he follows me.

HELENA: The more I love, the more he hateth me.

(1.1.194–9)

The rhetoric of this sequence converges to the third couplet, where the parallel structures and the use of the same word – 'me' – as the rhyme enact the same collapse of difference that the play develops elsewhere. Linguistic and rhetorical doubling, through parallel syntax and through the heavy use of rhyme, show us the way that Shakespeare's language is a microcosm of his wider dramatic art: what happens at the level of a sentence or speech often miniaturizes a wider theme or debate.

That larger-scale repetition includes the prominent use of actor doubling. Most of Shakespeare's plays have more characters than there were actors available to perform them and are therefore structured to allow efficient use of acting two parts to cover the roles (see *The Comedy of Errors* and *Hamlet* chapters for more examples of how this might have worked). But sometimes that doubling seems to have an interpretative, as well as a practical, payoff. Most notably, *A Midsummer Night's Dream* seems to be constructed to allow Theseus and Hippolyta, the rulers of Athens, to be doubled with Oberon and Titania, monarchs of the fairy realm. They're already cross-connected – Oberon and Titania each accuse the other of entanglements with Theseus and Hippolyta – but they also function as their doubles. The silenced Hippolyta might be recuperated in the fiery Titania, for instance, while the languorously authoritarian Theseus, as Oberon, meets a mischievously disrespectful servant Robin. There are technical consequences too. We can see, for instance, that Puck delivers an unnecessary speech when the stage has cleared after the performance of 'Pyramus and Thisbe': the purpose here seems to be less the content of his words than the time they take, in order to cover a challengingly quick backstage costume change for Theseus and Hippolyta to return as Oberon and Titania.

The doubling of the rulers of the two worlds has broader implications. The fairy world comes to stand as the nighttime to the court's day, with productions often also doubling Thesesus' master of ceremonies Philostrate with Oberon's sprite factotum Puck. It's also suggested that the Athenian workmen who are practising their play would have been the same actors as those playing Titania's fairy entourage – so that Flute and Snug and Snout would have played Peaseblossom and Mote and Mustardseed. Seeing these heavy-booted working men as the distinctly human-sized fairies is another challenge to romanticized ideas about the play's magical world.

Dreams, sex, death: *A Midsummer Night's Dream* is a comedy with unexpectedly adult themes. Comedy here is a displacement of illicit, transgressive or excessive sexual desire, ultimately regulated in marriages that we suspect will be less thrilling and less dangerous than the liminal woodland dreams they repress. Perhaps that's really a bit too much information for children.

CHAPTER 7

The Merchant of Venice

Bassanio is in a fix. This rakish spendthrift has mortgaged his best friend Antonio's credit back in Venice to finance a speculative trip to Belmont to woo a woman he describes, frankly, as 'a lady richly left' (1.1.161). His 'argosy' to win this 'golden fleece' (1.1.170) simply has to succeed. And when he arrives in Belmont he discovers another hurdle. He has to choose correctly between 'three chests of gold, silver, and lead' (1.2.29). One of them contains the prize – the image of Portia – that means the suitor has been accepted. There are hopeful suitors before Bassanio arrives. We watch, as first the Prince of Morocco chooses, unsuccessfully, and learn in passing that 'all that glisters is not gold' (2.7.65); next the Prince of Aragon also picks the wrong – silver – casket. Bassanio, by far the most indigent of these exotic suitors, cannily chooses the inauspicious lead casket and hits the marital and financial jackpot. The play itself gives over almost a quarter of its entire length to the lottery plot, and its longest speeches take place in contemplation of the weighty choice among gold, silver and lead. Nevertheless, readers and audiences have tended to minimize this part of the plot. Since at least the nineteenth century, the play's major interest, for good and ill, has been its representation of the moneylender

Shylock, Shakespeare's only central Jewish character. But the title page of its first edition places this theme in direct conjunction with the casket competition, advertising the play as 'The most excellent history of the Merchant of Venice. With the extreme cruelty of Shylock the Jew towards the said Merchant in cutting a just pound of his flesh: and the obtaining of Portia by the choice of three chests'. Understanding Bassanio's unlikely choice of the lead casket helps us see some important themes of *The Merchant of Venice*: its interplay of romance and realism, its structural dependence on debt, speculation and credit, and its understanding of the comic genre.

So why does the one man who is attracted to Portia precisely because she is wealthy choose the worthless casket? Well, of course, he's read his fairy tales. Anyone who is familiar with the genre knows that's the right one to choose. Folklore stories are preoccupied with testing their hero, often with a reiterated choice between three options (think Goldilocks and those bears, or Paris's judgement of the fairest goddess, or the common fairy gift of three wishes). Sigmund Freud noticed in his essay on the caskets in *The Merchant of Venice* that Shakespeare has shifted the gender roles from his source, the *Gesta Romanorum* – a popular medieval Latin collection of stories and legends – in which a woman has to choose among three caskets of gold, silver and lead to be allowed to marry the emperor's son. Freud argues that the three caskets represent different versions of woman, and that the three women they suggest are the classical Fates: Bassanio is choosing his own destiny by confronting a nightmarish vision of mortality. The lead casket confronts this Venetian playboy with a morbid decoration of 'crispèd, snaky, golden locks' ghoulishly bred 'in the sepulchre' (3.2.92, 96). The choice test is thus already deeply familiar in formal terms, and just as he models himself on mythology and the questing Jason seeking the golden fleece, Bassanio here recognizes the genre in which he is operating: fairy tale.

And he has to choose lead because the play has already shown us the two other caskets being chosen. Even though the mathematical probability of picking any one of the caskets is the same with each choice – that's to say, just because Morocco has picked gold it doesn't mean statistically that Bassanio is any less likely to pick gold – it is, of course, formally and structurally inevitable that three suitors each pick one of three available choices. Having already seen the revelation of the gold and silver caskets, it is time for us, like Bassanio, to see what is behind the lead casket's exterior.

So, like Bassanio, we know the drill: third time lucky. But maybe he also has a little help from Portia. The casket test is set up as a patriarchal attempt to control Portia's marriage choice. She tells her first suitor, Morocco, that 'In terms of choice I am not solely led / By nice direction of a maiden's eyes' (2.1.13–14). Instead, 'the lott'ry of my destiny / Bars me the right of voluntary choosing' (15–16). Portia's dead father has established her as a fairy-tale princess to whom suitor-knights must come to complete a quest. But this is also a scenario which enables Portia neatly to dispatch those suitors she doesn't want and to ally herself with the one we've already been told she likes best. (To underline this, the casket scenes are intercut with the elopement of Jessica against *her* father Shylock's will, and she too throws her portable dowry in the form of a valuable stolen 'casket . . . worth the pains' to her nogoodnik lover (2.6.33).) When Portia is reminded of 'a Venetian, a scholar and a soldier' who once came to visit her father, she recalls, 'Yes, yes, it was Bassanio', adding hastily to cover this apparent overeagerness, '– as I think, so was he called' (1.2.110–12).

Portia has thus already identified Bassanio as her preferred suitor, and her foreign suitors are established as clearly impossible marriage partners for her in a play so concerned with racial difference and intermarriage. Portia's reply when the Prince of Morocco withdraws, beaten, from the contest, is deeply uncomfortable: 'Let all of his complexion choose me so' (2.7.79). Critics who admire Portia have spent ages trying to suggest that 'complexion' does not mean skin colour here, but it's an effort, especially since Morocco uses the word himself in precisely that sense, in anticipating her racial antipathy: 'Mislike me not for my complexion, / The shadowed livery of the burnished sun' (2.1.1–2). Portia clearly has her own views about the husband she wants, under the guise of pliant submission to her father's authority. And when she calls for music to accompany Bassanio as he ponders the choice, might there be a particular emphasis on the final, heavily rhyming syllables of the lyric: to point Bassanio to the correct casket? 'Tell me where is fancy bred, / Or in the heart, or in the head? / How begot, how nourishèd?' (3.2.63–5). (We might also recall here her words to Morocco: 'I am not solely led' (2.2.13).) Again, Portia fans don't like to see her in this light, but would a woman who dresses as a lawyer and bosses the whole Venetian establishment really let her dead father's metallic fairy tale govern her choice of husband?

Despite the fact that, on the face of it, Bassanio seems

deeply unlikely to choose lead over gold and silver, he does. It's a miniature form – what the Elizabethans might have thought of as an emblem – of his own motives, and of the role of his romantic quest in the play's wider themes. The calculated risk of investing in lead is the romance version of the buccaneering mercantilism that structures the Venetian plot, a kind of high-risk financial gaming. Like the merchant of the play's title, Bassanio knows he has to speculate to accumulate. And that willingness to 'hazard' is the key to this play, in which human friendship and romantic love are consistently expressed through financial interdependence. Mercantilism and its twin, credit or moneylending, forms the connective tissue of *The Merchant of Venice*. Unusually among Shakespeare's deeply familial comedies of fathers and daughters, cousins and siblings, this play depicts no family relationships apart from the cheerless examples of Shylock and his daughter Jessica, and his servant Gobbo and his father. In the absence of blood ties, what binds is money: relationships are financial rather than affective. When, for example, Bassanio needs money, he goes to Antonio, who goes to Shylock, who goes to his business contact Tubal: what connects and implicates these people is a series of transactions constructed via intermediaries. Bassanio never meets Tubal, but his romantic quest is entirely dependent on his investment. In an otherwise sterile world, it is money that breeds and multiplies. 'Or is your gold and silver ewes and rams?' Antonio asks scornfully after Shylock's parable of Jacob's own astute financial management. 'I make it breed as fast', is the exultant reply (1.3.94–5).

Bassanio's marital plans for Portia combine the two worlds

of Venice and Belmont. The play's entire premise is based on his desire to appear wealthier than he really is, in order to gain more wealth, and he needs to borrow money to make this happen. Bassanio's expensive wooing of Portia is a kind of confidence trick, funded by the credit economy of Venetian moneylending and underwritten by expectations of mercantile gain. Like Antonio's argosies sent to the East to bring back valuable cargoes that will recover their costs and make a fat profit, Bassanio sails off to rich shores, supported by venture capital, hoping for large returns. He is, he admits, a credit risk. Bassanio tells us that he has 'disabled mine estate / By something showing a more swelling port / Than my faint means would grant continuance' (1.1.123–5): there's something wheedlingly evasive about this pompous diction, which over-promises, bigging up the statement just as Bassanio bigs up his own status. He persuades Antonio to support him by means of a childhood simile:

> In my schooldays, when I had lost one shaft,
> I shot his fellow of the selfsame flight
> The selfsame way, with more advisèd watch,
> To find the other forth; and by adventuring both,
> I oft found both.
>
> (1.1.140–44)

This same counsel of sending good money or arrows after bad, and the language of adventuring, is applied to his romantic quest. The down payment on Portia is 3,000 ducats – a sum that Shylock, like Antonio, 'cannot instantly raise up' (1.3.53) – and perhaps worth around £360,000 now. It is a substantial splurge, for Bassanio is pitching against some very wealthy men. The Prince of Morocco is described in the stage direction as 'a tawny Moor all in white, and three or four followers accordingly' (2.1): it's a cue for a showy entrance. At the moment when Aragon is dispatched for mistakenly choosing silver – the motto of the silver casket is, ironically, 'Who chooseth me shall get as much as he deserves' (2.7.7) – the messenger tells Portia that yet another suitor is at her gates, bringing 'gifts of rich value': 'A day in April never came so sweet / To show how costly summer was at hand' (2.9.90–93). That adjective 'costly' is apposite. Since we have witnessed the loan of the money, we know exactly what this grand arrival has cost: 3,000 ducats, with a pound of human flesh pledged as collateral. The bright, natural imagery of spring and summer clashes uneasily with this strategic display of conspicuous consumption.

The language of the caskets scenes echoes with hazard, speculation and investment. Romantic relationships here are monetized along with everything else. Perhaps in this sense, Bassanio takes seriously the motto on the lead casket: 'Who chooseth me must give and hazard all he hath' (2.9.20). The noble virtues of self-sacrifice and generosity suggested here have not been particularly prominent aspects of Bassanio's characterization. And indeed, his willingness – genuine or strategic – to commit himself to this motto takes on a different quality when we remind ourselves that he doesn't have anything of his own to hazard. If Bassanio is speculating, he is being bankrolled by others in a credit economy. Giving and hazarding all you have is easy to do when it's not yours to lose in the first place.

The play continues to trade in images of gambling and

risky investments, from Shylock's Old Testament story of sheep-breeding to his daughter Jessica's prodigal expenditure in Genoa, 'fourscore ducats at a sitting' (3.1.103). And although for Karl Marx Shakespeare's most powerful economic critique was in the morose fable *Timon of Athens*, perhaps he should have looked instead to *The Merchant of Venice*. There's very little 'use value' in the commodities and persons connected through financial speculation in this play. Salerio imagines the marketable 'spices' and 'silks' of Antonio's Venetian trade, but the main economic focus here is in investigating and negotiating exchange value. Is a turquoise worth a monkey? Is a pound of human flesh worth 3,000 ducats? Even the play's most powerful expression of humanity seems to partake of this bookkeeping morality. 'If you prick us do we not bleed? If you tickle us do we not laugh? If you poison us do we not die? And if you wrong us shall we not revenge?' (3.1.59–62). Extracted from its context, the speech is often used as a paean to fundamental humanity and equality. In context, amid Shylock's raging about Jessica's expensive elopement, and the first rumours that Antonio's business is in trouble, it emerges rather as a bargaining tool to negotiate equivalent values within this mercantile economy of profit, loss and speculation. If this, then that. Pay this, owe that. Shylock's parallel sentences 'if . . . do' all pivot with the syntactical equivalent of a merchant's weighing scale or moneylender's balance.

In this way we can see that Shylock's despised profession of moneylending is only the professional expression of a more thoroughgoing speculative economy in the play. He serves less as a real person, still less a real Jewish person, and more as a convenient personification of the play's fiscal energies. Perhaps, too, he is a kind of scapegoat. The opprobrium attached to him is the play's way of blaming him for its own thoroughgoing investment in financial matters. Everyone is doing it, but Shylock must carry the ethical can. And perhaps part of Shylock's implacable opposition to Antonio from the start is not only sectarian – 'I hate him for he is a Christian' (1.3.40) – but also economic:

> But more, for that in low simplicity
> He lends out money gratis, and brings down
> The rate of usance here with us in Venice.
>
> (1.3.41–3)

Shylock is often charged with the ultimate conflation of emotional and financial bonds – 'My daughter! O, my ducats! O, my daughter! / Fled with a Christian! O, my Christian ducats!' (2.8.15–16) – although it's worth remembering that this is an unsubstantiated and malicious report of the reaction of 'the dog Jew' (14) to news of Jessica's elopement, rather than something we actually witness him say. He is indeed clear about price, worth and value when itemizing her thefts: 'A diamond gone cost me two thousand ducats in Frankfurt . . . Two thousand ducats in that and other precious, precious jewels' (3.1.78–82). Marriage, as Jessica and Bassanio doubtless would agree, is an expensive business. But Shylock does also acknowledge another system of value – sentimental value – when he tells Tubal he would not have given the turquoise ring he 'had . . . of Leah when I was a bachelor' 'for a wilderness of monkeys' (3.1.113–14).

Shylock is not driven entirely by money – otherwise he

would have accepted Portia's offer. 'For thy three thousand ducats here is six', proffers Bassanio in the courtroom. Shylock is contemptuous:

> If every ducat in six thousand ducats
> Were in six parts, and every part a ducat,
> I would not draw them. I would have my bond.
>
> (4.1.84–6)

The play's structure makes it clear that the payoff for all this speculation – its accumulation – follows quickly from Bassanio's success in Portia's marriage lottery. News that Antonio's merchant ships have 'miscarried' is interleaved with the scene of Bassanio's successful casket choice; his friend Graziano married off to Portia's gentlewoman Nerissa as a kind of free gift, along with Bassanio's acquisition of Portia, immediately suggests another bet, conflating human and financial fertility: 'We'll play with them the first boy for a thousand ducats' (3.2.213). Immediately, Jessica and Lorenzo arrive in Belmont with Antonio's letter, and Bassanio admits himself utterly emotionally bankrupt: 'worse than nothing, for indeed / I have engaged myself to a dear friend, / Engaged my friend to his mere enemy, / To feed my means' (3.2.258–61). Portia is herself conscious of her new husband as a cost: 'Since you are dear bought, I will love you dear' (3.2.311). Her repetition of 'dear' tries to recuperate it away from being a financial term meaning 'expensive' to an emotional term meaning 'beloved', but despite this the word remains saturated with monetary meaning. Portia now needs to buy the bad debt undertaken by Bassanio to buy her in the first place. At least she shows no inclination to submit to her new, prodigal husband in matters of financial management.

The spectacular success of Bassanio's investment is coupled with the failure of Antonio's. 'What, not one hit?' Bassanio asks, disbelieving, 'From Tripolis, from Mexico, and England, / From Lisbon, Barbary, and India' (3.2.265–7)? But there are other connections between the worlds of romance and trade. Just as the merchant is a middleman in buying wholesale and selling retail, so too this merchant Antonio is a romantic intermediary, in the curiously triangulated relationship he has with Bassanio and Portia. Antonio's unexplained sadness at the beginning of the play has seemed to many critics and theatre directors all too explicable: he cannot speak his love for his beloved Bassanio (see the chapter on *Twelfth Night* for more on male homosexuality and same-sex desire in the plays, particularly related to characters called Antonio). He is both the enabler of their relationship – in taking out the fateful loan – and the impediment to it – in immediately intervening, at a distance, in their intimacy. Antonio's letter to his friend is a brief masterpiece in the passive-aggressive genre: 'all debts are cleared between you and I if I might but see you at my death. Notwithstanding, use your pleasure. If your love do not persuade you to come, let not my letter' (3.2.316-19). Bassanio does indeed come, armed with his new wife's treasury.

The wealthy Portia is astute – 'First go with me to church and call me wife, / And then away to Venice to your friend' (3.2.301–2) – and also munificent. The precise terms of her generosity are so tied to that initial debt of 3,000 ducats that her response to the summons reads as a fabulous return on an investment: 'Pay him six thousand and deface the bond. / Double six thousand, and then treble that' (3.2.297). 6,000 × 2 × 3 = 36,000 ducats. If the initial 3,000 was worth about $360,000, then this new sum approaches $4.4 million. These inflated sums are incredible – literally. The prudent calibration of investment and return so crucial to Bassanio's success with Portia has now become a bubble, in which the expansiveness of romantic love and the calculation of debts and bonds do not compute. The play is rapidly recalibrating exchange values, to prepare us for a new ethical vocabulary in the courtroom scene. The moral aim seems to be negatively to caricature Shylock in the play's fourth act as the sole figure driven by money. Having established all its characters and relationships as deeply and literally transactional, the play now changes course to pin this greedy self-interest on the Jew.

The play's financial entanglements come to their climax in the Venetian courtroom of Act 4. Unbeknown to Bassanio, Portia has presented herself disguised as the lawyer Balthasar, and she takes charge of the trial in which the plaintiff Shylock demands his bond, the pound of flesh agreed as guarantee for the loan. Shylock is implacable in claiming his due. In a bravura speech on 'the quality of mercy' (4.1.181), Portia uses her rhetoric to displace the financial self-interest of the Christian community and substitute a more rarefied glossary of abstract ethical terms. Mercy is a hyper-currency, above the earthly ledger of debit and credit, because it 'blesseth him that gives, and him that takes' (4.1.184) as 'an attribute to God himself' (192). Portia's intervention serves to establish the Christian community on the moral high ground and to back Shylock into a corner. He obliges, helpfully (for her plan) stereotyping himself as the vengeful Jew, stropping his knife blade on the sole of his shoe. Shylock is here completely isolated on ethnic, religious and legal grounds, as if he alone in the play was interested in money, profit and speculation, and is now being punished for it. It's striking that in the first printed text of *The Merchant of Venice*, dating from 1600, the speech prefixes – those abbreviated names that indicate to us who is speaking in a play text – change at this point in the play from 'Shylock' to 'Jew'. The character has lost his personal identity, or been robbed of it, under the pressure of the racial and ethnic stereotype. Some critics have read the courtroom scene as a kind of allegory of the defeat of Old Testament vengeance through Christ-like self-sacrifice. But for modern audiences, this court represents something simpler and more sickeningly familiar: a system of justice rigged on racial grounds, revealing the true limits of Venetian tolerance for religious difference. A Jew who sheds 'one drop of Christian blood' (4.1.307) must have his lands and goods confiscated, according to the laws of the state, and if there is a suggestion he plots to kill a Venetian citizen, his life can be ended on the Duke of Venice's command. Portia's disquisition on mercy starts to look a bit hollow. Shylock's life is saved, but barely: his money is confiscated, partly to fund his renegade daughter and her husband, and he is forced to convert to Christianity.

Like the moneylender, the merchant struggles to find a place in the play's whitewashed romantic world of Act 5: as so often, these adversaries are more similar than they initially appear. There is no place for Antonio at the end of the play, no marriage partner to bookend his opening declarations of sadness with contentment. One reason that there is no resolution of the play's central triangle may indeed be unrequited homosexuality in the character of Antonio – and perhaps of Bassanio too. Another might be the structure of mercantilism itself. Throughout the play its titular merchant adds middleman value to Bassanio, sold at a profit to the wealthy heiress Portia, just as Bassanio's credit-fuelled courtship of Portia lays out 3,000 ducats to win a fortune many times that sum. At the end of the play, Portia has the upper hand. Bassanio has learned, and earned, his lesson: his first allegiance must henceforth be to his wife, not his friend. But Antonio cannot quite accept his demoted role in Bassanio's life. He immediately offers himself again, in the play's closing lines, as physical surety: 'I once did lend my body for his wealth . . . I dare be bound again, / My soul upon the forfeit, that your lord / Will never more break faith advisedly' (5.1.249–53). The language of forfeit, credit and trust is, as we have come to expect, a vocabulary of financial transaction only imperfectly translated into the emotional realm. *The Merchant of Venice* emerges as a strikingly contemporary play about commodified relationships, romantic and business entrepreneurialism, and the obscure transactional networks of credit finance.

1 Henry IV

1 Henry IV is a history play that would prefer not to be. It has scant patience with heroics, fighting and politics, and little investment in its eponymous central character, the king. It is cavalier with historical facts and chronicles. It would rather be joking in the tavern than politicking in the court. These preferences create a new and compelling version of the history play. *1 Henry IV* tells the story of the king who, having taken the throne from his cousin Richard II, is now beset by conspiracy, civil war and insubordination. These take two substantive forms. The first is an insurgency led by the charismatic and chivalric Hotspur, supported by his father Northumberland; his brother-in-law Mortimer, who has a claim to be the rightful heir to the throne; the Welshman Glendower; and Douglas, a Scot. This political threat to Henry is a coalition of noblemen, representing constituent parts of the nation and its neighbours, who do not accept his right to the throne. But perhaps the more pressing challenge is the second, the rebelliousness of Henry's son, Prince Hal, who ignores the court and his obligations, preferring instead the company of a disreputable knight, Falstaff, in the taverns of London's Eastcheap. The play tells the story of the gradual reconciliation of father and son, culminating at the Battle of Shrewsbury, where Hal protects his father from attack and kills Hotspur in single combat.

The extended title of the first edition covers some of its appeal: 'The History of Henry the Fourth, with the battle at Shrewsbury, between the king and Lord Henry Percy, surnamed Henry Hotspur of the North. With the humorous conceits of Sir John Falstaff'. 'Humorous conceits' (meaning clever, entertaining ideas and expressions; wit) here, as in the play, threaten to undermine the high seriousness of political and military conflict. This play was one of Shakespeare's most popular in print, with seven editions in the following twenty-five years. More significantly, it generated two distinct sequels. One, entitled 'the second part of Henry the fourth', was published two years later, producing in its turn the designation of the previous play as 'Part 1'. For audiences and early readers the play we now call Part 1 was experienced as a stand-alone entertainment, although it looks backwards, to the reign of Richard II, as well as forwards, to the future reign of Prince Henry. We can judge that 1 *Henry IV* was popular because, like a modern film, it produced a sequel that essentially tried to repeat the success of the original (and again, like many modern equivalents, failed, because what we liked so much about the first one was that we had never seen anything like it before). But 'Part 2' is not the only spin-off from this popular play. Shakespeare turned away from the restrictions of the historical play to recast its non-aristocratic characters in the unexpectedly bourgeois milieu of Windsor, in the romp *The Merry Wives of Windsor*.

These opportunistic sequels tell us something about the way the early modern theatre industry was developing responsive, and recognizable, marketing techniques to cash in on successful productions. But they also tell us something more particular about the star quality of 1 *Henry IV*. The sequels share only one element. Not the king, not even the prince; not the battles or rebellions or disquisitions on the nature of government. Their common denominator is Falstaff. Fat, dodgy, cash-strapped, self-interested Falstaff. In inventing this anti-hero, Shakespeare had launched a cultural phenomenon that he milked in two further plays: the success of 1 *Henry IV* was the success of Falstaff.

So what made Falstaff so compelling? Why did Elizabethans recognize Falstaffs in the world around them, when they did not, for example, see Hamlets? Why did this character come alive for audiences in a way that no other Shakespearean character did? Crucial to Falstaff's characterization is his morbid obesity. Hal's first words to him in the play's second scene call him 'fat-witted' (1.2.2), and there is constant banter about his appetite for food and drink. Other names for Falstaff reiterate his size: 'fat-guts' (2.2.31), 'whoreson round man' (2.5.140), 'fat rogue' (2.5.548), 'a gross fat man' 'as fat as butter' (2.5.517). 'How long is't ago, Jack, since thou sawest thine own knee?' goads Hal, as Falstaff blames sighs and griefs for blowing him up like a bladder (2.5.330–31). When Hal advises him to hide on the ground during a trick, Falstaff asks if he has 'any levers to lift me up again' (2.2.34). In an important sequence in 2.5 where Hal and Falstaff rehearse in the tavern an interview between the prince and his father, Falstaff's fatness and its interpretation is their main topic of conversation. Ventriloquizing his father's disapproval, Hal (playing the king) addresses Falstaff (as if he were the prince): 'There is a devil haunts thee in the likeness of an old fat man; a tun of man is thy companion' (2.5.452–3). He extemporizes an extravagant sequence of similes for Falstaff's size: 'that trunk of humours, that bolting-hutch of beastliness, that swollen parcel of dropsies, that huge bombard of sack, that stuffed cloak-beg of guts, that roasted Manningtree ox with the pudding in his belly'(2.5.454–8). Falstaff sticks up for himself against this fat-shaming: 'If to be fat be to be hated, then Pharaoh's lean kine are to be loved' (2.5.477–8), referring to the cattle that are the biblical symbols of famine in Joseph's dream. Images of bulk, size and, above all, fatness, pepper the play. It is impossible to get away from the fact that Falstaff is fat.

It's worth stepping back a moment to see how unusual this level of physical description is in Shakespeare's writing. Very few characters in Shakespeare are given specific physical characteristics. We hear that Cassius in *Julius Caesar* has a 'lean and hungry look' (1.2.195), just as the apothecary in *Romeo and Juliet* has been worn to the bones by misery; we know that Juliet is just shy of fourteen years old; we know that one of Helena and Hermia is fair and the other dark and one is tall and the other short (but as with everything in *A Midsummer Night's Dream*, who can possibly remember which is which?). Beyond this handful of immediate examples, most of which have thematic rather than specifically personal resonances, there isn't much more. On some rare occasions a physical description is so at odds with the image we have of a character – Gertrude's description of Hamlet in the final fencing match with Laertes as 'fat and scant of breath' (5.2.240) is an example, or the idea that Caliban's witchlike mother Sycorax had blue eyes – that editors have tried to manipulate the reference away as a misreading of some sort. But for the most part, Shakespeare does not give his characters extensive physical descriptions, nor is their appearance of particular interest. While we know that Shakespeare writes with a definite group of actors in mind – the Lord Chamberlain's Men where he was actor, resident playwright and shareholder – he seems more interested in their acting ability than their physical appearance. So what? Well, Falstaff's fatness is the most thoroughgoing physical designation we ever get in Shakespeare, or, to put it another way, Falstaff is the most insistently physical character Shakespeare ever wrote.

The density of all these inventive signifiers of fatness is also significant when compared to Shakespeare's sources. Although Falstaff as he appears in the play seems to be an ahistorical character enjoyably adrift from the serious political and military business we associate with history plays, he does have a real and controversial historical source, the Lollard knight Sir John Oldcastle. Oldcastle was a soldier and companion to the young Henry V, who was executed as a heretic in the early fifteenth century. His life was included in John Foxe's extensive prehistory of English Protestantism, *Acts and Monuments* (known as the *Book of Martyrs*), and he was understood by Elizabethan England to be a heroic religious man who died for those beliefs. There is firm evidence that in the play's first incarnation, and possibly in its early performances, Falstaff's name was Oldcastle. Hal's phrase 'my old lad of the castle' (1.2.41–2) doesn't make sense without this name, for instance, and the Epilogue added to the end of 2 *Henry IV* teases the audience with the sense that Falstaff both is and is not Oldcastle: 'for anything I know, Falstaff shall die of a sweat – unless already a be killed with your hard opinions. For Oldcastle died a martyr, and this is not the man' (Epilogue 27–30). So the historical Oldcastle was a devout and principled man (nothing suggests that he was fat), and it is clear that his Elizabethan successors took exception to seeing their noble ancestor pilloried by Shakespeare, forcing the change of name. (The Oxford Shakespeare reinstates the name 'Oldcastle', which reminds us of the author's original association – but I've emended quotations to 'Falstaff' because I think that's how the character was known to audiences.) The Chamberlain's Men's great dramatic rivals, the Admiral's Men, capitalized on this tactlessness by producing a more acceptable and sycophantic version of the story in their own play, *Sir John Oldcastle*.

In part, then, Falstaff's fatness laughs in the face of Old-castle's piety, presenting a figure who is self-indulgent rather than ascetic, carnal rather than spiritual. He is a figure of feast-ing rather than fasting. In a joyous moment his itemized bar bill is winkled out of his snoring pocket and brandished for hilarity: 'O monstrous! But one halfpennyworth of bread to this intolerable deal of sack!' (2.5.543–4). And there's been a long history of criticism that has seen his insistent physical-ity as a marker of personality itself. In the history of Shake-spearean character study – even of Shakespearean criticism altogether – Falstaff is the weighty foundation stone. In 1777 Maurice Morgann's *An Essay on the Dramatic Character of Sir John Falstaff*, the first book-length study of Shakespeare, was published. Morgann attempted to defend his subject against Dr Johnson's withering moral judgement: '[T]he fat knight has never uttered one sentiment of generosity, and for all his power of exciting mirth, has nothing in him that can be esteemed' (1765). In responding to this character assassination, Morgann inaugurated an interpretative tradition that has informed actors from Henry Irving to Laurence Olivier and implicated critics from William Hazlitt to Harold Bloom. Claiming that Shakespeare invents what it is to be human, Bloom develops two characters as extended examples. Hamlet is a predictable enough choice, but the other is Falstaff. In an interview about his work, Bloom describes Falstaff as 'the most intelligent person in all of literature', but he also suggests something less personal and more general: 'Falstaff is life! Falstaff is the blessing.'

Falstaff's fatness is less an individualizing characteristic of his personality and more metaphorical, as if his bulk makes him exceed the individually human and take on a kind of symbolic function. That expansive meaning is something Falstaff himself aspires to. As he and Hal each pretend to be the disapproving king, they brandish different meanings. Is Falstaff 'reverend Vice . . . grey Iniquity' (2.5.458–9), the 'abominable misleader of youth' (467–8), or is he simply 'old and merry' (476)? Does he love the prince – one reading of the play sees him as an alternative father figure providing the human affection so lacking from the cold, troubled king – or is he merely exploiting him in expectation of later preferment and advantage? Falstaff-playing-Hal defends Falstaff against the charges: 'sweet Jack Falstaff, kind Jack Falstaff, true Jack Falstaff, valiant Jack Falstaff . . . Banish not him thy Harry's company. / Banish plump Jack, and banish all the world' (2.5.480–85).

Falstaff's claim to Hal's – and our – affections here is

in the claim that he is representative of 'all the world'. No wonder then, in that age newly fascinated by globes, that he is fat. The suggestion that Falstaff represents a physical, self-centred enjoyment of existence identifies him with popular archetypes such as the Lord of Misrule or the embodiment of carnival. These operate within structures of inversion or excess that challenge normal hierarchies and protocols of self-discipline. An analogy with Homer might be helpful. Not on this occasion the epic author, but the cartoon figure Homer Simpson. We all know that Homer Simpson is a loser, a wastrel, an inadequate father and a positively dangerous worker at the Springfield Nuclear Power Plant. Here's a few choice Homerisms: 'Lisa, if you don't like your job you don't strike. You just go in every day and do it really half-assed. That's the American way'; 'Son, when you participate in sporting events, it's not whether you win or lose: it's how drunk you get. If something's hard to do, then it's not worth doing'; 'Kids, you tried your best and you failed miserably. The lesson is, never try.'

These are funny because they are counter-cultural. Their rhetoric is to set up a statement that seems to demand a pious answer. We have all heard – perhaps even heard ourselves delivering – the standard line: it's not the winning, it's the taking part. If at first you don't succeed, try, try, try again. Homer's rhetoric is funny because it is anti-climactic. He sets up a cliché morality, but completes it with his own realist, bathetic conclusion. That makes him attractive, precisely because he is not up to the ideals with which our culture bombards us, and because he therefore allows us, too, the leeway to fail. Now let's compare these with one of Falstaff's musings at the end of Act 5.1. Amid the chaos of the battle between the forces of the king and the rebellion of Hotspur and his associates, Falstaff is alone for a brief soliloquy. We are prepared. This is the point heavily cued by a structure of repentance elsewhere in the play, when we expect that the no-mark, the selfish, the drunk is going to come good. Falstaff is going to find reserves of honour, courage, nobility. He will be like that alcoholic Vietnam vet pilot who takes the suicide mission in *Independence Day* (directed by Roland Emmerich, 1996): a man who grasps a final chance at redemption when he realizes what's really important, sets aside his selfishness and narcissism and goes out in a blaze of glory.

'What is honour?' asks Falstaff rhetorically, at this moment of anticipated moral renewal. And then the bathos. 'Can honour set-to a leg? No. Or an arm? No. Or take away the grief of a wound? No. Honour hath no skill in surgery, then? No. What is honour? A word. What is in that word "honour"? What is that "honour"? Air' (5.1.131–5). Falstaff ends this manifesto by describing it as his 'catechism' – a nicely ironic and subversive use of a statement of belief to puncture pious and clichéd definitions of honour and replace them instead with the pragmatic and selfish concerns of the vulnerable body. Like Homer, Falstaff sets up a rhetoric of piety and draws on our familiarity with the way we know we ought to behave; and like Homer again he deflates that expectation and tells the self-interested, taboo truth. Since this pragmatism would be so offensive to the martyr Sir John Oldcastle's memory, it is easy to see how his family took exception.

Falstaff's popularity, then, is in part related to the fact that he is unapologetic and unrepentant. He embodies the larger anti-moralistic energy of theatrical production in this period that so annoyed preachers fulminating against theatres as 'Satan's synagogue'. But Falstaff also features as one aspect of a structuring principle of repentance, apology and recidivism in the play. 1 *Henry IV* is organized, like a number of dramatic and prose texts from the 1590s, around the popular biblical theme of the prodigal son. The theme of the prodigal comes from a parable in Luke's Gospel. Jesus tells how the younger son of a rich man claimed his share of the inheritance before his father's death and spent it in profligate city living. Brought to absolute penury by his reckless spending, he realizes that his father's servants have a better life than he, and vows to return and throw himself on his father's mercy, not as his son but his servant. But on his arrival home his father is so overjoyed to see him that he orders a great feast and the killing of the fatted calf in celebration, much to the chagrin of the older brother, who has had no such reward for his loyalty and consistency. The theme is a prominent one in 1 *Henry IV*: the prince's impressive dedication to excess and riot rather than obedience to his father makes the paradigm clear. Implicit in the theme is the expectation of reformation: as in the parable, the prodigal will repent.

We get an early indication that Hal intends to use this theology entirely strategically. At the end of his first scene (1.2), the prince delivers an unexpected soliloquy. He has been laughing and joking in prose with his tavern companions, particularly Falstaff, their banter in pronounced contrast to the constipated formal verse of the opening court scene. But after the others have left, he stays on stage to deliver a long speech about his intentions:

I know you all, and will a while uphold
The unyoked humour of your idleness.
Yet herein will I imitate the sun,
Who doth permit the base contagious clouds
To smother up his beauty from the world,
That when he please again to be himself,
Being wanted he may be more wondered at
By breaking through the foul and ugly mists
Of vapours that did seem to strangle him.
If all the year were playing holidays,
To sport would be as tedious as to work;
But when they seldom come, they wished-for come,
And nothing pleaseth but rare accidents.
So when this loose behaviour I throw off
And pay the debt I never promisèd,
By how much better than my word I am,
By so much shall I falsify men's hopes;
And like bright metal on a sullen ground,
My reformation, glitt'ring o'er my fault,
Shall show more goodly and attract more eyes
Than that which hath no foil to set it off.
I'll so offend to make offence a skill,
Redeeming time when men think least I will.

(1.2.192–214)

It's a wonderful speech, riffing on the contrast between the prince's apparently dissolute lifestyle and his steely determination to change his 'loose behaviour' when the time comes. Like the sun – a traditional symbol of monarchy – he allows clouds to obscure his majesty so that he shines more brightly when people are eager to see him. Like precious metal set off against a dull background or foil to make it look more desirable, his 'reformation' will be all the more attractive. Like a holiday, or other rare occurrence, new Hal will be the more desirable because unusual. The language is part religious: 'reformation', 'redeeming', 'fault', offence' – Hal is thinking about the prodigal son narrative. It is also part mercantile: 'debt', 'promised', 'foil', 'attract'; Hal thinks of himself as a commodity needing its value inflating. It's a masterclass in manipulation. He is stage-managing his reformation for maximum effect, a self-conscious prodigal who knows that the worse his behaviour is now, the greater the sense of welcome when he turns over that new leaf. And this speech echoes the blank verse world of the court – established in the previous scene and in the scene immediately following this soliloquy – to align Hal with his royal birthright. I'm only slumming it in the tavern. I know my rightful place. In time I will emerge to claim it. We could read this as successional reassurance: no need to worry about the apparently unregal behaviour of the Prince of Wales; it's all under control; order will be restored. But it also has a chilly quality. The forgivably human element of the biblical prodigal son that's missing here is its authenticity. The original prodigal did both parts – the spendthrift years and the humiliating return – sincerely and wholeheartedly. Hal has it all planned out in advance.

In moral and structural terms the play probably needs to end with Hal's repentance and reconciliation with his father. And to some extent it does. Hal assumes the proper role of the Prince of Wales in the climactic battle at Shrewsbury against the rebel forces. He fights alongside his father and, in a Shakespearean invention not found in the historical sources, protects him against attack by Douglas. The terms of King Henry's gratitude are striking: 'Thou hast redeemed thy lost opinion' (5.4.47), a phrase that echoes 'redeeming' in Hal's earlier speech and suggests that the anticipated time of the Prince's reformation has now come to pass. In fact, the father-and-son Henrys have already showed themselves to be more similar than different (which, as in many families, is of course the root of their disagreements): King Henry berates his son for being too 'stale and cheap to vulgar company' (3.2.41), for being too visible and therefore not sufficiently respected. The language of strategic self-concealment as an attribute of effective authority is common to both men's understandings of their power. But in its final scenes, the play makes good on the promise of reformation and steps back from it. In King Henry and Falstaff, the play has established that there are two incompatible father figures with whom Hal needs to reconcile.

1 *Henry IV* is deeply concerned with real and imagined relationships between fathers and sons. There's Northumberland and his son Hotspur as well as King Henry and his son Hal. But when King Henry wishes, at the outset of the play, that the brave Hotspur were really his son, and 'that it could be proved / That some night-tripping fairy had exchanged / In cradle clothes our children where they lay' (1.1. 85–7), his wish for an alternative son legitimates Hal's own wish for an alternative father. Falstaff's court of misrule in Eastcheap is full of the warmth, wit and, yes, sack (a kind of

sherry) that is singularly absent from the war-wearied king's council. When Douglas fights first Henry IV and then Falstaff at Shrewsbury, we can see that the two figures are being brought together towards resolution (although they never appear on stage at the same time). What is striking is that while Hal does align himself with his royal father, he does not quite manage the related step of distancing himself entirely from Falstaff. He has the opportunity to reveal Falstaff as a shameless and dishonourable coward, who has claimed Hotspur as his own kill by stabbing his corpse callously and dragging it off to claim the reward. But Hal does not take this decisive chance. At the end of the play he is still caught between his two alternate fathers.

That Hal's own reformation is compromised by this ambivalence is made clear by the existence of the sequel: in Part 2, Hal reunites, temporarily, with Falstaff, and his behaviour continues to disappoint his royal father. And perhaps Falstaff's physical size and the difficulty of denying him come together here: Falstaff's bulk makes it more difficult for Hal to turn away from him. The moral thrust of the play and its dramatic energies are in conflict. A morally conclusive ending requires the rejection or defeat of Falstaff, whereas a dramatically satisfying one does not want to see him go. It may be that Shakespeare has been too successful: he has allowed the play's antagonist, Falstaff, to claim centre stage. Versions of the *Henry IV* plays that put him at their heart take their cue, perhaps, from Orson Welles' brilliant tragi-comic biopic *Chimes at Midnight* (1965), a combined adaptation of the plays organized around Falstaff, played by Welles himself. Such a focus on Falstaff substitutes for

Shakespeare's conflicted moral *telos* of the prodigal, a crowd-pleasing focus on the anti-hero.

The end of 1 *Henry IV* is no ending at all. Hal and his father have been reconciled, and, at least for now, Hal has behaved in a princely manner. He has dispatched his rival, the rebel Hotspur. One Henry down, one to go. But just as this battle is not the whole war, and just as the last lines of the play see the king reorganizing his forces to continue the fight against the rebels, so too Falstaff is an unresolved and perhaps unresolvable figure. To adapt a phrase from a different context, perhaps he is simply too big to fail. In the Shrewsbury encounter with Douglas, Falstaff falls down as if he were dead, and he lies among the battle casualties for some moments. Hal delivers a eulogy on the dead Hotspur and then on Falstaff himself, with a last nod to his size: 'Could not all this flesh / Keep in a little life?' (5.4.101–2). The prince leaves the stage, apparently believing his old acquaintance to be dead, at which point the stage direction reads, Falstaff 'riseth up'. The word 'riseth' is wonderfully descriptive – Falstaff takes on a kind of unkillable or immortal quality – here he is the spirit of life itself, as Bloom would have it. Striding away from the dead of the battle, he resists the historical process that would kill him too. Hal's opening remarks to Falstaff – 'What a devil hast thou to do with the time of the day?' (1.2.6) – have here their serious echo: Falstaff is not subject to time, or to history. Adapted beyond recognition from the Lollard knight Oldcastle, he is not really a historical figure. It is almost as if he operates in a different world from the other characters. Falstaff's fatness is, then, finally a challenge to historical pragmatism, the leanness of cause and effect. He is an anti-historical excess intruding on a history play, just as the character of Falstaff impedes the patterns of succession that structure historical progress. His bulk blocks historical progress, so we are not quite yet ready for the glorious redemptive reign of Hal as Henry V. The result? Even more Falstaff, in 2 *Henry IV*.

CHAPTER 9

Much Ado About Nothing

Shakespeare writes some fabulous villains. Richard III, Iago in *Othello* and Edmund in *King Lear* are all energetically amoral figures whose iniquity is elevated into a compelling personal credo. They are alluring and terrifying in equal measure, drawing other characters into their nihilistic world, demonstrating the awful entranced complicity of villain and victim. They represent a horrifically plausible evil that is always one step ahead of goodness, and they are brilliant, bravura, charismatic stage presences. Well, sometimes. But not in this case. The villain of *Much Ado About Nothing*, Don John, seems to be phoning it in. Criticisms of Keanu Reeves's performance of the role in Kenneth Branagh's sunny film (1993) as 'wooden' really miss the point: it's not Reeves who is wooden but Don John himself, and in capturing that peculiar stiltedness, his is actually a brilliant performance. So why is everyone in the play world of Messina taken in by this poor man's Iago, this wannabe Edmund, this budget Richard – and how might their collective credulity help us understand the specific undercurrents of romantic comedy in *Much Ado*?

Let's start with some analysis of Don John's role in the play. *Much Ado About Nothing* opens by bringing together two distinct gendered worlds, when the returning soldiers under

Don Pedro's command billet in Messina, home to old men and young women. A declarative stage direction names 'John the bastard' as one of the brigade (1.1.90). He is largely silent, until he is welcomed by Leonato, Governor of Messina. This silence comes straight from the Shakespearean villainy play-book: in other plays, we see Iago and Edmund as taciturn onlookers in long scenes to which they hardly contribute but from which they gather intelligence to furnish their traps. We discover that there has been bad blood between Don John and his legitimate brother, Don Pedro, but that they are now reconciled (it's not clear whether this argument between the brothers was the substance of the wars, or a sideline, since we never hear about their cause). John's reply professes in-eloquence: 'I thank you. I am not of many words, but I thank you' (1.1.150–51). The play's attention shifts to the matchmak-ing of Claudio and Leonato's daughter Hero, and to some jockish bantering with Benedick, a prominent soldier in Don Pedro's army.

We then see Don John in full villainous mode talking to his henchman, Conrad. John defines himself here by a kind of saturnine melancholy, claiming that his 'sadness is with-out limit' (1.3.4). Disdaining the silencing 'muzzle' (30) of the peace terms with his brother, Don John commits himself instead to a radical policy of self-revelation. In contrast to those Shakespearean villains who admit they are not what they seem (or even, Iago-like, 'I am not what I am' (*Othello* 1.1.65)), Don John states that he is incapable of dissimulation: 'I cannot hide what I am. I must be sad when I have cause, and smile at no man's jests' (1.3.12–14). He's a curious kind of vil-lain, characterized by disclosure rather than concealment: 'I am a plain-dealing villain' (29–30). News arrives that Claudio, described as Don Pedro's 'right hand' (45), is to be married. Don John sees that 'this may prove food to my displeasure': 'That young start-up hath all the glory of my overthrow. If I can cross him any way I bless myself every way' (60–63). Because Claudio has substituted for Don John in Don Pedro's affections, Don John will plot to undermine the wedding.

As we've seen before, the boy-meets-girl structure of romantic comedy doesn't quite capture Shakespeare's approach. Often it's girl-meets-boy for starters, but then there are the boy-meets-girl-and-this-really-messes-up-his-boy-pals or even boy-meets-girl-who-will-have-to-do-since-the-boy-he-really-wants-is-off-limits versions. That's to say that romantic comedies, produced by Renaissance dramatists including Shakespeare for a largely male audience, major on male-male relationships. *Much Ado About Nothing* is a fine example of this Shakespearean genre of bromantic comedy, as Don John reveals. His plot is established within a network of rivalrous male bonding that structures the entire play. Don Pedro has already told Claudio that he will woo Hero on his behalf, and this courtship is a negotiation between Claudio, Don Pedro and Leonato, with Hero herself barely figuring. The couple are never seen speaking together on stage until the scene of their marriage ceremony, and Don Pedro's triumphant declaration, 'Here, Claudio, I have wooed in thy name, and fair Hero is won. I have broke with her father and his good will obtained. Name the day of marriage' (2.1.279–81), seems to miss out something important, not least Hero's unambiguous consent. In part, at least, Hero is silent because she's irrelevant: her existence merely seals the deal between the powerful men and secures the network of male relationships at the heart of the play.

The masked ball gives Don John further chance for mischief. He pretends he thinks the masked Claudio is in fact Benedick, telling him that Don Pedro is really wooing Hero for himself. Claudio's gullible response to this fiendishly clever manipulation means not only that he immediately believes it – ''Tis certain so, the Prince woos for himself' (2.1.164) – but that he quickly excuses the prince for this betrayal: 'for beauty is a witch / Against whose charms faith melteth into blood' (169–70). Hero is to blame. Claudio is rationalizing the situation so that his relationship with Don Pedro can sustain this alleged breach of faith. While this particular malign misinformation is soon cleared up, Don John is not defeated, attacking Claudio to heal his own psychic agonies: 'any impediment will be medicinable to me' (2.2. 4–5). This time the proposed intervention targets Hero's virtue more directly. Don John will bring Claudio and Don Pedro to see her gentlewoman Margaret performing 'Hero' apparently in a nocturnal assignation with a lover. He whips Claudio up with the idea that 'the lady is disloyal' (3.2.93– 4) and promises to show him the proof. Claudio vows to 'shame her' (115) at the wedding if these allegations prove true, and Don Pedro agrees, confirming that the relationship between Claudio and Hero is in fact a relationship between Claudio and Don Pedro: 'And as I wooed for thee to obtain her, I will join with thee to disgrace her' (116–17). Neither raises a murmur of suspicion about why Don John should so trouble himself with their joint honours, nor does either of them recall his dubious past behaviour. Don John the bastard is here behaving like a bastard, in both the early modern and modern senses, but the characters all seem to have forgotten this conveniently legible marker of his true nature.

Given that Don John scarcely troubles to hide his malevolence, that he bears the useful shorthand 'bastard' like an accusing finger as part of his name throughout the play and that his first attempt to screw Claudio over at the ball fails, then why do Claudio and Don Pedro believe him so implicitly? One possible answer is generic rather than psychological. The classical New Comedy, associated with Plautus and Terence, on which Shakespeare often bases his own dramas, delivers a stock cast of lovers, wily servants and boastful soldiers. New Comedy also involves a prominent role for a blocking figure, often a patriarch who does not want the young couple to get married. We can see how this operates in *A Midsummer Night's Dream* or *The Two Gentlemen of Verona* or in *The Merchant of Venice*, for instance, where the circumvention of the father figure is a significant part of the comic plot. In *Much Ado About Nothing,* this blocking figure is more displaced. Leonato, the supposed patriarch, could not be happier that his daughter is to be married off to Claudio. And everyone in the plot wants Beatrice and Benedick to get together. (We might observe in passing that *Much Ado* is probably the first Shakespearean comedy in which the crucial blocking element to romance is actually psychological rather than circumstantial: the obstacle that needs to be overcome to bring the couple together is, here, significantly an internal, not an external, one. That's what makes this part of the play seem so modern – it doesn't rely on elaborate plot, but on recognizable relationship congestion caused by emotional scarring, fear of commitment and so on.) In the absence of any other blocking figure, Don John takes up the role: his rivalries with other men express themselves by trying to divert the play's impulses away from heterosexual conclusion. And so, he is believed because the play needs a blocking figure: a kind of generic speed bump to slow down its progress, delaying and deferring its movement towards marriage.

If the blocking figure is a conventional element of Shakespearean comic structure, Don John is given a slightly different role from that found by Shakespeare in his sources. While the tale of the slandered-but-virtuous woman is a popular trope in early modern literature (and one to which Shakespeare is repeatedly drawn in plays from *The Merry Wives of Windsor* to *The Winter's Tale*), the plot from Shakespeare's source, the Italian poet Ariosto's *Orlando Furioso*, took male jealousy as its motivation. The source material shows us Don John equivalents who have been rejected by Hero and who therefore seek to destroy her reputation. Shakespeare is not averse to these plots of male sexual rivalry – titular pairs in *The Two Gentlemen of Verona* and *The Two Noble Kinsmen* are exemplary – but he doesn't give us one here. George Bernard Shaw called Don John a 'true natural villain . . . having no motive in this world except sheer love of evil', but perhaps motive in Don John's case is not entirely absent. Don John activates a plot in which bonds between men are the real blocking structure in this play: his destructive behaviour is related explicitly to the play's wider depiction of male relationships and the threat these pose to comic resolution.

Almost all of Shakespeare's comedies dramatize the developmental movement in which young people forgo primary attachments to their own sex in favour of exclusive romantic attachment to an opposite-sex partner. Elizabethan young men got part of their education about this rite of passage from the theatre. So, in the last scene of *The Merchant of Venice*, when Portia makes Bassanio squirm as she forces him to confess he gave away his wedding ring, we see her imposing a message on her new husband and on the young men of the audience: you're with me now. In the chapter on *Twelfth Night* we see that this choice is helpfully muddied for Orsino, whose love for the cross-dressed Cesario shifts across into marriage: Orsino is fortunate in not having to choose between his male friend and his female lover. But nowhere in the plays is this drama of male torment more explicitly painted than in *Much Ado About Nothing*. After spending more than half the play flirting and bantering, while maintaining that they cannot stand each other, Beatrice and Benedick finally acknowledge their mutual feelings amid the shock of Hero's broken nuptials. 'I protest I love thee,' says Benedick. 'I was about to protest I loved you,' replies Beatrice (4.1.280–81, 284–5). Just as each makes him- or herself vulnerable to the other, there comes immediately a terrible choice. 'Come, bid me do anything for thee,' offers Benedick in the heady expansiveness of acknowledged love. Beatrice's reply is deadly: 'Kill Claudio' (289–90). To be sure, the context of Claudio's cruel denunciation of Hero has made this explicable, but we could reverse the causal relationship: the romance plot is the vehicle for Benedick's absolute break with Claudio, rather than the other way around. To be with Beatrice means to kill Claudio.

Benedick's realization of this cost is sharp but not unprecedented in the play. That romance and marriage signal an end to certain sorts of male relationship is part of the wistfulness of *Much Ado*. Military camaraderie outside the play is replaced within it by the 'merry war' (1.1.59) of words between Beatrice and Benedick, and violent plots and ambushes are recast in the play's repeated tropes of overhearing. In 'The Last One' (2004), the final episode of the longrunning romantic sitcom *Friends*, the establishment of the heterosexual couples which will bring narrative closure is simultaneously seen to cut out the same-sex friendships. Their loss is symbolized by the poignant dismantling of the table foosball which has been such a symbol of male bonding in the guys' apartment. Something similar happens in *Much Ado*. From the beginning of the play, problems emerge among the men as they shift their interest from masculine friendship to romance. Benedick bemoans Claudio's moonish preference for the effeminate 'tabor and . . . pipe' and 'new doublet' over 'drum and . . . fife' and 'good armour' (2.3.15, 18, 14, 16), as their shared male pursuits are displaced by Claudio's engagement in the female sphere. Under provocation from Don John, Claudio suspects that his friend Don Pedro is wooing Hero for himself. The 'bros before hoes' ethic of the military is at odds with the momentum of romantic comedy.

Don John is believed because the world of the play makes men implicitly more likely to believe other men than they are to believe women. When Claudio accuses Hero of infidelity before her father at the altar, he does so in shocking terms of sexual disgust which identify marriage primarily as a relation between men ('Give not this rotten orange to your friend' (4.1.32)). The shame is the broken contract between male friends, rather than the broken marriage itself. Leonato immediately believes his daughter's accuser, crying out in an ecstasy of shame that is as vehement as it is short-lived: 'Do not live, Hero, do not ope thine eyes' (4.1.124). Only Beatrice believes absolutely in her cousin's honesty.

Perhaps it's worth observing here one character who is absent from this scene in which sexual politics are at their most tribal. There are clues in the early texts of *Much Ado About Nothing* that Shakespeare originally conceived of a role for Hero's mother in the drama, and that he went so far as to give her a name, Innogen. The opening stage direction of the first edition of the play, printed in 1600, reads: 'Enter Leonato, governor of Messina, Innogen his wife, Hero his daughter and Beatrice his niece, with a messenger', and there's another stage direction in which Innogen's ghostly presence is registered. Innogen never speaks, however, and most scholars assume that during the course of writing the play her role atrophied and was no longer relevant. The stage directions inadvertently record an earlier remnant of the drafting process. It's interesting in the larger scope of Shakespeare's attitude to mothers (generally absent: think Queen Lear, Duchess Senior, Mrs Prospero as candidates for a second volume of Carol Ann Duffy's revisionary feminist poems *The World's Wife*), but whatever the reasons, the effect of this excision is to isolate the two young women of the play. The failed wedding scene accentuates their vulnerability within an essentially patriarchal structure. What would Innogen have said to a husband who denounced their daughter on the say-so of a callow young soldier and a saturnine malcontent? Presumably this challenge to the gendered balance of power at this crucial point was precisely what Shakespeare did not want: the incompletely erased Innogen shows us the play's own gender politics at work.

Although the straightforwardness of relationships between men is irreparably damaged in the play, it could be argued that male camaraderie prevails. *Much Ado* is a play profoundly uneasy about female sexuality and its assumed duplicity. Leonato begins with a joke about whether he is really Hero's father, answering Don Pedro's innocent 'I think this is your daughter' with the unnecessary 'Her mother hath many times told me so' (1.1.98–100). Even after Hero's infidelity has been revealed as a piece of Don John's Machiavellian theatre, these jokes about cuckoldry (and cuckoldry is another form of relationship between men: the husband and the lover, rather than the lover and the wife) are still the dominant currency of male interchange. 'Prince, thou art sad,' Benedick notes of the redundant matchmaker Don Pedro in the play's closing scene, 'get thee a wife. There is no staff more reverend than one tipped with horn' (referring to the supposed horns of the cuckold) (5.4.121–2). The play ends by equating marriage with the inevitability of female unfaithfulness, even as these attitudes have been so dangerous in trying to divert the play from its romantic conclusion.

As if in acknowledgement of these tensions, the play's very last lines turn back to Don John, 'ta'en in flight, / And brought with armed men back to Messina' (5.4.124–5). Some stage productions bring him on stage in chains at this point to show that his malignancy has been curtailed and contained. But Don John merely represents a more general mistrust in the play – he is not its sole source. After all, his is a tiny part (no sniggering at the back): he has only 4 per cent of the play's lines. He does, however, symbolize something larger than himself. And perhaps this is why he is given the identity of bastard. His own malevolent illegitimacy might be thought a kind of proof that women can – and some do – sleep with men not their husbands. Don John the bastard is himself the very certification to stabilize the play's paranoia about women's faithlessness. His status as a bastard thus confirms the play's worst fears.

No wonder then that his plot promises characters and audience alike the pornographic voyeurism of Hero's chamber window at night, a spectacle to confirm the stereotype of women's infidelity. 'Leonato's Hero, your Hero, every man's Hero' (3.2.96–7). But in fact we do not see the scene of this illicit encounter, backlit at an upper window or balcony – a shop-soiled, post-romantic *Romeo and Juliet*. Don John's taunting: 'I will disparage her no farther till you are my witnesses. Bear it coldly but till midnight, and let the issue show itself' (118–20) is, for the theatre audience, an empty promise. We move from the tight-jawed responses of Claudio and Don Pedro into a scene in which the comic watchmen, led by their pompously foolish chief Dogberry, undergo their inept training, then to Hero's wedding preparations with her womenfolk, then back to Dogberry, and from thence to the chapel where the marriage is to take place. The pivotal scene of Hero's apparent deceit is not staged. There's no practical reason not to show us, and we can see from the prose sources of the play that careful choreography with ladders and an upper window is a constant in the story as it is transmitted across genres. So, as with Innogen left on the cutting-room floor, the scene is deliberately omitted.

And, as with Innogen, there are consequences to this choice. It's worth thinking about what happens when we do see a scene interpolated in stage productions, since this can help us understand why it's not there. Broadly speaking, those productions of *Much Ado About Nothing* which want the play to end happily tend to show us this missing scene. The directorial motivation seems to be to suggest that Claudio's was a plausible mistake, that Don John's plot was convincing, and that Claudio's credulous acceptance should not reflect too badly on him. We too see what he sees, or thinks he sees, and recognize that it is indeed a convincing piece of stage business. He cannot therefore be blamed too harshly for his conduct. This particular reading is often accompanied with other cuts or additions – a scene in which Claudio's own mental anguish at Hero's apparent death is somehow conveyed, or the excision of the uncomfortable scene in which an untroubled Claudio and Don Pedro joke at the expense of Hero's elderly father and uncle. The trembling Adam's apple of a boyish Robert Sean Leonard in Branagh's film did much to excuse that Claudio's over-hasty denunciations.

As Shakespeare has actually written the play, without any scene at Hero's window, Claudio's readiness to believe Don John goes without visual 'proof'. In this, Shakespeare departs decisively from his sources: Claudio is a much more compromised figure than the lover-equivalent Shakespeare read about. Claudio chooses to shame Hero publicly on her wedding day rather than confront her with his suspicions and, tellingly, he imagines himself doing this even before he has any reason: 'If I see anything tonight why I should not marry her, tomorrow in the congregation where I should wed, there will I shame her' (3.2.113–15). Thus, while Beatrice and Benedick's offbeat relationship seems recognizably modern, the dynamic between Claudio and Hero is much more difficult to make acceptable for contemporary audiences. For its series of updated plays for television, *ShakespeaRe-Told* (2005), the BBC reworked *Much Ado* in a modern newsroom setting. Everything worked in this radically different context: Bea and Ben as the bickering news anchors; Claude, laddish on the sports desk; Hero the self-possessed weathercaster. But the one thing that couldn't be transposed was Hero taking Claude back at the end – or, rather, that outcome could no longer be a 'happy' ending. (So the BBC gave us the following dialogue: CLAUDE: But when you've had some time, maybe you would think about carrying on where we left off? HERO: What, get married to you? Never in a million years. CLAUDE: Okay, maybe not in the short term, but . . .)

But however imperfect and fearful a prospect, marriage, as Benedick ruefully acknowledges, is a social inevitability: 'The world must be peopled' (2.3.229–30). As in a Hollywood screwball comedy such as *Bringing Up Baby* or *His Girl Friday* (directed by Howard Hawks in 1938 and 1940), the bantering interplay between Beatrice and Benedick functions as a kind of verbal foreplay. We feel we know they ought to get together, because their playful dialogue bespeaks deep intimacy. They just need a little help to change roles. But it is also striking how much social pressure is exerted to resolve these two confirmed singletons, these potential misfits, into a couple. Their initial refusal of convention is a challenge to everyone around them. Each says they do not want to marry, and the community swings into action to prove them wrong. And, relatedly, the world of Messina is one in which private actions and individual behaviours are all closely monitored. Almost everything in the play is overlooked or overheard, from the opening rumours that Claudio intends to woo Hero, to the inadvertent confession of the plot in Borachio's loose talk which brings about the play's resolution. Our presence as audience adds another level to the surveillance culture which governs social codes and sacrifices privacy to a potentially coercive version of 'community' – a kind of comic Sicilian *Nineteen Eighty-Four*.

The means by which romantic resolution is achieved are remarkably similar in type, if not in motive, to those of Don John. That is to say, both Messina's fixers and blockers are using the same techniques. Like Claudio and Don Pedro at Hero's window, Beatrice and Benedick each think they are accidentally overhearing a scenario which has, in fact, been manufactured expressly to transmit particular (mis)information. Beatrice, in particular, hears herself accused of 'pride and scorn' (3.1.108) in her refusal to marry (we might recollect in passing that choosing to remain single is never an option for Shakespearean comic heroines: think of Olivia in *Twelfth Night* or Isabella in *Measure for Measure* or Katherine in *The Taming of the Shrew* – all female characters who express their opposition to marriage and all characters whose plots make damn sure that their resolve is circumvented): in part, at least, what she hears is that she should behave in a more conventionally feminine way. The scene in which she overhears her faults enumerated by her cousin is therefore the flipside of the imagined scene of Hero's balcony transgression. Both scenes work by implicitly establishing a norm of femininity against which it measures its female characters. Hero's self-abnegation when she contritely accepts Claudio once again as her husband shows how obediently she has taken her lesson from an act she never committed but nevertheless seems to own: 'One Hero died defiled, but I do live, / And surely as I live, I am a maid' (5.4.63–4). Both Hero and Beatrice are brought to heel by these deceptions.

So Don John is believed by the characters and by the plot because two contesting storylines run through *Much Ado* and give it narrative torque. One impulse reinstates male bonds and is therefore, implicitly, anti-comic; the other educates men into accepting primary allegiances with women, and thus conforms to comic necessity. Don John spins the play towards tragedy, and momentarily it obeys, bringing out a friar and a crazy plan to make a difficult marital situation better by pretending a woman is dead. That worked so well in *Romeo and Juliet* – a play already well known by the time of *Much Ado*. Like other villains, and not just in comedy, Don John represents an alternative worldview from that which comes to dominate. But as these alternative visions fight it out, we can see that Don John's version does have some traction on the play's psyche. The play's men are anxious for the excuse that lets them off the obligation and commitment of marriage: Don John proffers that excuse. Ultimately he's believed because the play's male characters all – Benedick excepted – have a weakness for his particular misogynistic view of the world.

In the end, Don John's plot is foiled by the most unlikely agents – the buffoonish Dogberry, played by the Chamberlain's Men's favourite clown, the actor Will Kemp, and his dim assistants. In some ways they are unworthy opponents – but in another way, their very foolishness is the triumph of comedy. Don John knows that his blocking misogyny is on the losing side in this romantic comedy. He needs to bide his time and beef up his villainy. There's not long to wait before another Italianate world, more hospitable to his particular anti-romantic malevolence, will present itself, and this time there will be no pesky watchmen to interrupt: *Othello*.

CHAPTER 10

Julius Caesar

Shakespeare's tragedies tend to follow certain rules. First, they're named after their prominent hero: *Macbeth*, *King Lear*, *Othello*. Occasionally they have double protagonists: *Romeo and Juliet*, *Antony and Cleopatra*. The shape of a tragedy is essentially biographical, ending in the death of this central character or characters. We instinctively know when Macduff kills Macbeth, or when Lear's heart breaks, that there are only minutes left before the play is over. The play cannot last without its eponymous life force. Not so *Julius Caesar*. In this play, Shakespeare experiments with a tragedy organized around a decentred titular figure, who is killed right in the middle of the drama. What's more (or less), Caesar himself appears in only five scenes of the play, although he returns, both as a ghost and as the abiding memory for the other characters, after his death in Act 3. The climax of this play is in the middle. *Julius Caesar* builds up to and then explores the aftermath's shock waves of a climactic event – a political assassination. The shape of this play is unusually unteleological, that's to say, it's not the end it is trying to get to, but the middle.

That may seem pretty obvious, but it is a quite different structure from that employed by Shakespeare for similar story types in other plays. Shakespeare deals with regicide, or the assassination of a political leader, repeatedly, but two examples, one earlier and one later than *Julius Caesar*, will serve here. *Richard II*, the earlier play, ends with Richard's own death, which, as discussed in Chapter 4, has two immediate effects on the play's politics. First, it constructs the narrative as a tragedy, organized around the life and death of the title character. And second, it means that there are no immediate consequences of the regicide. Although the new king Henry professes himself guilty and repentant – 'my soul is full of woe' (5.6.45) – there is no time left in the play to unpick the aftermath of the coup. So *Richard II* is all about the build-up to the assassination of a leader. *Macbeth*, a later play, gives us an alternative look at the same kind of myth, in a play all about consequences. King Duncan is murdered at the beginning of Act 2, and the rest of the play traces, unflinchingly, the unravelling of both political and psychological integrity. *Macbeth* is a play about assassination which is all about its aftermath, so it forms the structural and ethical opposite of *Richard II*. In between these two narratives of political murder we have *Julius Caesar*, balanced around its own central depiction of the corpse of Caesar as a kind of fatal pivot, between anticipation and aftermath.

Related to these structural questions is the question of titling. Both *Richard II* and *Julius Caesar* are named for the murdered ruler; *Macbeth*, of course, takes its name from the assassin. Mid-twentieth-century critics were curiously preoccupied with the question of whether *Julius Caesar* ought more properly to be called 'The Tragedy of Brutus', and certainly the scene in which Brutus muses in soliloquy on the murder that is to come anticipates Macbeth in some interesting ways. Alone in his orchard, Brutus begins his speech about Caesar with its conclusion: 'It must be by his death' (2.1.10). He goes on to justify the killing, not by what Caesar has already done, but by what he might go on to do:

> therefore think him as a serpent's egg,
> Which, hatched, would as his kind grow mischievous,
> And kill him in the shell.
>
> (2.1.32–4)

If Brutus is hatching the murder of Caesar at this minute, Shakespeare is hatching the play *Macbeth*. And like that later regicide, Brutus cannot bring himself to name the deed: 'It must be by his death' (2.1.10) compares directly with Macbeth's 'If it were done when 'tis done, then 'twere well / It were done quickly' (1.7.1–2), where the prominent use of the pronoun 'it' completely elides the unsayable noun that he is planning. As Brutus puts it:

> Since Cassius first did whet me against Caesar
> I have not slept.
> Between the acting of a dreadful thing
> And the first motion, all the interim is
> Like a phantasma or a hideous dream.
>
> (2.1.61–5)

The insomniac Macbeth who 'does murder sleep' (2.2.34) is already in Shakespeare's sights. Brutus' wife Portia aspires to political partnership, to Lady Macbeth-dom, but she is caught in the role of women in the English history plays: pushed out from political life, like Hotspur's wife in *1 Henry IV*. Part history, part tragedy, the very structure of *Julius Caesar* propels its wider ethical equivocation. Like the Roman populace it dramatizes, the play itself shifts, away from the conspirators and towards their revengers. The balance of dramatic power changes like the balance of political power, and no individual character rises to displace Caesar as the play's central focus.

One of the standard classroom exercises for Elizabethan schoolboys was to argue *in utramque partem*, or both sides of an issue (as discussed on *Richard II*), and it was probably a wonderful inadvertent training for playwrights. One such set topic was whether Brutus was justified in killing Caesar. Dante had placed Brutus at the very centre of Hell, along with Cassius and Judas, in his *Inferno*. So the question of the ethics of Julius Caesar's assassination was already a live issue in the reception of classical history at the end of the sixteenth century. And this moral dilemma is already self-consciously in the minds of Caesar's killers: the play, that's to say, knows about the reception of its story even as it purports to be running through it in real time. We all – characters and audience alike – know this story before it begins. Caesar, Brutus and the rest are subject to a particular form of overdetermined fame – and so the play embodies a kind of double perspective or parallax view. It is both now – present tense – and then – past; it is both a history, meaning the events in the past, and a present retelling of that past. 'Let's be sacrificers, but not butchers' (2.1.166), Brutus tells his fellow conspirators. The question of how to present and interpret the act is intrinsic to its planning and commission. The murder of Caesar was always a piece of political theatre, a series of sound bites, something always already staged.

Julius Caesar is both event and commentary on that event, as the assassins acknowledge over Caesar's bleeding corpse:

> BRUTUS: Stoop, Romans, stoop,
> And let us bathe our hands in Caesar's blood
> Up to the elbows, and besmear our swords;
> Then walk we forth even to the market-place,
> And, waving our red weapons o'er our heads,
> Let's all cry 'peace, freedom, and liberty!'
> CASSIUS: Stoop, then, and wash. How many ages hence
> Shall this our lofty scene be acted over,
> In states unborn and accents yet unknown!
> BRUTUS: How many times shall Caesar bleed in sport,
> That now on Pompey's basis lies along,
> No worthier than the dust!
> CASSIUS: So oft as that shall be,
> So often shall the knot of us be called
> The men that gave their country liberty.
>
> (3.1.106–119)

No sooner has the assassination of Caesar taken place than it is subject to narrative and interpretive retelling. The murder is immediately repackaged as a play. Those states unborn and accents yet unknown are the England and the English in which the play is being performed in 1599: present and future are ironically collapsed, as the bloodstained assassins pose like trophy hunters for the camera of history.

From the very beginning of the play, *Julius Caesar* has been deeply conscious of how its events need to be interpreted. Calpurnia, Caesar's wife, has a portentous dream which is a striking example of this expository process:

> She dreamt tonight she saw my statue,
> Which like a fountain with an hundred spouts
> Did run pure blood; and many lusty Romans
> Came smiling and did bathe their hands in it.
> And these does she apply for warnings and portents
> And evils imminent, and on her knee
> Hath begged that I will stay at home today.
>
> (2.2.76–82)

Our own knowledge that Caesar will indeed be murdered gives this dream the curious quality of simultaneous prophecy and recall that comprises visions of the future in historical drama. But within the play, Decius nimbly reinterprets the dream as metaphor:

> This dream is all amiss interpreted.
> It was a vision fair and fortunate.
> Your statue spouting blood in many pipes,
> In which so many smiling Romans bathed,
> Signifies that from you great Rome shall suck
> Reviving blood, and that great men shall press
> For tinctures, stains, relics, and cognizance.
> This by Calpurnia's dream is signified.
>
> (2.2.8, –90)

His interpretation is deliberately wrong, aiming to persuade Caesar that he should indeed go to the Capitol, where he will be turned into exactly that fountain of blood in which his murderers bathe their hands. But Decius is persuasive. Interpretations are not so much correct or incorrect, as persuasive or ineffectual: what is important is what is believed.

Decius' retelling of Calpurnia's dream shows us how interpretations cloud and eclipse their apparent actions. We're somewhere in the territory of the provocative post-modernist Jean Baudrillard's famous contention that the Gulf War did not take place: what we all saw on television was merely a stand-in, endless media simulacra behind which there was nothing at all. And often Shakespeare stages that very nothingness behind our interpretations, refusing to give us any access to the event itself, only its subsequent and contested readings. The play opens in this mode. Brutus and Cassius' discussion of Caesar's tendency towards tyranny and despotism is punctuated by offstage shouts and cheers. The two men interpret this soundtrack as the people offering the crown to their leader. Caesar – offstage – rejects the repeated offer, but this does not reassure Brutus and Cassius about his ambitions. Since we don't see the scene for ourselves, we can't judge whether this is simply politic on Caesar's part – he wants the crown but knows he must be seen not to want it – or genuine – he does not want to be king. When Casca gives his own gloss on events, reporting that 'to my thinking he was very loath to lay his fingers off' (1.2.241–2) the crown, the impossibility of adjudication has been replaced with unnecessity: what do people (want to) believe?

So, these insistent interpretative examples – what we might call the play's hermeneutic consciousness – mean we are already primed for the play's most famous act of reinterpretation,

Mark Antony's 'Friends, Romans, countrymen' speech in Act 3. Antony's skill is to persuade the crowd away from Brutus' explanation of the murder by introducing new information about Caesar. He tells them about Caesar's will, which has left 75 drachmas to each Roman citizen, as well as his parks and villas by the Tiber as a recreation ground. Interestingly, we never get corroboration of this – the will that Mark Antony brandishes is a prop, rather than a proof. We cannot see for ourselves, but, as Mark Antony's speech itself enacts, we can be persuaded that it is true. This long scene slows the play down after the violence of the murder. Mark Antony sets out the incompatibility of the evidence of Caesar's generosity against the claims made about his ambition by Brutus, all the while famously emphasizing that 'Brutus is an honourable man' (3.2.83). Simple repetition of that phrase enacts the work of reinterpretation here, as each time the phrase is uttered it seems to mean something slightly different, until it has completed the 180-degree turn to mean its opposite: Brutus is, for Antony, very far from honourable.

Julius Caesar's self-consciousness about interpretation gets a final twist in a scene often cut in modern performance. After the death of Caesar, the next on stage murder is very different from the choreographed tableau of weighty historical significance in the Capitol. A character that we have not previously met or heard of is intercepted by four plebeians. He is interrogated briefly about who he is and why he is abroad. He gives his name and vocation: Cinna the poet. The name Cinna already echoes in the play as the name of one of the conspirators: the man's hapless attempts to escape by saying he is Cinna the poet not Cinna the conspirator are ineffectual. He is set upon by the mob with cries of 'Tear him, tear him!' (3.3.35). There is no stage direction, but it's generally assumed that Cinna the poet is murdered in an act of pointless communal bloodletting that symbolizes the depravity of the times.

It's easy to see, perhaps, why this play about the self-conscious retelling of Roman history might have a cameo role for a poet. Cinna the poet has his brief stage moment within a context of contested interpretation, irrupting into the play in a short, choppy sequence that contrasts sharply with Mark Antony's deliberately extended, dilated oratory of the previous long scene. After the overdetermined death of Caesar, about which characters within the play and in a much more extensive cultural discourse have talked and interpreted so much, we get a bewilderingly random death. Cinna's death is thus part of a structural contrast. It is about action without words, or about the failure of language to effect action. Cinna's attempts to plead for his life are shortened and abrupt – far from the measured eloquence of what we have just witnessed. But the immediate result of Antony's clever and elevated rhetoric before the Roman citizenry is presented as the barbarity of mob violence; the plebeians who heed his reinterpretation of Caesar's murder are the same men who attack Cinna.

Cinna's is also a death that recaps what we have just seen in miniature. His first words about a dream align him with Caesar and Calpurnia:

I dreamt tonight that I did feast with Caesar,
And things unlucky charge my fantasy.

I have no will to wander forth of doors,
Yet something leads me forth.

(3.3.1–4)

The plebeians set upon him as a pack and 'tear him', just as the conspirators set on Caesar. In some ways, then, this scene echoes what we've just been through: a minor aftershock after a cataclysmic political earthquake. The echo may be parodic in effect. There is a humour in the scene, as well as, or in conjunction with, its abrupt or absurd horror. The plebeians fire a sequence of questions at Cinna: 'What is your name?' 'Whither are you going?' 'Where do you dwell?' 'Are you a married man or a bachelor?'; followed by a series of mutually contradictory instructions: 'Answer every man directly', 'Ay, and briefly', 'Ay, and wisely', 'Ay, and truly, you were best' (3.3.5–12). The stage business is bleakly comic. It's easy to see that it is scripted with no gaps for his answers so that Cinna can't get a word in edgeways. When he replies to all the questions in one speech, he looks superior, and the plebeians look foolish, even farcical. Karl Marx's dictum on how history repeats itself seems to work well here. Marx recalled that 'Hegel remarks somewhere that all great world-historic facts and personages appear, so to speak, twice. He forgot to add: the first time as tragedy, the second time as farce.' Does Cinna the poet represent the repetition, as farce, of the tragic Caesar? Is the humour of this scene a kind of relief after the extended stress – for actors and audience – of what has gone before, or does it establish the serious jesting savagery of mob rule? Is it, that's to say, a contrast with, or a clarification of, what has gone before? Does the senseless butchery of Cinna make Brutus and his co-conspirators look more like sacrificers, or does it echo their wild bloodlust? The death of Cinna the poet is cued by those previous interpretative acts as symbolic – but of what? The scene misses that explanatory analysis and commentary so carefully elaborated in other scenes of the play. No one has time to interpret its significance, so the murder of Cinna is left hanging, an emblem without its motto, a parable without the gloss.

It's clear that Cinna's death is the consequence of an unfortunate coincidence: it's because he has the misfortune to share his name with one of the conspirators that he is killed. The plebeians are unwittingly carrying out an act of dramatic hygiene: after all, it is confusing when a play has two characters with the same name. Something similar happens at the end of that contemporaneous play, also from this highly productive year of 1599, with which *Julius Caesar* may seem otherwise to have almost nothing in common – *As You Like It*. One dominant theme of this pastoral comedy is the quarrel between the de Boys brothers: Oliver (the older, bad brother) and Orlando (the younger, good one). But early on in the play there is a mention of a middle sibling, Jaques. Something has gone awry here, for the play already has a prominent Jaques, the melancholic courtier who is a member of Duke Senior's Robin Hoodish court in the forest. When Jaques de Boys finally enters at the end of the play, there is a funny, momentary standoff between him and the other Jaques. The message is a self-conscious one about dramaturgy: one name = one character. And where there are two characters with the same name, one must cede, as the Prince tells Hotspur at the end of 1 *Henry IV*. There isn't room in this play for another Henry. So there isn't room in *Julius Caesar* for another Cinna. Sometimes when watching a play we don't actually pick up what characters are called – perhaps because it doesn't matter, or perhaps because they are being left more shadowy for some purpose. But in *Julius Caesar* the names are particularly emphatic, in that they are repeatedly spoken aloud. These are already familiar names, and Cinna's is not the only one that carries a fatal message. Historical awareness means that all the characters in the play suffer from nominative determinism, part of the monumentalizing notoriety of their stories.

If Cinna is killed partly for his name, he is also killed because he is a poet. Shakespeare's poet is innocent, and when the plebeians claim to tear him 'for his bad verses' (3.3.30), there's no reason to think they know anything about his poetry. In this scene the play suggests that to be a poet is by definition apolitical: the poet is self-evidently a mistaken target. Shakespeare emphasizes Cinna's occupation more than his sources do. For *Julius Caesar* he uses an English translation of the Greek essayist and historiographer Plutarch's *Lives of the Noble Grecians and Romans*, but his immediate source for this scene seems to be another favourite text, Ovid's *Metamorphoses*. The story of the death of the legendary poet Orpheus is a clear parallel to Cinna, as Arthur Golding, in the English translation favoured by Shakespeare, describes how 'rash / And heady ryot out of frame all reason now did dash, / And frantik outrage reigned.' Orpheus too was torn to pieces by a mob with 'with bluddy hands':

As when a Stag by hungrye hownds is in a morning found,
The which forestall him round about and pull him to the
  ground.
Even so the prophet they assayle . . .

So Cinna is a bystander, caught up in events he seems to have
no part in. Is that really Shakespeare's view of the poet? A
number of references to poets and poetry in the cluster of
plays of this period seem to poke fun at this pursuit, from Orlando's lame poetry in the forest of Arden in *As You Like It*
and the wish of the foppish French nobleman in *Henry V* to
write a sonnet to his horse, to the 'halting sonnet of his own
pure brain, / Fashioned to Beatrice' (5.4.487–8) triumphantly
produced by the matchmakers at the end of *Much Ado About
Nothing* as the last nail in the coffin of Benedick's bachelor-
dom. All these poets and poems are gently mocked: poetry is
hardly a heroic pursuit. But these images of poetry must also
have a self-reflexive quality, an element of the self-portrait.
It's around this period, after all, that Shakespeare's own name
begins to appear on the title pages of his printed plays: his own
identity as a named author is being consolidated.

If Shakespeare's own poetic identity is being cemented
around the time of *Julius Caesar*, the wider social and political role of the poet is also centre stage. If the role of the
poet had ever been to be an innocent bystander on the political scene, it was hard to maintain that disengaged fiction in
1599, the year of increased literary censorship known as the
Bishops' Ban. This piece of Elizabethan legislation imposed
much stronger censorship of printed material in specified
genres. The first was satire, where a number of titles were

publicly burned at the heart of the publishing industry, at Stationers' Hall in St Paul's Churchyard: works by John Marston, Joseph Hall and Thomas Middleton were among those named, and the entire work of Thomas Nashe and Gabriel Harvey was banned. The second was to restate in stronger terms restrictions on drama: 'that no plays be printed except they be allowed by such as have authority'. Finally, English history became a proscribed genre, referred to an authority higher than the Archbishop of Canterbury and Bishop of London: 'that no English histories be printed except they be allowed by some of Her Majesties' Privy Council'. No doubt this had a direct impact on Shakespeare's work: moving, after nine plays based on English historical material, to the classical world for *Julius Caesar*, seems one immediate response. Unusually for a Shakespeare play, we have a pretty close idea of when *Julius Caesar* was performed because a Swiss tourist called Thomas Platter saw it at the Globe towards the end of September 1599. (He has disappointingly little to say about it except that it was 'pleasingly performed' and that at the end 'they danced together admirably and exceedingly gracefully, according to their custom, two in each group dressed in men's and two in women's apparel' – it's an interesting coda to the solemnity of the victorious Mark Antony and Octavius Caesar acknowledging Brutus as 'the noblest Roman of them all'.) Platter's eyewitness account puts the performed play only a couple of months after the date of the Bishops' Ban in early summer of 1599. Perhaps, then, the cameo of the poet Cinna is some kind of gesture towards the new climate of poetic censorship. That the first casualty of the post-Caesar regime in the play is a poet – or poetry itself, perhaps – may have had a particular resonance in the climate of literary censorship at the end of the century.

Even though the Cinna scene is so short, then, it seems burdened with trying to say something about the role of the poet in contemporary political life. Even the poet as bystander is brought, resistantly, into politics. And in case we miss it, the play has another go at the same suggestion. It has a second poet, too – a figure called in modern editions with wonderful superfluity, 'Another Poet'. We've already had another Cinna – now we have another poet. Something is going pear-shaped in the second half of the play: just as it all unravels for Brutus and Cassius after the death of Caesar, so too it unravels a bit for Shakespeare. Conspirators and playwright alike are preoccupied by tactics – how to kill the leader, how to write that brilliant 'Friends, Romans, countrymen' set-piece oratory – rather than strategy – so what will we do next? Repetitions, perhaps farcical ones in Marx's sense, abound in the second half of the play, with two versions of Portia's death, Cassius' coinciding birthday and death day, and those two random poets. A figure simply called 'Poet' interrupts Brutus and Cassius just at the point when they have reconciled from their quarrel, showing off his vocation in a da-dah rhyming couplet: 'Love and be friends, as two such men should be, / For I have seen more years, I'm sure, than ye' (4.2.183–4). Cassius dismisses the 'jigging fool' (189) poet scornfully: 'Ha, ha! How vilely doth this cynic rhyme!' (185). Another poet, that's to say, is unnecessarily brought into the play. Like poor old Cinna, he gets no chance to effect anything, or do anything. But if he is so impotent, why is he there at all? Poets keep pushing at the door of this play and that duplication must be saying something about the contested role of poetry in a political play. In a play self-consciously about interpretation, Cinna the poet and his unnamed colleague draw attention to the role of poetry in political conflicts past and present: the aftermaths of both the assassination of Julius Caesar and the declaration of literary censorship in the Bishops' Ban.

CHAPTER 11

Hamlet

Hamlet is Shakespeare's most filmed play, from Laurence Olivier's claustrophobic black-and-white Elsinore (1948) to Michael Almereyda's moodily alienated Ethan Hawke in contemporary corporate New York (2000). Asta Nielsen played a secretly female Hamlet on film in 1921 (Horatio gets a bit of a shock when he inadvertently grabs the dying Hamlet's breasts and suddenly recalibrates his feelings for his fellow student); the politics of Kashmir shape Vishal Bhardwaj's adaptation as *Haider* (2014); and even Disney's *The Lion King* (1994) draws on this most famous of stories. One of my favourites is the avant-garde film directed by Celestino Coronado in 1976. Coronado went on to be a significant dancer, choreographer and theatre-maker, but this surreally inventive adaptation of *Hamlet*, made on a shoestring for his Royal College of Art diploma portfolio, has been unfairly overlooked. Even its casting is provocative. A young Helen Mirren plays both Gertrude and Ophelia. Quentin Crisp is Polonius. And Hamlet is played by twins, David and Anthony Meyer, who also play Laertes. Hamlet's doubts and uncertainties are magnified into a literally split personality: one Hamlet excoriates Gertrude's faithfulness while the other tries to suckle her breast, and in the final duel with Laertes it is clear that Hamlet is fighting against a part of himself.

If this all seems a bit of pretentious art-school campery (it is too, and nothing wrong with that), like all worthwhile adaptations it sends us back to the play anew. For there were always two Hamlets in *Hamlet*. Not quite the cloven prince literalized by the Meyer brothers, but Shakespeare's play significantly duplicates his Hamlets by giving the dead king and his troubled son the same name. The first Hamlet we hear about in the play is not the young prince but the former monarch, 'our valiant Hamlet' (1.1.83). This Hamlet is already slain when the play begins, a dead man who will not lie down: 'through the ghost of the unquiet father the image of the un-living son looks forth', as James Joyce put it in *Ulysses*. The guards on the castle battlements who encounter an apparition 'In the same figure like the King that's dead' (1.1.39) decide that one person in particular needs to know of this. Horatio reassures them:

> Let us impart what we have seen tonight
> Unto young Hamlet; for upon my life,
> This spirit, dumb to us, will speak to him.
>
> (1.1.150–52)

Hamlet, our Hamlet, the Hamlet we imagine the play is named after, is actually 'young Hamlet' – Hamlet 2, Hamlet Jr. His name requires a modifier to avoid confusion. He bears the name of a dead man. His very identity is caught up in the past. This apparently incidental decision by Shakespeare, to give father and son a shared name, turns out to open up a retrospective cast to this most modern-seeming of plays.

To call *Hamlet* a nostalgic play or a play preoccupied by the past may seem perverse, given the many, many ways it has seemed to capture Shakespeare at his most modern. For Sigmund Freud and for Karl Marx, Shakespeare was the textual exemplar for their theories of psychological and economic modernity. Big-hitting philosophers like Lacan, Nietzsche and Adorno have all used Hamlet to theorize modern selfhood, even as T. S. Eliot's Prufrock declared 'I am not Prince Hamlet.' In *Shakespeare Our Contemporary*, the Polish theatre director Jan Kott imagined a black-sweatered Hamlet reading Sartre and Beckett. Since a bewigged David Garrick played Hamlet to delighted eighteenth-century audiences (everyone wore wigs, so he was effectively in contemporary dress, but Garrick's had a hidden mechanism to stand Hamlet's hair upright in fear at the Ghost's entrance), every age has re-costumed Hamlet himself as a modern individual, from a studenty David Warner in long stripy scarf at Stratford-upon-Avon in the 1960s to David Tennant in jeans and Converse sneakers in 2009. Hamlet's soliloquies have come to represent the ultimate articulation of a fraught, reflective consciousness: modern man captured in the process of emotional and intellectual formation. We are so used to seeing a *Hamlet* that anticipates modernity, a play that is more popular and more appreciated four centuries after its composition than it ever was at the time, that it is hard for us to register the ways it is deeply retrospective in tone. But the name Hamlet is key to a more backward-looking play caught up in its own history. For a play that has had so vital an afterlife, that's to say, *Hamlet* itself is morbid and memorial, and the name Hamlet registers that pull to the past.

As so often, Shakespeare takes his names from his sources. Although some of the sources for *Hamlet* are obscure – scholars disagree about a so-called 'Ur-Hamlet', a lost earlier version of this play – we do know that Shakespeare read a history of the Danes by Saxo Grammaticus. There he found the story of a prince who feigns madness after his uncle kills his father, who is sent to Britain and who returns to take revenge on the king. And we know that the name Amleth comes from this story, probably via a French translation in the 1570s. If the name Hamlet comes from the play's sources, one thing that is distinctive about Shakespeare's naming in the play is the doubling of the name Hamlet for both the dead father and the living son. In none of the sources is the burden of the past, the psychic overlap between the two generations, so stressed as in the play. In Saxo Grammaticus, for instance, Amleth's father is called Horwendil. Shakespeare repeats the technique to be sure we've noticed: Hamlet's military foil Fortinbras is another avenging son of a heroic dead father who shares the same name. So good, as Gerard Kenny famously sang of New York, they named him twice.

The play's first Hamlet is a ghost (and perhaps the one the play is really named after). On encountering that ghost for the first time, Hamlet addresses it with his own name: 'I'll call thee Hamlet, / King, father, royal Dane. O answer me!' (1.4. 25–6). The ghost jerks the beginning of the play backwards. From the outset, *Hamlet* is preoccupied with the past. In the tense opening, Marcellus asks 'has this thing appeared again tonight?' (1.1.19): that word 'again' tells us the ghost is doubly reiterative, symbolizing the recurrent past. Horatio informs us that the ghost represents a more martial Denmark, and a nostalgic world of sledding Polacks and other feats of derring-do. But the later description of the ghost as he lay sleeping in his orchard evokes a kind of biblical golden age. This prelapsarian past is for ever lost by Cain's murder of his brother Abel, as Claudius acknowledges when he tries unsuccessfully to pray in the middle of the play: 'It hath the primal eldest curse upon't, / A brother's murder' (3.3.37–8). Old King Hamlet, then, symbolizes the past: familial, political, cultural and temporal. And his appearance pulls Hamlet away from the future and into the past.

In the play's second scene we see two young men setting off on different courses. Laertes, son of Polonius, requests permission to go to France and is granted it (his father imagines him spending his time 'drinking, fencing, swearing, / Quarrelling, drabbing [whoring]' (2.1.26–7)); Hamlet, by contrast, allows himself to be persuaded to stay at home rather than return to university, and in that decision he fixes himself as for ever a child. 'For your intent / In going back to school in Wittenberg, / It is most retrograde to our desire' (1.2. 112–14). Hamlet's arrested development is a continued theme. In Gregory Doran's Royal Shakespeare Company production of 2009 with David Tennant as Hamlet, the ghost's appearance in Gertrude's chamber is played as an affectionate family portrait, with parents sitting companionably on the bed and their son arranged happily at their feet, more like a child than a young adult. The ghost's repeated encouragement to 'Remember me' (1.5.91) is a command for his son to join him in the past. The trap is that the play's own structure has made clear that the past is unreachable, a place beyond the compass of the play, where the murder of the old king took place before the play started.

In sharing a name, father and son cannot be entirely distinguished: young Hamlet cannot form an autonomous identity for himself. This psychological overlap has sometimes been literalized in stage productions: one review of Richard Eyre's 1980 production at the Royal Court in London described how 'Jonathan Pryce, in what is effectively his first soliloquy, plays both sides of the conversation between Hamlet and his dead father, adopting for the latter a deep voice wrenched from his stomach'; Laurence Olivier also voiced the ghost's lines in his 1948 film. Such doublings suggest the strong psychic overlap between dead father and troubled son. The repeated names link *Hamlet* more closely than we often allow to the concerns with political and psychological succession that characterize Shakespeare's history plays of the 1590s. In many ways *Hamlet*'s closest canonical neighbour is not the later tragedies of *Othello* and *Macbeth* but the earlier 1 *Henry IV*, another story of a prince trying to escape the burden of a father with whom he shares the same name (and we can see that that play goes to considerable onomastic lengths to hide the fact that the prince – variously dubbed Hal or Harry – is, like his father, 'Henry', a name he can only really inherit, like the crown itself, on the death of his father).

So when Claudius tells Hamlet that mourning for his father's death is unnatural, he is not merely callous. He articulates a quite different worldview, a different understanding of teleology. Claudius looks forward, Hamlet backward. Nature's 'common theme / Is death of fathers' (1.2.103–4), he tells the black-clad prince – 'you must know your father lost a father; / That father lost, lost his' (89–90). Stuff happens, time passes, the son outlives the father. Get over it. Move on. Claudius's pragmatic approach to succession and progress is quite different from the impeded and circular 'Remember me' which structures Hamlet's role in the play. Hamlet's actions tend towards undoing and negation rather than doing or progress: he breaks off his relationship with Ophelia; he does not return to university; he wants the players to perform an old-fashioned speech 'if it live in your memory' (2.2.450–51); his primary attachments are to the dead not the living. The play's iconic visual moment – Hamlet facing the skull of the jester Yorick – epitomizes a drama, and a psychology, in thrall to the past.

Since at least Sigmund Freud's *The Interpretation of Dreams* (1900), the idea that Hamlet cannot make progress in the play has been understood psychoanalytically. Freud's own view of Hamlet as a repressed and 'hysterical subject' who 'is able to do anything but take vengeance upon the man who did away with his father and has taken his father's place with his mother – the man who shows him in realization the repressed desires of his own childhood' gives one influential account of why the play's action is impeded: the so-called Oedipus complex. But there are other ways, also, to see this less as an individual or personal property of Hamlet himself, and more as a cultural one, bound up with the specific moment of *Hamlet*'s own composition.

Part of the charge of this play written around 1600 must have been the issue of succession. Elizabeth I was approaching seventy, and childless. Most people in England could not remember another monarch, but the question of who would succeed her preoccupied late Elizabethan society and theatre, as discussed in the chapter on *Richard II*. It is particularly explored on stage in history plays, and *Hamlet* has some particular affinities with this genre. Shakespeare's history plays interweave patrilineal and fraternal rivalries within the family and state, marginalizing women and rehearsing versions of regime change. Seen in this context, *Hamlet* exists as a belated history play, and a rather apocalyptic one. Mysteriously, Hamlet himself, despite being evidently old enough, does not inherit the throne on his father's death. The play itself does not adequately explain why he is supplanted by his uncle, but in a cultural atmosphere in which succession was such a hot topic, it's hard to imagine that this puzzling element would have gone unnoticed. What unfolds is the self-destruction of a royal dynasty, leaving the kingdom to fall into foreign hands: one nightmare scenario for England at the end of Elizabeth's long reign. Fortinbras marches on Denmark and is able, suavely, and without shedding a single drop of his own soldiers' blood, to enter the throne room and take over. He does so on account of a past political claim: 'I have some rights of memory in this kingdom' (5.2.343). We saw in *Richard III* how little creative investment that play put into its eventual victor, Richard's nemesis Richmond: he wins the battle for the kingdom but barely figures in the battle for the play. We might say something similar of Fortinbras, a figure often, and rather easily, cut from *Hamlet*, and one in whom it is hard to take much interest. The future is hardly presented in *Hamlet* as something to look forward to. As an image of late Elizabethan political anxieties, it's a bleak ending.

Like Elizabethan culture more widely, the play prefers to look backwards rather than forwards: to dare to think forwards, to a time post-Elizabeth, was a crime. Connected to this backward-looking is the issue of religion. One big question about *Hamlet* focuses on what a Catholic ghost talking about a Catholic purgatory is doing in an apparently Protestant play. After the religious turmoil of the middle years of the 1550s, Elizabeth's accession marked the establishment of Protestantism as the religion of England: Catholicism was outlawed and driven underground. Two particular doctrinal differences are often used to focus the theological disagreements between Catholicism and Protestantism. The first is the question of transubstantiation and the physical presence of Christ in the Eucharist. The second is more obviously stageworthy: the presence, provenance and reliability of ghosts. In *Hamlet*, the ghost's description of his imprisonment 'confined to fast in fires / Till the foul crimes done in my days of nature / Are burnt and purged away' (1.5.11–13) describes the outlawed theology of purgatory, just as the ghost's very presence is anathema to Protestant doctrine, which could not allow that anyone returned from the dead. Horatio, alumnus of a distinctly Protestant university in Wittenberg, a place indelibly associated with Martin Luther's radical challenge to the Catholic Church in 1517, expresses more orthodox reformed views. He questions what the ghost intends, warning Hamlet not to follow: it 'might deprive your sovereignty of reason / And draw you into madness' (1.4.54–5). Shakespeare's own religious allegiances have been the source of much inconclusive speculation: we know little about the playwright's own allegiances, but we do know that his father was fined for not attending church (often the sign of Catholic adherence). Perhaps Hamlet, too, is a Protestant son haunted by the ghost of a Catholic father, as the critic Stephen Greenblatt has memorably explored in his book *Hamlet in Purgatory*. Hamlet certainly represents a peculiarly generational predicament for children of the Reformation overshadowed by the Catholic past. The murder of old Hamlet isn't a religious allegory for doctrinal upheaval. That's not really how Shakespeare's imagination works, unlike, say, his contemporary Edmund Spenser, whose epic poem *The Faerie Queene* (1590) begins with the knight Redcrosse encountering the beautiful pure Una, or the true Church, menaced by the monstrous Error, or ignorance or misinformation, and fiendishly impersonated by the scarlet woman Duessa, signifying Catholicism. These ciphers for big ideas are a long way from Shakespearean forms of characterization and circumstantial detail. Nevertheless, something of *Hamlet*'s nostalgia might be attributed to this specific kind of religious retrospection at the end of the sixteenth century.

One final component of the play's thoroughgoing nostalgia is theatrical. *Hamlet* draws extensively on one of the Elizabethan theatre's great blockbusters, Thomas Kyd's *The Spanish Tragedy*: the name Horatio, the appearance of the ghost, the image of a woman running mad, the murder in a garden, and the device of the play within the play all come wholesale from this popular revenge predecessor. We are used to seeing Shakespeare as a creative alchemist turning his sources into treasure, and to appreciating *Hamlet* as one of the undisputed masterpieces of world literature. But these are later assessments: in 1600, Shakespeare's relationship to his predecessors was less effortlessly superior. Kyd's play was more popular than Shakespeare's. *The Spanish Tragedy* haunts *Hamlet*: even the word 'stalking', used of the ghost in the opening scene, is one strongly associated with the particular stage aura of Edward Alleyn. Alleyn was the chief tragedian with the rival company, the Admiral's Men, and played Kyd's central character, Hieronimo. Since Freud, it's been hard to ignore the Oedipal theme in considering Hamlet's own relationship with his parents; thinking about the overbearing theatrical 'father', Thomas Kyd pushes that issue onto *Hamlet*'s relationship with its literary parents.

The play's theatrical nostalgia also looks back further, to the pre-history of the London theatres that were newcomers to the Elizabethan entertainment scene. The court drama of the mid-sixteenth century typically separated out a dumb-show of the action from a formal verse presentation. A play such as Thomas Norton and Thomas Sackville's *Gorboduc*, performed before Queen Elizabeth in 1561, does exactly that: action is mimed and described in stage directions at the beginning of each act, and then the speeches are declaimed. We can see this influence on the dramaturgy of the inset play 'The Murder of Gonzago'. In *Hamlet* the travelling players come to Elsinore and Hamlet shows himself a connoisseur of their performances. They recall together the lost heroics of Troy and they enact a close parallel to old Hamlet's description of his own murder. An extended stage direction spells out in considerable detail the mimed stage action: '*The dumb show enters. Enter a King and Queen very lovingly, the Queen embracing him. She kneels and makes show of protestation unto him. He takes her up and declines his head upon her neck. He lays him down upon a bank of flowers'* (3.2.129). The description continues with the king's poisoning, and the poisoner's wooing of the queen, who *'seems loath and unwilling a while, but in the end accepts his love'*. The play then repeats this mimed action, this time verbally. This dramaturgical split between saying and doing is rather apt for the whole play of *Hamlet*, in which the relationship between speech and action is so famously fraught. More immediately relevant to the issue of retrospection is that the players preserve, in theatrical amber, an older form of drama. In Kenneth Branagh's 1996 film of the play, these professional players are cameo roles for older actors: in a kind of backlist homage to the cinematic and theatrical past, John Gielgud, Judi Dench and Charlton Heston are among the recognizable faces. Branagh offers a modern equivalent for the nostalgia in *Hamlet* for older forms of staging, and a particular elevated and stilted language. The past of old Hamlet and Yorick, or of Priam and Hecuba, or of Kyd and Alleyn: *Hamlet* keeps reinforcing the notion that things were better in the past.

Succession politics, religious upheaval and technological change in the theatre, then, add up to a cumulative nostalgia. Reading the play in this way helps us to see *Hamlet* as a symptom of its own historical moment rather than, as is more usual, thinking about it solipsistically as the anticipation of ours. Hamlet's name connects him to the past: it hobbles him from moving forwards and condemns him to a life shaped by verbs prefixed by 're-': remembering, revenging, repeating. The echoing name Hamlet activates a wider sequence of echoes from which the play's nominal hero struggles to free himself.

One last point. What, then, are we to make of connections

between Hamlet's name and something more obviously intrinsic
to Shakespeare's own individual biography – the idea that Hamlet's name might actually recall Shakespeare's own young son
Hamnet? Shakespeare's twins Hamnet and Judith, born in
1585, were named after their neighbours (and probably god-
parents) Hamnet and Judith Sadler. Scholars have noted that
when Hamnet Sadler is mentioned in Shakespeare's will, his
name is spelt 'Hamlett'. Hamnet Shakespeare died in 1596,
aged eleven. Freud made the connection with Hamnet with
considerable certainty, suggesting that *Hamlet* was written
under the double bereavement of Shakespeare's own father
(who died in 1601) and son. In his approach, as in much else
of his work on Shakespeare, Freud is heir to Victorian notions of biographical criticism. The nineteenth century had
invented a narrative of Shakespeare's plays that was closely
mapped against his perceived emotional life, so that the turn
from comedies to tragedies was a consequence of his own
darkening mood (probably, some speculated, caused by that
minx, the Dark Lady of the *Sonnets*). The character of Prospero in *The Tempest* became a self-portrait. As a corollary,
nineteenth-century biographical scholarship also produced
the so-called authorship controversy – a feeling that Shakespeare's life could not adequately explain the plays and created an interpretative dissonance which logically precluded
Shakespeare from having written Shakespeare (a view Freud
also espoused). Shakespearean biography continues to fas-
cinate us as we try to invent an emotional life for Shakespeare as a back projection from the plays.

So can authorial biography help us with *Hamlet*? Clearly
this is a play preoccupied by grief and by mourning, a play

that looks backwards to something painfully unrecoverable. The idea that Hamlet's name registers Hamnet encourages us to see that lost something as personal, rather than a general mood at the end of the sixteenth century. The gains of this reading are twofold. First, it authenticates the play's emotional landscape by connecting it to familial grief, and second, it helps to humanize Shakespeare, whose apparent abandonment of his young family in Stratford as he pursued his career in London has long been a problem for sympathetic biographers. We do not have any actual evidence of whether Shakespeare even attended Hamnet's funeral in Stratford on 11 August 1596, but the useful idea that his grief produced a literary masterpiece goes some way to excusing him from any accusation of paternal neglect. Both *Hamlet* the play and Shakespeare the writer, that's to say, derive a kind of benefit from the association of Hamnet with Hamlet.

But there is counter-evidence too. From his earliest plays, long before the death of Hamnet, Shakespeare envisages the bond between father and son as crucial. One of his first history plays, *3 Henry VI*, distils the horrors of civil war in a specific tableau described in its first printed edition: '*Enter a Son that hath killed his Father, at one door: and a Father that hath killed his Son at another door*'. Shakespeare's most famous depiction of grief for a lost child comes from *King John*, where Constance laments her son Arthur:

> Grief fills the room up of my absent child,
> Lies in his bed, walks up and down with me,
> Puts on his pretty looks, repeats his words,
> Remembers me of all his gracious parts,

Stuffs out his vacant garments with his form;
Then have I reason to be fond of grief.

(3.4.93–8)

We are so invested in the phantom of Shakespeare's emotional biography that many critics date *King John* to 1596 or later, solely because they think this speech could only have been written after Hamnet's death (compelling evidence about the play proves it was written earlier). Shakespeare the imaginative writer can access grief without the immediate stimulus of Hamnet's death. To elide Hamlet and Hamnet may be to underestimate the inventive, creative powers of the dramatist on the one hand, and to overestimate the claims of confessional emotional writing on the other. Shakespeare doesn't, I think, write autobiography, much as we might wish him to. *Hamlet* gets its emotional punch from the context of late Elizabethan culture, not from the inner landscape of its author. That public context is what has allowed us to reinvent the play so insistently ever since.

CHAPTER 12

Twelfth Night

'If music be the food of love, play on' (1.1.1). The opening line of *Twelfth Night, or, What You Will* makes clear that this is a play all about desire. The central protagonists all yearn, deliciously, for the unattainable. Orsino desires Olivia, Olivia desires Cesario; Malvolio desires Olivia, Olivia desires Sebastian; Orsino desires Cesario; Viola desires Orsino. This chapter on the play approaches these networks of desire via an apparently minor character, Antonio, to help reveal how *Twelfth Night* works and what we might understand by its teasing subtitle 'What You Will'. As with the blurred skull in Hans Holbein's anamorphic sixteenth-century painting *The Ambassadors*, a sidelong look at *Twelfth Night* brings the play's themes into three-dimensional focus. Viewing the play from an angle helps us to see how Shakespeare crafts his plays for the theatre, how he engages with conventions about comedy, and how potential meanings of *Twelfth Night* shift over time.

We first meet Antonio at the beginning of the play's second act, where he and his companion Sebastian look like the convenient final jigsaw pieces needed for its comic resolution. What's happened so far is that we have met the lovesick Count Orsino, who is languorously in love with being in love, rather like the passionate speaker in an Elizabethan sonnet, whom we suspect would actually run a mile if the idealized object of his affections stepped off her pedestal and gave him the eye. Olivia disdains him, ostensibly because she is in extended mourning for her dead father and brother. We have also encountered a shipwrecked woman – let's call her Viola, although if we were watching the play we wouldn't know what to call her (of which more later) – whose brother has been drowned, and who has decided to enter Orsino's service in male disguise. Her male persona, Cesario, has been such a hit with Orsino that he has sent this new servant to woo Olivia on his behalf, but as Cesario reveals to us, he/she is in a difficult position since he/she is actually in love with Orsino himself/herself. The encounter with Olivia complicates things further, as she is clearly attracted to the messenger's assured confidence. In addition to this love triangle, the play has established the tensions within Olivia's household: her strict steward Malvolio has clashed with her fool Feste, and it is clear that her drunken uncle Sir Toby Belch, his friend and her would-be suitor Sir Andrew Aguecheek, and her sassy waiting woman Maria are a riotous comedic problem waiting to happen.

So into this play world – part yearning, part mourning, part wassailing – comes Sebastian, Viola's twin brother, supposed drowned in the shipwreck. It's easy to see why Shakespeare would introduce Sebastian at this point. He is the reassurance of a comic conclusion, a fourth eligibly single character who will enable the triangle of Orsino–Cesario–Olivia to reconcile into two romantic pairs. He is also the embodiment of the fictional Cesario, who will enable Viola to return to herself. After all, Viola's assumption of male dress in the play is rather under-motivated: it is an odd decision for a young noblewoman, shipwrecked on a shore where she knows by reputation a prominent local man, not to send a message saying 'bring blankets and hot soup to the beach', and instead to decide to dress herself in male clothes and present herself as his servant. Such commonsensical exceptions to Shakespeare's plotting are often unhelpful, since his plays are not always, or only, realistic, and, importantly, characters often serve their plots rather than the other way around (see the chapter on *Measure for Measure* for more on this idea). Viola has to dress as a man because otherwise there would be no play: it's the enabling condition for everything else that follows.

But there is also a more compelling psychological explanation for Viola's behaviour. In becoming her dead brother, she keeps him alive, as she tells us later at the end of Act 3:

> I my brother know
> Yet living in my glass. Even such and so
> In favour was my brother, and he went
> Still in this fashion, colour, ornament,
> For him I imitate.

$$(3.4.371-5)$$

If comedy is about the triumph of vitality over mortality, and about life rather than death, which is the proper business of tragedy, then Viola's doublet and hose is the very life-support system for comedy.

Sebastian, then, is a necessary introduction for the plot – but, since his only purpose is to wait to be substituted effectively for someone he looks like (his twin sister), it is important that he be as individually underdeveloped as is possible. He isn't really allowed to be a character, because that would disrupt the comic ending. He's effectively a duplicate, but of the 'right' sex. That makes the question of his companion, Antonio, more puzzling. Since Antonio's role in the play is in relation to Sebastian, he is therefore in a difficult position, as it is their relationship that undermines the attempt to retain Sebastian's character as a blank sheet. It is Antonio who prevents Sebastian from being simply the spare male twin who pitches up to resolve the play's romantic entanglements, and he does that by complicating, rather than resolving, its erotic muddle.

When Antonio and Sebastian enter in Act 2, they are already on the verge of parting from each other. Antonio is the first to speak: 'Will you stay no longer, nor will you not that I go with you?' (2.1.1–2). Sebastian's answer is negative: he needs to bear his evils alone. He reveals to Antonio that he is not who Antonio has thought, but is actually Sebastian, son of the Sebastian of Messaline who was the father of twins, the girl now drowned. Antonio's responses as this story unfolds suggest that their past relationship has been one of equals, but what has now been revealed is that Sebastian's social status is in fact much higher than his: 'Pardon me, sir, your bad entertainment'; 'let me be your servant' (29–32). Sebastian rebuffs him and leaves: alone on stage, Antonio gives a short blank-verse soliloquy. This form contrasts with the workaday prose of the rest of the scene to suggest passionate emotion, and so does the content:

> The gentleness of all the gods go with thee!
> I have many enemies in Orsino's court,

Else would I very shortly see thee there.

But come what may, I do adore thee so

That danger shall seem sport, and I will go.

(2.1.39–43)

This short scene echoes the associations between household service and romantic love that have already been established by the play in the complicated interactions between Orsino and his page Cesario, and between Olivia and her messenger Cesario – and which will be replayed again, more bitterly, when the steward Malvolio is tricked into believing his mistress is in love with him. The intersection of the erotic and the servile in this scene is a striking one. One way to read what's happening is as a lovers' breakup. Listen to Sebastian: don't come with me, it's not you it's me, I still haven't got over my father and sister's death, I'm not the person you think I am. And now the plaintive Antonio: don't you want me anymore? Tell me where you're going, I'll do anything for you, I'm so sorry that I didn't understand how things were for you. No wonder that Lindsay Posner, directing the play for the Royal Shakespeare Company in Stratford-upon-Avon in 2001, had the two men talking as they got dressed across a rumpled double bed.

Scholars have tended to be more cautious than theatre directors, and two related historical trajectories should make us wary of reading the intensity of this scene between Antonio and Sebastian as a gay relationship in the modern sense. The first is the history of sexuality, which suggests that before the eighteenth century, sexual practices did not constitute the identity of hetero- or homosexual (perhaps the twenty-first century is returning to this scepticism). You might do things, but you don't become them: a man having sex with another man is a verb, not a noun. Historians of sexuality tell us that binary models of sexuality, and of identity defined by sexual practice, postdate the Renaissance period. In this way, then, the identity of 'gay' is simply not available in Shakespeare's time. The second important historical context is the high value placed on male–male friendship in the early modern period. Humanist theories of male friendship drew on a long tradition dating back to Cicero, which idealized it in the very terms we would now allocate to heterosexual marriage. For the essayist Michel de Montaigne, the perfect emotional equivalence between male friends far exceeded the pragmatic alliance with a wife. Montaigne described marriage as typically 'forced and constrained, depending elsewhere than from our will, and a match ordinarily concluded to other ends', whereas friendship is a true 'sacred bond', 'a knot so hard, so fast, and durable'. Elsewhere, a short pamphlet on friendship designed to spread this concept beyond the elite designated the true friend as 'an Alter ego, that is another himself'. Shakespeare engages with this prevalent cultural tradition across his comedies (see also the chapter on *The Merchant of Venice*) and in particular in two plays whose titles indicate that their primary concern is with male friendship rather than romantic courtship: *The Two Gentlemen of Verona* and the collaborative work with John Fletcher, *The Two Noble Kinsmen*.

So, Antonio and Sebastian are just good friends. Well, perhaps. It's also true that Antonio's line 'I do adore thee so' is unexpectedly fervent. The word 'adore' turns up again in the play in the supposed letter of Olivia to Malvolio, where it is clearly in a context of erotic love: 'I may command where I adore' (2.5.103). Sir Andrew Aguecheek's poignant recollection 'I was adored once, too' (2.3.175) (Shakespeare is brilliant at these glimpses of backstory that make even minor or two-dimensional characters resonate with emotional possibilities) follows Sir Toby's acknowledgement that Maria is 'one that adores me' (173–4), again implicating the word with romantic or erotic love. A glance at Shakespeare's use of this word across his works – via an online text search or a print concordance – makes clear that it has two possible connotations: religious devotion or idealized romantic love. So Antonio's language has connotations of *eros* rather than *philia* – useful Greek terms distinguishing erotic love from deep friendship. For some critics it has been self-evident that Sebastian does not, could not, requite these feelings, perhaps based on the rather unimaginative assumption that a man who willingly marries a woman could not possibly also desire another man. But the play itself is not so sure.

Let's look at Antonio and Sebastian again, this time in Act 5. A lot has happened between their initial leave-taking scene and this reunion. Entering the stage to clear up the misapprehension that Olivia has married Cesario and that Cesario has beaten Sir Toby (in both cases it is not Viola but Sebastian who is responsible), Sebastian addresses his new bride formally and courteously: 'I am sorry, madam, I have hurt your kinsman' (5.1.206). He then ignores Viola, and turns to greet Antonio in altogether more enthusiastic terms: 'Antonio! O my dear Antonio, / How have the hours racked and tortured me / Since I have lost thee!' (215–17). So why would this be important? Well, it's important because it is unnecessary. Antonio has a very small number of lines in the play and appears in just four scenes. In two of these, comprising about three-quarters of his lines, he is with Sebastian, expressing his love for him and giving him money. In his other two scenes, Antonio serves to unravel the plot of the two twins. His intervention when Sir Andrew is reluctantly duelling with Viola in the mistaken belief that she is Sebastian, and his subsequent arrest when he asks Viola for his purse back, are the means by which the play world comes slowly to unpick the confusion caused by the presence of the two twins. It is Antonio addressing her angrily as Sebastian that gives Viola the first wonderful intimation that perhaps her brother is not dead after all. So Antonio does have a role in the plot, but his passion for Sebastian is quite unnecessary and in excess of that role. If Shakespeare often puts plot before character, here we have something different. Antonio is a character not really needed by the plot.

Except, that is, thematically. Antonio's desire for Sebastian resonates with Orsino's for Cesario and with Olivia's for Viola, which is to say that however hard we might want to try, it is hard fully to straighten out this play and reconcile it to the conventional drive towards heterosexual marriage. In this light, the play's tongue-in-cheek subtitle, *or, What You Will*, has a decidedly saucy ring to it: anything goes, whatever you like, every which way – or, as the beautifully ambiguous ending of Billy Wilder's analogous cross-dressing film *Some Like It Hot* (1959) has it, 'nobody's perfect'. Critics have tried hard to suggest that Orsino is attracted to Cesario's obscured femininity: 'thy small pipe / Is as the maiden's organ, shrill and sound, / And all is semblative a woman's part' (1.4.32–4). In this interpretation, when Viola is revealed at the play's conclusion, there is a kind of relieved recognition. This is the take we get in Trevor Nunn's highly enjoyable film of the play (1996), where Toby Stephens as Orsino and Imogen Stubbs as Viola/Cesario find themselves ineluctably drawn together, almost kissing during one of Feste's songs, before Orsino pulls back, bewildered at his own homoerotic desire. Finding out Viola is a woman reconciles his feeling of erotic dissonance: so that's why he fancied her – or him.

Of course, in a modern film in which Viola is played by Imogen Stubbs there is a reassuring gender stability throughout: we all know that Cesario is really ultimately female because 'he' is played by a woman, and thus the character of Viola is always in evidence. Not so on the Elizabethan stage where there was no underlying physical femininity to sort out the play's queer moments. All parts were played by men, so underneath Cesario's pretence of maleness is – uh-oh – real maleness: the body of the young male actor underwrites not Viola's femininity but the authentic masculinity of Cesario. Within the fiction of the play, it's the male Cesario that is the pretence, but on the all-male stage, the female character of Viola seems the unreal one. We get only a few minutes of the shipwrecked Viola in 1.2, and for the rest of the play we see 'her' entirely in male disguise. No one, until her reunion with Sebastian at the end of the play, knows her name, and so watching the play we would have no female identity to attach to her. Even at the denouement she does not reappear as a woman, and her lover Orsino seems happy to continue to address her as 'his fancy's queen' Cesario (5.1.384).

But even if we are convinced, or prefer to believe, that Orsino falls for a woman underneath unconvincing male disguise, that can't help us with Olivia, who also does. Or rather, it moves the frisson of same-sex desire across, mobilizing the relationship between the two women – or even the two male actors playing women – as a further instance of homoerotic attraction. And just as looking at the word 'adore' across Shakespeare's works helped to pin down its meanings, so too we might look at his use of the name Antonio – used in *The Merchant of Venice* to name another man whose primary emotional attachment is to another man to whom he gives money and whose marriage he too witnesses in conclusion. Something of Antonio in *Twelfth Night* echoes with this earlier picture of male friendship, that 'sacred bond', in Montaigne's terms, that is structurally and affectively opposed to heterosexual marital coupling, yet is co-opted to bring about that romantic conclusion.

Sexual transgression, then, is part of *Twelfth Night*'s queer comedy, and Antonio's role enables us to see that more clearly, making it harder to dismiss or de-authenticate the play's other expressions of same-sex desire. The name of the Southwark tavern Shakespeare has transplanted to Illyria is irresistible in this context: the relationship between Antonio and Sebastian is, for romantic comedy, the room in the Elephant, their lodging symbolizing an alternative homoerotic landscape.

Antonio's role in Act 5 also helps identify the way endings function in Shakespearean comedy. In a useful summary of the differences between comedy and tragedy, Jacobean playwright and theatrical apologist Thomas Heywood described them in these terms: 'Tragedies and comedies . . . differ thus: in comedies, *turbulenta prima, tranquilla ultima*; in tragedies, *tranquilla prima, turbulenta ultima*: comedies begin in trouble and end in peace; tragedies begin in calms and end in tempest.' It's all about how things end, Heywood diagnoses: in comedy, the so-called happy ending is constitutive. For Shakespeare (if not in life generally), that happy ending is in multiple marriages, a truism that he mocks in his arch, self-conscious comedy *Love's Labour's Lost* by ending with marriages deferred, by the women, for a year:

> Our wooing doth not end like an old play.
> Jack hath not Jill. These ladies' courtesy
> Might well have made our sport a comedy.
>
> (5.2.860–62)

Twelfth Night is clearly heading towards ending in marriage, with Olivia and Sebastian, Orsino and Cesario, and even Maria and Toby paired off 'in recompense' (5.1.361) for her work in writing Malvolio's trick letter. But alongside these couples, the play is more than usually concerned with bringing into its long final scene the characters for whom no such ending is possible. It is very noticeable in *Twelfth Night* that not everyone gets a happy ending, and the particular prominence of these outsiders has identified the play as markedly dark, postfestive, heading towards the so-called problem plays that Shakespeare was to write over the next two or three years (see the chapter on *Measure for Measure* for more on this subgenre).

Most prominent of these anti-comic figures is, of course, Malvolio. The steward's worldly aspiration to marry Olivia, mercilessly exploited by Maria's hoax penmanship, is depicted in unforgiving detail. Malvolio's fantasy aligns possession of his mistress with possession of a range of high-status consumer goods indicative of luxury and breeding: a daybed, a branched velvet gown (Elizabethan sumptuary laws meant that the wearing of velvet was forbidden to all but the highest echelons of society) and that latest miniaturized technological Renaissance gizmo, a watch. The letter supposedly from Olivia explicitly incites these dreams of social mobility in its encouraging formula: 'Some are born great, some achieve greatness, and some have greatness thrown upon them' (5.1. 367–8): 'great' here means 'of persons: eminent by reason of birth, rank, wealth, power, or position; of high social or official position'. Amid all the playfulness around sexual identity, therefore, Malvolio's transgression is a different and more dangerous one. He is roundly punished for his dreams of social elevation. The play moves from the ritual hilarity of his humiliation in yellow stockings and cross-garters, face contorted into an unfamiliar rictus smile, to the terrifying prison, via one of my favourite jokes in all of Shakespeare. Concerned that he must be ill, Olivia asks solicitously: 'Wilt thou go to bed, Malvolio?', to which he replies with brilliantly inappropriate gusto: 'To bed? Ay, sweetheart, and I'll come to thee' (3.4.27–9). But the laughter becomes crueller. When Feste visits the imprisoned Malvolio to try to persuade him he is mad, the joke seems, perhaps, to have gone too far. Malvolio's return, swearing to be 'revenged on the whole pack of you' (374), acknowledges the way the community, including the theatre audience, have turned on him and his ambition. 'What You Will' takes on a more savage air of communal violence. No such punishment, of course, is handed down for sexual, rather than social, transgression. Viola is the only person at the end of the play who really gets what she wants, and is therefore rewarded for her male disguise. It's a good reminder that, for all the outcry it caused among contemporary moralists, playing with gender is less fraught on the Shakespearean stage than playing with status or rank.

Malvolio is one prominent outsider in the play's conclusion, but there are others. Feste, the fool, is also outside the unions that structure the ending of the comedy. He provides a melancholy epilogue in the form of a song about 'the rain it raineth every day' (5.1.388), but then Feste has been an outsider throughout, an observer of events rather than a participant. But most interesting, and most alienated from the comic denouement because he has so few lines to speak, is Antonio. Antonio has his longest speech of the play in Act 5 when he expresses the pain of his betrayal by Sebastian – a 'most ingrateful boy' (73) who has repaid him for saving his life with rejection, 'false cunning' (82). He directs the speech mistakenly to Viola, but that doesn't neutralize its wounded power. Then, spent, he looks on as the plots unravel. In three hundred lines, or about twenty minutes' stage time, he has only four further lines.

Here it's useful to think practically about logistics. Employing an actor to do so little could seem rather extravagant. Analyses of the casting of Shakespeare's plays suggest fourteen actors could play *Twelfth Night*. Three of these men would double two or more smaller roles, but Antonio's part cannot easily be doubled, because he is present in the final scene, which requires twelve actors on stage at once. So while he doesn't say much, his presence has real dramaturgical costs. In other plays doubling is used efficiently to make full use of the company personnel, sometimes requiring some adjustment to the plot for practical purposes. The Fool in *King Lear*, for instance, disappears without comment in the play, most likely because he is needed for another role, probably Cordelia; at the end of *As You Like It*, Duke Frederick never arrives for the showdown in the forest, probably because the actor playing him is already present as another character, Duke Senior. For Shakespeare, a playwright who uniquely in this period wrote all his plays for a stable company of known actors, the drafting of Antonio's role looks somewhat inefficient. The only logical explanation is that Antonio's silent presence in this final scene is crucially important.

Silences in plays are easy to miss on the page. It is easy to forget who is present in the scene if they are not speaking. But on the stage, silences are impossible to ignore: the actor is still full of meaning. Actors act even when – especially when – not speaking. Elsewhere in Shakespeare's plays there are some important silences that have become critical cruxes: Silvia's response to Valentine at the end of *The Two Gentlemen of Verona* when he offers her up to the rapey Proteus; Isabella's silence after the Duke proposes marriage to her at the end of *Measure for Measure*; the failure of another Antonio, this time in *The Tempest*, to reply to Prospero's overture of forgiveness. How Antonio should behave in this scene is worth thinking about: is he attentive? jilted? well-wishing? angry? sad? Shakespeare leaves us no stage directions as clues, but he's put the character there for a reason.

Northrop Frye, an important structuralist critic of

Shakespeare's plays who brings out their mythic contours and parallels, notes that the end of comedy is always tinged with something darker: 'This sense of alienation, which in tragedy is terror, is almost bound to be represented by somebody or something in the play . . . We seldom consciously feel identified with him, for he himself wants no such identification: we may even hate or despise him, but he is there.' It seems a good description of the indefinite Antonio in this scene: present, not inviting conspiracy or identification (no scripted asides, for example), again monitoring the genre boundary. Just as in saving Sebastian from the waves he enables the plot to resolve, so here he becomes the figure of alienation whose presence, according to Frye, secures the comedy.

Antonio, then, is a character who seems unnecessary, even extravagant in theatrical terms, but turns out to do important thematic and structural work for *Twelfth Night*. His presence at the end of the play gives a different, oblique perspective on its resolution, and his irreconcilability into the married world of the finale complicates *Twelfth Night*'s movement from queer to straight, from homoeroticism to heterosexuality. His is the desire that cannot be contained in the marital conclusions typical of romantic comedy. The seventeenth-century diarist and theatregoer Samuel Pepys grumpily thought the play 'silly' and 'not related at all to the name or day', but he was missing something important. Although it doesn't address it directly, the play is named for the last day of the Christmas festivities, and there's something wistful about the ending, a sense that the party is over, rather than, like the marriages, just beginning. 'The clock upbraids me with the waste of time' (3.1.129), Olivia notes as she hurtles through her heady interview with the beautiful Cesario. The play's conclusion calls time – almost – on the erotic alternatives with which it keeps flirting. But, as Antonio witnesses, it is a bittersweet conclusion, shot through with losses as well as gains.

Measure for Measure

'That Shakespear made a wrong Choice of his Subject, since he was resolved to torture it into a Comedy, appears by the low Contrivance, absurd Intrigue, and improbable Incidents he was obliged to introduce, in order to bring about three or four Weddings, instead of one good Beheading, which was the Consequence naturally expected.' Charlotte Lennox, one of the earliest female commentators on Shakespeare, did not like *Measure for Measure* at all. In her *Shakespear Illustrated* of 1753, she condemned its contrived plot, which had no purpose 'but to perplex and embroil plain Facts, and make up a Riddle without a Solution' that was ultimately 'absolutely defective in a due Distribution of Rewards and Punishments'. The idea that the subject matter of the play – enforced, commodified and otherwise transgressive sex – was unsuited to a comedy and could be effortfully reconciled into this shape only by torture is a recurrent theme in the reception of *Measure for Measure*. Ending in marriage, this play may look like a duck but doesn't quite quack like one: what sort of play is it, then?

There's an easy answer to this question. It's a comedy. *Measure for Measure* was not published at the time of its first performances in the early Jacobean period, and had to wait until the posthumous collected edition of Shakespeare's plays in

1623. Among other innovations, this volume divides the plays into three genres: its title is *Mr William Shakespeare's Comedies, Histories & Tragedies*. *Measure for Measure* is listed among the comedies, and therefore for its first readers it was clearly generically allocated. Read within this framework, its allegiances are clear: like *Twelfth Night* or *A Midsummer Night's Dream*, *Measure for Measure* concludes with multiple marriages; like *As You Like It* or *The Two Gentlemen of Verona*, it has themes of disguise; like *The Comedy of Errors*, it deploys a *deus ex machina* figure to bring about its final reconciliations; like *The Merchant of Venice*, not everyone is happy at the end; like *Much Ado About Nothing*, it deals with high-born families and their interactions with comic low-life; like *The Taming of the Shrew*, it ends with a woman forced, or agreeing, to say the opposite of what she previously espoused. Comedy: full square. But on the other hand, as in *Hamlet*, it has musings about what death might be like; as in *Richard II* and 1 *Henry IV*, it is about the nature of good government. Its locations are not the green world of comedy but the distinctly urban scenes of the prison, the courtroom, the brothel and the city gates. Sex here is most definitely before, and instead of, marriage – not the implied post-play culmination of those romantic comedies ending, decorously, at the newlyweds' bedroom door. *Measure for Measure* borrows, that's to say, from Shakespeare's creative experience across different genres, to create a play that butts up against generic limitations and explores the elasticity of notions of comedy.

To start with, Shakespeare selects a plot that was never comfortably comic. He takes the story of Isabella, who refuses to have sex with the city governor Angelo to release her brother Claudio from prison, from two related kinds of source. The first is a sort of general, folkloric one which appears in many cultures and offers what the formal analysis of myth calls a mytheme, or plot function. The second are more direct sources: a play by George Whetstone called *Promos and Cassandra*; and the English version of an Italianate story by Giovanni Battista Giraldi, usually known as Cinthio, which also provided the source for *Othello*, written in the same year – 1604. The first sort of source is sometimes known as the story of the 'monstrous bargain': sleep with me, and someone – usually a brother or husband – will be saved. In the twenty-first century we might call this out as a #MeToo plot. In most versions of this story before Shakespeare, the woman accepts this terrible choice and does sleep with the governor or authority figure, and in most cases this is not enough to save her imprisoned brother or husband. Often the story ends with an emperor or higher authority coming in and making the bad man marry the woman he has slept with, thus making a sort of reparation for his behaviour. In Cinthio's version of the story, Epitia's sixteen-year-old brother is in prison for rape. This is a crime punishable by death, despite the fact that he agrees to marry his victim. Epitia sleeps with the official in order to save her brother. When this is revealed, the official is forced to marry her, and then she successfully pleads for his life.

We can see in this outline something of Shakespeare's play, but with some key differences. First, whereas Cinthio's character is in prison for rape, Shakespeare makes it clear that Claudio is not a habitual fornicator, and that he and Juliet were engaged to be married, or had even undergone a civil but not a church marriage ceremony (depending on how we interpret his claim that 'Upon a true contract, / I got possession of Juli-etta's bed. / You know the lady; she is fast my wife' (1.2.133–5)). Juliet also makes clear that her pregnancy is 'mutually com-mitted' (2.3.29), not the result of coercive violence, in a scene with the Duke/Friar that seems to have the sole purpose of establishing this fact. Shakespeare's change makes Claudio much more sympathetic than he might have been if he had been guilty of rape, and thus the severity of Angelo's inter-pretation of the law here seems all the more unreasonable. If the job of the deputy is to sort out civic morality and to close down Vienna's brothels, he seems to have picked the wrong case (although Claudio's familiarity with the bawd Mistress Overdone might suggest he is indeed a part of the city's red-light district culture). Second, Shakespeare has made his Isabella into a nun, or at least a novice nun. The extent of her religious scruples about sleeping with Angelo is a key axis in the play. Her strong statement of rebuke: 'More than our brother is our chastity' (2.4.185) has earned her scant appre-ciation from readers and theatregoers. But Shakespeare has deliberately made Isabella into more than a woman of upright moral character; rather, she is one about to devote herself to strict religious principles (this slightly obscures the eth-ical point for modern viewers: whether she is a sex worker or a nun, Isabella surely has our support when she refuses unwanted sex?). Third, Shakespeare develops the charac-ter of the Duke, who, in the disguise of a friar, observes much of what is happening – he calls himself 'a looker-on . . . in Vienna' (5.1.314) – and plots to engineer a rather complicated denouement. In the sources, the Duke figure comes in at the end to sort things out, but has no larger role in the unfolding story. All three of these changes – the substitution of consensual sex for rape, making Isabella into a nun, and developing the role of the Duke – could also be said to bring moral questions to the fore of Shakespeare's drama – and the evidence that these have been introduced deliberately makes it difficult to explain them away as somehow incidental or irrelevant to the plot. In *Measure for Measure*, then, Shakespeare seems to have systematically complicated and darkened the ethical dilemmas at the heart of the 'monstrous bargain' plot.

There's one other significant change to Cinthio's source which bears on the question of genre. Cinthio's Isabella-figure, Epitia, is the main character in the story, and this isn't quite so clearly the case in *Measure for Measure*. Cinthio's emphasis aligns his story more closely with comedy, the Shakespearean genre which is most hospitable to women: whereas Shakespeare's tragedies tend to be structured around male experience, in comedies women take on agency, and their story quest structures the narrative. They use this agency in different ways: in *The Merchant of Venice* Portia bests the Venetian lawyers to save her husband's friend; in *As You Like It* Rosalind escapes her tyrannical uncle and makes a life in the Forest of Arden; in *All's Well That Ends Well*, Helen sets her sights on marrying Count Bertram and follows him across Europe to trick him into bed. That's not to say that women are always dominant quantitatively. In *Much Ado About Nothing*, for example, we may feel Beatrice and Benedick are evenly matched in their verbal sparring, but they most certainly are not in terms of their stage presence: not only Benedick but also Leonato, Don Pedro and even the vapid Claudio all have more lines than Beatrice. Antony out-talks Cleopatra. And while everyone in *The Taming of the Shrew* may feel that Katherine is an exhausting scold, she has only a third of the lines of Petruchio, and fewer even than the servant Tranio. As the Scottish poet Liz Lochhead puts it in her rap 'Men Talk', 'Women prattle, woman waffle and witter/Men Talk. Men Talk': women, and women characters, are often perceived to talk more than they actually do. *As You Like It* is the only Shakespeare play where the largest role is female, although women's roles across the comedies are proportionately much larger than in the tragedies. In *Measure for Measure* the Duke speaks the largest proportion of the lines by far: 30 per cent. Isabella comes next, with 15 per cent; with Lucio, the play's commentator and observer figure, and Angelo speaking about 11 per cent each of the play's lines.

Isabella, then, speaks half the number of lines of the Duke; but perhaps it's more interesting to break these figures down. She speaks much more in the first half of the play than in the second; these proportions are reversed for the Duke, who becomes much more talkative in the second half. Perhaps these are causally connected: the Duke asserts himself by diminishing Isabella. By silencing a previously dominant female character and turning the plot away from Isabella's agency, *Measure for Measure* seems almost to dramatize its own retreat from the conventions of comedy. It moves from a world at the beginning where women characters are vocal and dramatically powerful, to a world by the end in which women are virtually silenced or puppeted by male directors. Isabella changes from the character Claudio calls upon for help with his imprisonment and describes as eloquent, with 'prosperous art / When she will play with reason and discourse, / And well she can persuade' (1.2.172–4). By the end of the play she is forced to read a script effectively prepared for her by the Duke, and then to hear, without giving any verbal response, his unexpected proposal of marriage to her:

> Dear Isabel,
> I have a motion much imports your good,
> Whereto, if you'll a willing ear incline,
> What's mine is yours, and what is yours is mine.
>
> (5.1.533–6)

That Isabella does not answer this proposal in the play's final lines produces one of the most pregnant silences in Shakespeare. The first attested reader of *Measure for Measure*, an early-seventeenth-century Scot, observed in a marginal note to his copy of the plays: 'The Duke takes Isabella to wife', apparently assuming that her consent can be taken for granted. Directors and readers who want a neat comedy ending likewise rush to some gloss or wordless choreography to indicate Isabella's delight at this turn of events. But for others the failure to direct Isabella's assent is a gap that strikes at the heart of romantic comedy, leaving the question hanging that other comic heroines like Olivia (in *Twelfth Night*) or Beatrice (in *Much Ado*) flirt with but ultimately suppress – do I even want to get married? We can read Isabella's silence psychologically as the plausible response to an extraordinary sequence of events, including pleading for the life of the man who abused her, and discovering that the brother she thought was dead because of her own choices is in fact alive after all. But we can also read it generically. She has been beaten as the play's central character, bested by the Duke, and the individual gender politics of their roles can be read out into the genre politics of comedy and tragedy. On the one hand, that's to say, the marriages at the end of *Measure for Measure* affirm one of the prominent traditions of comedy endings; on the other hand, by silencing one of the genre's most prominent characters – the active woman – they seem to negate comic expectations.

Perhaps it's worth pausing to think about what those comic expectations might reasonably have been for the play's first audiences familiar with Shakespeare's own previous plays and those of his company. *Measure for Measure* dates from the end of the sequence of comedies Shakespeare had produced during the 1590s, so theatregoers were probably well schooled in what to expect: interrupted courtship, inadvertent humour from low-born characters, disguise, marriages in conclusion. Fashionable playgoers who were au fait with more modern kinds of comedy (Shakespeare's Never-Never Land comic worlds were beginning to look a bit outdated in the theatre economy of the early Jacobean period) might have been more comfortable with the play's frankly unromantic designation of sex within an economy of civic transactions: looked at in the context of non-Shakespearean comedies of the period, *Measure for Measure* is more recognizable. This is the closest Shakespeare comes to a popular genre of contemporary city comedy, with its cheerfully dog-eared cast of prostitutes, bawds, young lovers, corrupt patriarchs – and, unsurprisingly, modern scholars believe that it was partly written by the master of the genre, Thomas Middleton. City comedy takes some of the fairy tale out of comedy, re-situating it in the contingent and commercial world of getting and begetting, revealing virtue as a commodity and marriage as a business transaction. It also has its own values: acceptance or forgiveness rather than punishment, an awareness that the moral high ground is dangerously vertiginous, that grown-up sense we've all been round the block a time or two, and it's probably best not to ask too many questions about the past. All these are features, and not altogether negative ones, of *Measure for Measure*'s compromised urban world.

But there's an awareness of mortality in *Measure for Measure* that exceeds city comedy, which is often characterized by a sense of the teeming fecundity of contemporary London (Middleton's brilliant comedy *A Chaste Maid in Cheapside*, for example, offers a reproductive frenzy fuelled by a potency elixir). In the middle of the play we get an extraordinary speech from the imprisoned Claudio, urged to prepare himself for his execution for the crime of fornication. Isabella explains that the one thing that would save him, her sacrificing herself to Angelo's demands, is impossible. At first Claudio accepts this advice, but with the realization 'Death is a fearful thing' (3.1.116), he breaks out into an existential cold sweat that continues to send shivers down the play's spine:

> Ay, but to die, and go we know not where;
> To lie in cold obstruction, and to rot;
> This sensible warm motion to become
> A kneaded clod, and the dilated spirit
> To bathe in fiery floods, or to reside
> In thrilling region of thick-ribbèd ice;
> To be imprisoned in the viewless winds,
> And blown with restless violence round about
> The pendent world; or to be worse than worst

Of those that lawless and incertain thought
Imagine howling – 'tis too horrible!
The weariest and most loathèd worldly life
That age, ache, penury, and imprisonment
Can lay on nature is a paradise
To what we fear of death.

(3.1.118–32)

This really isn't the stuff of comedy. All Isabella can proffer in reply is the despairing 'Alas, alas!' (133) and an outburst abusing her brother as a 'faithless coward' (138): no one in the play can begin to engage with Claudio's nihilistic post-mortem imagination. In a world where the central characters are, respectively, a novice nun of the order of St Clare, and a duke disguised as a friar, there is precious little Christian comfort for the disconsolate prisoner. Condemned by his horrified sister for even contemplating a moral recalibration of the monstrous bargain – 'Sure it is no sin,' Claudio ventures, 'Or of the deadly seven it is the least' (109–10) – Claudio wishes instead for death: 'I am so out of love with life that I will sue to be rid of it' (173–4). And although he does not actually die, he never speaks again in the play, which, in theatrical terms, is essentially the same thing.

Stand-up comedians describe an act during which they don't get any laughs as 'dying' on stage. Dying literally, metaphorically and proleptically (in advance), as here in Claudio's prison cell, is a failure of comedy. Claudio's encounter with death at the heart of *Measure for Measure* is a real challenge to the play's generic dues. Immediately, *Measure for Measure* gets to work to get comedy back onto the agenda – and the disobliging shock troops of this generic realignment are led by the unlikely commander, Duke Vincentio.

The Duke is a distinctly ambiguous character. We don't even know his name save for the list of characters appended to the first printed text. We meet him when he is handing over power to his deputy, Angelo, and leaving Vienna in haste, for reasons that are never made clear. He tells his courtiers: 'I love the people, / But do not like to stage me to their eyes' (1.1.67–8), sometimes seen as a reference to the public reticence of the new king, James I. But the Duke has not left Vienna: he borrows friar's robes (he says he will explain why 'at our more leisure' (1.3.49), but that time never comes, at least not in our hearing), and suggests that he has delegated to Angelo the task of reinstating the law which has become 'more mocked . . . then feared' (1.3.27) under his rule. Some part of the Duke's motivation seems to be to test Angelo: 'Hence shall we see / If power change purpose, what our seemers be' (1.3.53–4). He withdraws from the play for much of its first half, reappearing to visit the pregnant Juliet and offer her moral guidance. Before Claudio's great prison valediction, therefore, the Duke's main role in the play has been to make the arrangements for his own absence. But after this point, he is newly revitalized. He takes on the role of ringmaster to the play's ragtag human circus, choreographing its acrobats and clowns, often against their own will, into an uncomfortable comedy.

Immediately after they leave Claudio, the disguised Duke makes his own proposal to Isabella, that she 'may most uprighteously do a poor wronged lady a merited benefit, redeem your brother from the angry law, do no stain to your own gracious person, and much please the absent Duke' (3.1. 201–5). In order to snatch this marvellous victory from the unpropitious moment in the plot, he quickly summons into being a new character: 'Have you not heard speak of Mariana'? (210). Sketching out Mariana's backstory as Angelo's jilted fiancée begins to establish the new coordinates of a comic resolution (rather as the entrance of Sebastian in *Twelfth Night* opens up the solution for that play's romantic entanglements). Elaborate plots of trickery are associated with comedy, and projecting a tawdry scenario in which Mariana will take Isabella's place in Angelo's bed seems a shot in the arm for the reticent Duke, who speaks more and more freely here, when organizing how Mariana will be deployed to resolve the plot, than he has at any point hitherto. Significantly, Isabella is reduced to short statements of assent. The Duke is in the play's next scene too, this time giving moral instruction to two of the play's low-life characters and hearing from the irrepressible Lucio some home truths about his own reputation. Lucio contrasts the upright and cold Angelo, who, 'when he makes water his urine is congealed ice' (3.1.374), with the humanly carnal absent Duke, who 'had some feeling of the sport' (383) and, in a lovely phrase with an obscure suggestion of friskiness, 'had crochets in him' (391). Later the Duke prompts his loyal lord Escalus to describe their ruler, and hears himself judged 'a gentleman of all temperance' (3.1.494–5). At the end of the scene he delivers a curious, incantatory soliloquy of general wisdom and plot summary, seeming, momentarily, to be in an old folktale or nursery rhyme:

Craft against vice I must apply.
With Angelo tonight shall lie
His old betrothèd but despisèd.
So disguise shall, by th' disguisèd,
Pay with falsehood false exacting,
And perform an old contracting.

(3.1.533–8)

The Duke's hyperactivity in resolving the play out of its distinctly un-comic generic doldrums reaches its feverish climax in *Measure for Measure*'s long final act. He runs on and off stage, alternating speeches in his own person and his friar's disguise. He prompts the other characters to their lines, arranges them in scenes and revelations and delivers judgement on their conduct. He threatens Angelo with death, forces him to marry Mariana and then commutes his death sentence; he maintains that Claudio is dead and then reveals him, living and mute; he punishes the loose-tongued Lucio with marriage to his pregnant 'punk', Kate Keepdown (5.1.511); he threatens to sack the Provost; he agrees to pardon an unrepentant murderer on death row. The scene lasts about forty-five minutes in the theatre, and its sheer length and demands on the actor playing the Duke are an index of what hard work it is to get the play back on track. This final bravura effort to bring the play under control has to move it from punishment, abandonment and death (the terrain of tragedy) into forgiveness, reconciliation and marriage (the world of comedy). The Duke's determination to produce a comedy from this generic train crash runs roughshod over his characters. Like Claudio earlier in prison, Angelo resolutely declares: 'I crave death more willingly than mercy' (5.1.475); his last chance for dramatic dignity is to end as the tragic hero of his own play, felled by his fatal flaw of concupiscence. No such luck! He is to take his allotted place, married, in a forced comic ending. Claudio and Juliet are brought together on stage, but given no words to help the Duke's relentless drive to a happy ending. Nor are brother and sister reconciled after their rift in the prison. The pardoned reprobate Barnardine has no words of repentance or gratitude. Lucio strongly resents his allocation: 'Marrying a punk, my lord, is pressing to death, whipping, and hanging' (5.1.521–2); the Duke is clear that his marriage is designedly punitive: 'Slandering a prince deserves it' (523). Charlotte Lennox's description of the play's content tortured into comedy with which we began is here literalized. The conventional ending of romantic comedy – marriage – here becomes the dramatic equivalent of the torturer's rack.

That marriage might be punishment rather than reward is the upshot of the Duke's manic generic stage management. It is an end to the comedy that is indeed an end of comedy. *Measure for Measure* is post-romantic in its unflinching depiction of a disconnect between tone and form. It places un-comic characters in un-comic settings and then works overtime to bring them to a comic conclusion. How much do you want a comedy? Shakespeare seems to be asking, and how far will you go to get one? At the play's queasy conclusion, the Duke attempts a cheerful tableau of romantic comedy, lining up his couples for a final smiling snapshot. But there is nothing to laugh at here: Claudio is silently traumatized by prison and self-loathing; Mariana has committed herself to a man desperate to escape her; Kate Keepdown gets no say at all in being palmed off on Lucio; and as for Isabella – she is abused and manipulated throughout this sequence of reversals and fiats by the Duke, who then tries to coerce her into marriage. Like the contemporary play *All's Well That Ends Well*, the end of *Measure for Measure* shows us that a comedy is more than its ending.

CHAPTER 14

Othello

Interviewed by the apartheid state police about his performance of Othello at the Market Theatre, Johannesburg, in 1987, the black actor John Kani defended a number of interpretative choices in his passionate scenes with Desdemona, played by the white actor Joanna Weinberg. The police chief accused him of piggybacking on Shakespeare to foment 'a communist plot to attack the State's racial segregation policies. You people deliberately broke the Immorality Act on stage, in front of a white audience, who were disgusted by all the love and kissing scenes you put in the play.' Recalling this brave production, directed by Janet Suzman, Kani later identified *Othello* as 'a play that is woven into the struggle for equality in South Africa', and its title character 'one of the most important roles for an African'. He added, 'Even today, *Othello* still makes people uncomfortable.' He located his own particular discomfort with the play in the character of Iago, who is alive and resistant at the end of *Othello*: 'that bothers me, that Shakespeare leaves racism alive in some way'. For Kani, both Shakespeare's play and Suzman's apartheid-era production were on the side of racial equality, on the side of the central couple whose love, temporarily at least, crosses a racial divide. Suzman's was the necessary *Othello* for its time and place, just as the *Othello* burlesques that flourished around abolitionist controversies in early-nineteenth-century England, Paul Robeson's New York performances during the Second World War, and the 2015 Royal Shakespeare Company production that cast both Othello and Iago as black, were the necessary versions for theirs. In its ongoing encounters with changed racial and sexual politics, *Othello* has always been able to transform itself.

One of Shakespeare's most extraordinary claims on our modern attention is the capacity of his plays to anticipate our contemporary worldview. To some extent, of course, this is confirmation bias: we are taught that Shakespeare is humanely and timelessly relevant and therefore we are primed to discover it in his works. But it also seems to be an intrinsic quality of his opaque characterization, capacious plotting and ambiguous poetry. Shakespeare's gappy dramaturgy appears to allow a particular space for us, now, with our current concerns hatched in a world far from the narrow London streets and wooden stage boards of his early modern imagination. This sense of a Shakespeare 'not for an age', as his contemporary Ben Jonson confidently predicted in 1623, 'but for all time' has done much to reify Shakespeare's contemporary reputation as a prophet of our age. It also suggests that in part Shakespeare's appeal is a narcissistic one, reflecting back to us our own anxieties and preconceptions. Shakespeare appeals to us because it is about us. This mirror model of relevance can overemphasize empathic similarity over historical distance. *Othello* is a vivid example of this tendency. Because attitudes to race, difference and belonging continue to reverberate across our cultures, *Othello* has been subject to extraordinarily divergent interpretations; because the play has been so culturally significant, it has itself become a founding document in cultural difference and racialized identities. It is already implicated in the formulation of the categories and assumptions that we might want to use to investigate it.

Othello is the tragedy of a black man in a white world, persuaded that his innocent wife has been unfaithful to him, and prompted by jealousy to murder her. Recent criticism has been preoccupied by the meaning of Othello's race for the modern academy. Is this a racist play in which a black man is driven to homicidal rage, revealing that his civilization is only skin-deep? Or a plea for a more tolerant society in which Othello and Desdemona's marriage might flourish? Most contemporary critics have been more comfortable arguing that the play interrogates racism and racist categories, and that it shows us an Othello whose race is significant not because it makes him essentially savage, but because it exposes him to the terrible psychic vulnerability of being an outsider. In these readings, race functions as a social construct – an issue for a society rather than a defect of an individual. We might see that Othello's own apparent equation of black skin and moral failure – 'My name, that was as fresh / As Dian's visage, is now begrimed and black / As mine own face' (3.3.391–3) – registers his internalization of racist norms in Venetian culture, a society in which he is initially welcome at Brabantio's house, until he steps over the line and marries his daughter. Characters in the play repeatedly denigrate Othello (the word 'denigrate', not coincidentally, comes from Latin *denigrare*, or 'to blacken'), or describe him in racial terms. It is made clear to him that he does not belong, so the play reveals, and makes us sympathize with, this isolated outsider position.

But the play's dramaturgy is marked by its own institutional racism too. In focusing our attention on Iago, rather than on Othello, it makes us complicit in the Moor's downfall. In giving us, from the very beginning, a clear view of Iago's malignity, it presents as credulous Othello's implicit trust in his ensign: we never ourselves experience that blokeish charm of 'Honest Iago' (2.3.170 and repeated throughout). This means we observe rather than empathize with Othello's 'free and open nature / That thinks men honest that but seem to be so' (1.3.391–2). A voyeuristic preoccupation with Othello and Desdemona's sex life structures the entire drama, from the vividly pornographic image of the tupping 'black ram' presented to her horrified father (1.1.88), to the final scene in the couple's wedding sheets with a bed brought onto the stage. It is striking that every time the couple seem to be offstage in bed together, some plot convulsion is manufactured to disturb them. In the opening scene, Iago's nocturnal rant to Brabantio results in an armed party searching 'where we may apprehend her and the Moor' (1.1.179); news of the Turkish armada requires Othello's 'haste-post-haste' (1.2.37) appearance before the consuls; on Cyprus, a drunken brawl between former friends described by Iago as 'like bride and groom' (2.3.173) rouses first Othello and then Desdemona: ''Tis the soldier's life / To have their balmy slumbers waked with strife' (2.3.251–2). The play is fascinated and disturbed by its own spectacle of interracial sexuality as it homes in on the ultimate object of its erotic obsession, that bed. And although Othello is a much more complex character than a previous

Shakespearean Moor, the saturnine Aaron in the early tragedy *Titus Andronicus*, that play is more able to contemplate the fruits of interracial sex. It's not clear what happens at the end of *Titus* to the baby born of the relationship between the Moor and his white lover Tamora, but it is a sign of *Othello*'s more constrained imagination that some critics have even wanted to wonder whether or not Othello and Desdemona ever consummate their relationship – perhaps with the underlying racist feeling that it would have been preferable if they hadn't.

Let's look back at how Shakespeare structures the first act of his play to show just how problematic the marriage between his Othello and Desdemona is. The whole of Act 1 takes place at night. In the first scene, Iago and Roderigo rouse the sleeping senator Brabantio with coarse revelations about his daughter's elopement. In the second scene, Othello is talking with Iago, who is disingenuously warning him about the 'raisèd father' (1.2.29). A party with lights approaches Othello, and naturally we, like Iago, assume that this is Brabantio's armed posse. But no, it is the Duke's servants summoning Othello for an urgent military conference on Cyprus to which he is 'hotly called' (44). In the next scene these two stories come together: in one narrative, the elopement of a daughter without her father's permission, Othello is potentially at fault; in the other, the attack on Cyprus by the Turkish fleet, Othello is potentially the saviour. A sardonically rhyming exchange makes the equivalence clear: as the Duke tries to cheer Brabantio up after the news that Desdemona has willingly chosen Othello for her husband, he urges him to accept the inevitable. 'When remedies are past, the griefs are ended /

By seeing the worst which late on hopes depended . . . The robbed that smiles steals something from the thief; / He robs himself that spends a bootless grief' (1.3.201–8). The sing-song tone of the couplets is patronizing: the very form of the verse here attempts to gloss the disharmony of the transgressive marriage into neatly aligned pairs. Brabantio's reply is telling: 'So let the Turk of Cyprus us beguile, / We lose it not so long as we can smile' (209–10). If I'm to accept the loss of my daughter, then you accept the loss of Cyprus.

That the elopement of Desdemona and Othello is a microcosm, or metaphor, for a broader geopolitics is hinted at but never developed. Should we see these lovers as caught in a wider conflict not of their own making – a cross-cultural Romeo and Juliet, or a bourgeois Antony and Cleopatra? Is the conflict between Venice and the Ottomans an exotic background for a domestic tragedy about the violent breakdown of a marriage, or is the marriage the crucible for the broader discussion about the fundamental and savage incompatibility of different cultures in the play's imagination?

Shakespeare wrote the part of Othello for the same leading actor who played Lear, Hamlet and Macbeth and numerous other roles: Richard Burbage. An anonymous elegy on Burbage's death in 1619, which plays with the idea that now all his roles have finally died with him, mentions among them 'the grieved Moor'. Othello's passionate decline would have given the virtuoso Burbage a chance to show off his talents: another obituarist observed 'no man can act so well / This point of sorrow'. We know from evidence relating to other contemporary entertainments that various prosthetics were used on stage to create the illusion of blackness, including woolly wigs and face paint. That Othello is racially different from the rest of the cast on the stage would have been an important element of the visual experience of seeing the play performed, and it is also made prominent in the early printed editions, which carry the prominent subtitle or alternative title 'The Moor of Venice'.

'Moor' is a word with dense historical associations. Two meanings jostle. One is geographical: the Moor is an inhabitant of Mauritania in North Africa (present-day Morocco and Algeria). The second, associated but not entirely identical with this, is a more general religious designation – Moor meaning 'Muslim'. Much critical ink has been spilled on whether Shakespeare intended Othello to be understood as an ethnically marked inhabitant of North Africa, like the noble and exotic Arab trade delegation of Barbary ambassadors who visited the Elizabethan court in 1600, where Shakespeare, performing with the Chamberlain's Men, may well have encountered them. An alternative is that the repeated epithet 'black' – Iago's 'black ram' or his sneering toast to 'the health of black Othello' (2.3.28–9) – coupled with Roderigo's description of 'thick-lips' (1.1.66) suggests later racial typing of sub-Saharan Africans. Critics trying to pin this ethnography down often had an ulterior motive: for generations of readers brought up on the implicit inferiority of black people in America and of the indigenous populations of the British Empire, the question of which kind of 'Moor' Othello should represent was crucial to the sympathy we were to feel for him, and thus to the whole notion of tragedy in the play. Arguments that Othello was more the noble Moor of North Africa were implicitly tied with arguments about his sympathetic character; arguments that he was recognizable as a black man, a negro, tended historically to find him less sympathetic. Clearly this tells us more about racial attitudes now than then. It is impossible to pin down what Shakespeare might have had in mind, and also irrelevant: what is striking is the way Othello's race has continued to matter in new and disturbing ways.

Part of *Othello*'s discomforting charge in the twenty-first century is the connotation of Islam, the primary meaning of the designation 'Moor'. There are very few references in the play to Othello's religion, although those there are may suggest that he is a Christian convert. He uses the phrase 'by heaven' (e.g. 2.3.197; 5.2.67), particularly when he accuses his brawling soldiers of having 'turned Turks' (2.3.163), and he bids Desdemona pray before her murder. Iago vows to make him 'renounce his baptism' (2.3.334), and for some productions Othello's decline into jealous inarticulacy is figured as a visible turning away from his adopted Christianity. Laurence Olivier, for instance, had Othello rip a prominent cross from his neck at the point he turns renegade. It's easy to see how this problematic symbolism works: Christianity is associated with self-control, social integration, lucidity, rationality; Islam with madness, isolation and murderous rage. In an essay on the play published only weeks after the attack on New York's Twin Towers, Jonathan Bate saw how contemporary 'battle-lines reinflect those of the sixteenth-century Mediterranean, waging the forces of global capitalism against the imperatives of Islamic fundamentalism' and concluded that 'few literary questions will be more significant than that of how best to interpret and perform this play'. *Othello* has found a new and edgy topicality, as Cyprus again features as a base for Western military action in the Middle East.

Crucial to a religious interpretation of the play is Othello's final long speech, as he is cornered by the Venetian authorities in the chamber where the body of his murdered wife lies on their bed:

> Soft you, a word or two before you go.
> I have done the state some service, and they know't.
> No more of that. I pray you, in your letters,
> When you shall these unlucky deeds relate,
> Speak of me as I am. Nothing extenuate,
> Nor set down aught in malice. Then must you speak
> Of one that loved not wisely but too well,
> Of one not easily jealous but, being wrought,
> Perplexed in the extreme; of one whose hand,
> Like the base Indian, threw a pearl away
> Richer than all his tribe; of one whose subdued eyes,
> Albeit unusèd to the melting mood,
> Drops tears as fast as the Arabian trees
> Their medicinable gum. Set you down this,
> And say besides that in Aleppo once,
> Where a malignant and a turbaned Turk,
> Beat a Venetian and traduced the state,
> I took by th' throat the circumcisèd dog
> And smote him thus.
>
> (5.2.347–65)

It's a wonderful speech, melodiously orientalist in its catalogue of exotica. And it is a rhetorical performance that encapsulates Othello's estranged position as both a Moor *and* 'of Venice', the commander of Venetian forces *and* the un-acceptable son-in-law, the Christian citizen's defender against a malignant Turk *and* that turbaned and circumcised Turk himself. Othello compares himself to distant tribes such as the Indian (one early text here reads 'Judean') and the Arabian; and then turns his dagger on himself as an alien. Thus the play, and its main character, ends on a fissure, an incompatible religious and ethnic split played out on the impossible identity of its central protagonist, who is destroyed by its unbearable cognitive dissonance.

That's all true, but what's complicated is the way this speech establishes Othello as a victim or scapegoat rather than (or at least as well as) a murderer. His dead wife is not mentioned except in the passing metaphor of a discarded pearl, a conventional image for femininity associating it with purity and exchange value, rather than with individuality. Instead, the focus is on Othello. Four first-person pronouns and a breathtaking self-exculpation portray him as 'one that loved not wisely but too well' (5.2.353). This is my epitaph, Othello tells the on stage and theatre audience. 'Speak of me as I am' (351). Keep talking about me. Look, I am the broken hero of my own play. It's difficult to reconcile our sympathies at this point: with Othello, abused and destroyed by a racist society, or with Desdemona, dead at the hands of a man she loved and trusted?

Twenty-first-century feminisms have been rightly concerned with the analytical concept of 'intersectionality': an understanding of oppression and disadvantage as multi-faceted along lines of class, race, sexuality and gender. As you might by now expect, our contemporary *Othello* is there already. The plot of the play shows us different outsiders struggling with their own disempowered status in the majority society. Othello's race may seem the most obvious point of difference, but that shouldn't obscure others. Iago, for instance, articulates his disdain for Cassio on grounds that we might unpick as based on rank or social status. In the highly stratified world of the military, Cassio is 'a great arithmetician' (1.1.18), and 'Mere prattle without practice / Is all his soldiership' (1.1.25–6). Iago, by contrast, is a tough squaddie. A world organized by racial categories sees Othello as 'the other'; one organized by rank – and this sense of personal status may well have been the identity category most significant and pressing to early modern audiences – marginalizes Iago. Both these models of community are closed to the play's other prominent misfit: Desdemona. Taken from her home in Venice to the garrison at Cyprus, Desdemona is isolated and marginalized. Like *Much Ado About Nothing*, this play shows how closely the male characters are bonded by military discipline and experiences. Desdemona herself is thus the final outsider: the play's last terrible scene shows intersectionality not as the property of an individual character but as the shared dynamic of a play that is sympathetically attentive to the destructive internalization of stereotype, wherever it is found. Othello, Iago and Desdemona all struggle to be autonomous selves within the confines of what is expected and assumed about them by others. The flip side of this observation is that the enemy in one context is the victim in another.

At the end of the play, Othello 'smothers' his wife in her bed (5.2.92). This literal violence is the culmination of considerable cruelty imposed on Desdemona's character throughout the drama, which turns her from a spirited and eloquent woman into a passive object in her husband's own tragedy. She goes from being a person to being a prop. And she goes from a Venetian world in which she has her own story into one in which a male narrative, 'of one not easily jealous' (5.2.354), is dominant. It is instructive to see her as a sister to Isabella in *Measure for Measure*, a play written in the same year as *Othello* and sharing the same Italian source material. Like Isabella, Desdemona starts the play with her own voice and her own trajectory; like Isabella, she is steadily silenced by an abusive male authority figure; and like *Measure for Measure*, *Othello* transforms a proto-comic heroine into a puppet for a male story. Shakespeare's other related attempts at the story of male sexual jealousy – in *Much Ado About Nothing* and in *The Winter's Tale* – all recast the narrative as comedy, bringing a woman apparently killed by the unwarranted suspicions of her husband back to life along with his renewed faith in her innocence. *Othello* teases us with a perverse version of this trope. As Emilia forces her way into the bedchamber, the smothered Desdemona revives momentarily to utter a few words of vindication. It is the last gasp of a comic resolution in which the misunderstanding can be rectified and all can be – almost – well. But without any further intervention, Desdemona expires, a tragic victim rather than a comic heroine.

With *Measure for Measure* and *Othello*, Shakespeare seems to be in a period of conscious generic experimentation. Having written ten comedies during the first decade of his career, he is pushing the possibilities of the genre in *Measure for Measure*, and he is also building his tragedy on comic frameworks in *Othello*. There are many aspects of comic structure in *Othello*. Iago is a version of the witty servant, a type from the comic playwright Plautus, and often depicted on stage laughing at his own diabolic cleverness. W. H. Auden called him 'the joker in the pack', a version of Iago played memorably in film by Bob Hoskins: the BBC television adaptation ends with his mirthless laugh echoing through the empty room. Iago seems a figure of improvisatory flair rather than a malign plotter: he uses what the characters inadvertently offer him to weave 'the net / That shall enmesh them all' (2.3.352–3). Part of his attractiveness is his clever plotting, but intricate plotting has tended to be a feature of comedy rather than tragedy. Ever since the eighteenth century, when an early and unimpressed reader called Thomas Rymer was scornful about the 'Tragedy of the Handkerchief', the world of *Othello* has been seen to be domestic rather than cosmic. Even Othello thinks there should be some heavenly anger at the death of Desdemona – 'Methinks it should be now a huge eclipse / Of sun and moon' (5.2.108–9) – but no. There is nothing more or less than this. At one level, despite Othello's elevating rhetoric, this is the tediously ordinary story of a man murdering his partner because he thinks she has been unfaithful: 'Yet she must die, else she'll betray more men' (5.2.6).

Stage-managed intrigues make Othello believe Cassio is discussing Desdemona when he is in fact talking about Bianca; the handkerchief is a comic prop. These aspects align the play's dramaturgy less with the ineffable workings of fate and more with the energetically human interventions of, say, the characters in *Much Ado* who are determined to bring the unwilling lovers Beatrice and Benedick together, or the dropped letter purporting to be from Olivia with which Malvolio is snared in *Twelfth Night*. Elsewhere in Shakespeare and his contemporaries, the figure of the jealous husband, paranoid about cuckoldry and over-interpreting the most innocent of details to corroborate his desperate fantasies of his wife's infidelity, is firmly comic. Act 1 of *Othello* is a miniature comedy of lovers overcoming differences or circumstances to be together in spite of the blocking figures (discussed in Chapter 9 on *Much Ado*). Verdi's opera *Otello* does away with the whole of the first act, beginning instead with the storm which brings the couple to Cyprus – it's a neat interpretation of the opening as an extended storm which, in *Twelfth Night* and in *The Tempest*, ushers in a comic calm. Perhaps this is what the contemporary playwright Thomas Heywood was thinking about when he distinguished between comedy and tragedy: 'comedies begin in trouble and end in peace; tragedies begin in calms and end in tempest.' A father who does not approve of his daughter's romantic choices – that's how *A Midsummer Night's Dream* begins. But all these indicators turn out to be deceptive. This is a comedy that goes horribly wrong. It is a tragedy cruelly created out of comedy's greatest human insight: that the individual is incomplete without their partner and thus forever vulnerable to them.

CHAPTER 15

King Lear

An early performance of *King Lear* is recorded on the title page of its first edition – before King James I at the Palace of Whitehall. On Boxing Day. It's a curiously bleak choice for the festive season: *King Lear* is perhaps Shakespeare's most desolate tragedy. It retells the biblical Book of Job, but without the ultimate redemption that rewards Job's acceptance of the many trials to which God subjects him. It's a perverse Cinderella story complete with innocent young princess and two ugly sisters, but one in which our heroine, rather than being whisked off to the ball, is instead savagely mown down by that pumpkin coach, drawn by mice coachmen of the apocalypse. Shakespeare's story of filial ingratitude and self-interest takes a heavy toll. At the end of the play, not only Lear but also his daughters Goneril, Regan and Cordelia lie dead; so, too, do Gloucester and his son Edmund, and even, apparently, the Fool. It is an unremitting story. In ancient Britain, life's a bitch (not to mention your daughters), and then you die.

Because of this gloomy trajectory, *King Lear* has been an object lesson in attempts to understand the ethical value of Shakespearean tragedy. Just as Terry Eagleton uncovers from the two millennia of tragic theory since Aristotle only the bathos that 'no definition of tragedy more elaborate than "very sad" has ever worked', so too the critical history of *King Lear* circles around the question 'How sad is this play?' Since the earliest recorded engagement in the seventeenth century, readers and critics, including, as we'll see, Shakespeare himself, have been attempting to excavate something positive or optimistic as an antidote to the misery of the play. Broadly, these responses trace three movements: 1) Shakespeare's play is just too cruel; then 2) Shakespeare's play is actually quite hopeful at the end; and thence 3) No, it really is cruel, but so is life. Related to this is *Lear*'s historical place in ideas of Shakespeare's canon. For the nineteenth century, *Hamlet* was identified as Shakespeare's greatest tragedy, as clever, modishly alienated men saw themselves reflected in its cerebral and isolated protagonist. But as the twentieth century unleashed its mad cruelties at Passchendaele, Auschwitz and Hiroshima, *King Lear* insinuated itself in the cultural imagination instead. The play registered as the ultimate modern tragedy of desolation in which, as the Duke of Albany recognizes, 'Humanity must perforce prey on itself, / Like monsters of the deep' (4.2.32.19–20). Changing attitudes to this play tell us something about ideas of tragedy, about what we want from our Shakespeare, and from art more generally. Beginning his book *Why Does Tragedy Give Pleasure?* with this perennial question, A. D. Nuttall traced the shift from art as moral to art as provocation: 'It is now virtually unimaginable that a reviewer of a new play should praise it by saying that it offers solace or comfort. Conversely the adjective "uncomfortable" is automatically read as praise': the newly cruel *King Lear* whispers its siren song of nihilism into our willing post-modern ears.

The earliest sustained critical responses to Shakespeare come when his plays are adapted to the newly restored theatres after 1660 (the London theatres had been shut during the Protectorate of Oliver Cromwell, and were reopened when Charles II returned from Holland to take up the throne). The Restoration period saw a number of Shakespeare plays reworked to suit the linguistic, structural and moral tastes of the new age. What happened to *King Lear* in this dispensation is famous and exemplary. Nahum Tate, Irish poet dramatist, and later Poet Laureate, rewrote the play in 1681 as *The History of King Lear*. Shorter and more cheerful than Shakespeare's, this version notably reworks the ending of *King Lear*. Tate leaves a chastened but restored Lear and Gloucester alive at the end, men who have learned from their experiences of doubting those who truly love them. The two faithful children of these parallel fathers, Cordelia and Edgar, are married. Tate concludes with Lear's invitation to 'pass our short reserves of Time / In calm Reflections on our Fortunes past, / Cheer'd with relation of the prosperous Reign / Of this celestial Pair'. It's easy in hindsight to see that these alterations are partly motivated by aesthetic taste and partly by politics. Tate explained that he had alighted on 'one Expedient to rectifie what was wanting in the Regularity and Probability of the Tale, which was to run through the whole a Love betwixt Edgar and Cordelia'. This also 'necessarily threw me on making the Tale conclude in a Success to the innocent distrest Persons': this new narrative thus conforms to artistic norms of 'regularity' and to moral norms about how 'innocent' characters should be treated. The theme of the king restored to his throne is clearly a major topical theme for Tate, writing in the restored monarchy of Charles II's reign (seeing how Restoration authors routinely rewrote Shakespeare clarifies that his plays are much more interested in dethroning than restoring kings). Although it's become a parodic byword for flat-footed historical adaptations of Shakespeare, Tate's *The History of King Lear*, like all adaptations, is also a revealing form of criticism. He's engaged in a more confident or extreme version of what we all do when we read: rewriting the text as we engage with it.

Implicit in Tate's reworking is the idea that Shakespeare's original ending, in which Lear bears on stage the body of Cordelia and, heartbroken, dies at her side, is unbearable. His amelioration of that conclusion gained its critical stamp of approval when it was quoted by Samuel Johnson in the General Introduction to his important 1765 edition of Shakespeare's plays. Johnson is also offended by Shakespeare's conclusion, which 'has suffered the virtue of Cordelia to perish in a just cause, contrary to the natural ideas of justice, to the hope of the reader, and, what is yet more strange, to the faith of chronicles'. He therefore endorses Nahum Tate's century-old adaptation: 'the public has decided. Cordelia, from the time of Tate, has always retired with victory and felicity. And, if my sensations could add any thing to the general suffrage, I might relate, that I was many years ago so shocked by Cordelia's death, that I know not whether I ever endured to read again the last scenes of the play till I undertook to revise them as an editor.' For Johnson, and for the public, Tate's version was preferable to Shakespeare's, because it ameliorated the shock of the ending. Johnson firmly locates his objection to Shakespeare's *Lear* in the figure of the martyred Cordelia, arguing that Shakespeare has over-stepped the boundaries of artistic and ethical expectation, boundaries reinstated by Tate's reworking. To be 'so shocked' by Cordelia's death is, for Johnson, a reason to abjure the play. For eighteenth-century tastes, Shakespeare's play was too unwarrantedly cruel, contrary to ideas of justice, artistic pleasure and historical accuracy. The answer to that old chestnut 'Why does tragedy give pleasure?' is, in this case – actually, it doesn't, so let's rewrite it so that it can.

Inevitably, Dr Johnson's discomfort at Shakespeare's *King Lear* was on precisely the grounds that the next generation found so electrifying. Neoclassical preoccupations with 'regularity' and 'probability' and the moral obligation to reward virtue and punish vice were swept away by the Romantic embrace of emotional extremity as a version of the sublime. As Edmund Burke wrote in his 1757 treatise on aesthetics, *A Philosophical Enquiry into the Origin of Our Ideas of the Sublime and Beautiful*, 'whatever is in any sort terrible, or is conversant about terrible objects, or operates in a manner analogous to terror, is a source of the sublime; that is, it is productive of the strongest emotion which the mind is capable of feeling'. That shock that was so unwelcome to Johnson on reading the end of *King Lear* is here elevated into a state of philosophical and physiological fulfilment; the job of great art is to approach that excess of feeling through its encounter with 'terrible objects'. Burke observes that 'there is no spectacle we so eagerly pursue, as that of some uncommon and grievous calamity'. While the theatre retained its preference for Tate's revisionist *Lear*, Romantic readers began to rediscover the delicious terrors of Shakespeare's original.

The German critic and translator August Schlegel led the way (German scholars were the pioneers in the serious reappraisal of Shakespeare's works, giving rise to the claim of *unser* [our] Shakespeare'). For Schlegel, *King Lear* had the sublime natural force of a huge waterfall or thunderstorm. It delineates 'a fall from the highest elevation into the deepest abyss of misery, where humanity is stripped of all external and internal advantages and given up a prey to naked helplessness'. In this play, Schlegel wrote, 'the science of compassion is exhausted'. The English essayist William Hazlitt drew a direct analogy with nature: 'the mind of Lear . . . is like a tall ship driven about by the winds, buffeted by the furious waves, but that still rides above the storm, having its anchor fixed in the bottom of the sea; or it is like the sharp rock circled by the eddying whirlpool that foams and beats against it, or like the solid promontory pushed from its basis by the force of an earthquake'. For the poet S. T. Coleridge, lecturing on Shakespeare as Napoleon prepared his disastrous invasion of Russia, *King Lear* shows how its author had 'read nature too heedfully not to know . . . that to power in itself, without reference to any moral end, an inevitable admiration and complacency appertains, whether it be displayed in the conquests of a Buonaparte or Tamerlane, or in the foam and the thunder of a cataract'. For the Romantics, then, natural forces are key to the scale and effect of *King Lear*. Their critical reappraisals serve as a microcosm of Romanticism's radical revisionism: the idea of the sublime is an absolute value, in the monumental and awesome scale of nature unconstrained by petty social notions of morality and justice.

King Lear has thus transitioned in the critical imagination, from being a play morally and aesthetically deficient and in need of remedy to a play too awesomely big in its vision to trouble with such bourgeois concerns. Asking why Cordelia has to die at the end of *King Lear* would be for Coleridge like asking the thunderstorm if it would mind keeping the noise down a bit.

In this whistle-stop tour of responses to *King Lear* we stop next in the early twentieth century, where critics redrew the play's ethical coordinates to produce a play that was recognizably Christian in sympathy. If for the Romantics *Lear*'s sublime imagination was its own justification, for A. C. Bradley, lecturing at the University of Oxford at the turn of the twentieth century, the effect was more clearly didactic. Bradley argued that the play's ending 'unlike those of all the other mature tragedies, does not seem at all inevitable. It is not even satisfactorily motived. In fact it seems expressly designed to fall suddenly like a bolt from a sky cleared by the vanished storm.' We all desire that Lear should enjoy 'peace and happiness by Cordelia's fireside' – but that is denied him. And Bradley argues that this is because of the play's particular depiction of a wild and monstrous world – and its particular interrogation of what makes its world so wild and monstrous. Noting that 'references to religious or irreligious beliefs and feelings are more frequent than is usual in Shakespeare's tragedies', Bradley discusses the way in which the play forces on its characters the question 'What rules the world?' The play's final outcome, Bradley argues, is 'one in which pity and terror, carried perhaps to the extreme limits of art, are so blended with a sense of law and beauty that we feel at last, not depression and much less despair, but a consciousness of greatness in pain, and of solemnity in the mystery we cannot fathom'.

In a reading of the play which has become almost commonplace, Bradley argues that *King Lear* is thus not fundamentally pessimistic. Rather, it depicts the transformative powers of torment. Because Lear recovers some of his former sympathy, 'there is nothing more noble and beautiful in literature than Shakespeare's exposition of the effect of suffering in reviving the greatness and eliciting the sweetness of Lear's nature'. Bradley suggests an alternative title: 'The Redemption of King Lear', declaring that 'the business of "the gods" with him was neither to torment him nor to teach him a "noble anger", but to lead him to attain through apparently hopeless failure the very end and aim of life'. Bradley interprets Lear's dying words, as he looks for vital signs on the body of Cordelia, as a final 'ecstasy' of 'unbearable *joy*' because he thinks his beloved daughter is still alive. For Bradley, Lear's heart, like that of the parallel 'foolish, fond old man' Gloucester, 'burst smilingly'.

Bradley's book *Shakespearean Tragedy* is perhaps the most influential work of twentieth-century Shakespearean criticism, and this redemptive *King Lear* has cast a long shadow. A more explicitly Christian framework was elaborated in the following decades by G. Wilson Knight, who understood the play's depiction of suffering as part of a 'purgatorial progress . . . to self-knowledge, to sincerity'. For Wilson Knight, 'at the end the danger of evil-doers is crushed. The good forces, not the evil, win: since good is natural, evil unnatural to human nature.' We might demur: it is surely a pyrrhic victory (the good forces may have won but they are also, save the colourless Edgar, dead), but the Christian idea that death is not the final end is also invoked. For Wilson Knight, the play emerges as an allegory of redemption through love, encouraging us to endure life's vicissitudes and to look to a life after death rather than pleasure on earth.

History, though, is at Wilson Knight's shoulder. The critical impulse to harmonize the play into a theologically consistent parable of human salvation was being chased down by a more unflinching eye for human savagery. Post-war critics tended to see *King Lear* less as the antidote to human suffering and more as its instruction manual, a play deliberately and resolutely depicting the terrible emptiness of the modern world. Work by Barbara Everett and W. R. Elton in 1960 converged on the conclusion that attempts to create meaningful and life-affirming understanding out of *King Lear*'s horrors were self-deluding and wilful misreadings of a play which had taken every opportunity systematically to snuff out hope and optimism. And so criticism of the play turned from the spiritual to the materialist.

Jan Kott's *Shakespeare Our Contemporary* (also cited in the chapters on *Richard II* and *Hamlet*) did much to influence British Shakespearean theatre directors such as Peter Brook. The title of Kott's chapter makes clear his Beckettian interpretation: '*King Lear* or *Endgame*'. Kott takes an existentialist view of the tragedy as the absurdist machinations of a world drained of providential intent. If for Wilson Knight *King Lear* is a kind of bad-weather *Pilgrim's Progress*, for Kott it is a blank verse *Waiting for Godot*: inevitably, Godot never arrives, and the time between the curtains is filled with absurdist humour, violence, abjection and grim bonding. Only in the mid-twentieth century could this play, long suspected of being unperformable, actually find its place on the stage, because Kott argues that it has now found its moment: 'neither the romantic nor the naturalistic theatre was able to show that kind of cruelty; only the new theatre can. In this new theatre there are no characters, and the tragic element has been superseded by the grotesque. The grotesque is more cruel than tragedy.' By realigning the play with the grotesque rather than with the morally overdetermined genre of tragedy, Kott is able to develop his view of a deterministic, mechanistic universe: 'In the world of the grotesque, downfall cannot be justified by, or blamed on, the absolute. The absolute is not endowed with any ultimate reasons; it is stronger, and that is all. The absolute is absurd.' 'All that remains at the end of this gigantic pantomime is the earth – empty and bleeding. On this earth, through which a tempest has passed leaving only stones, the King, the Fool, the Blind Man and the Madman carry on their distracted dialogue': the characters of the play lose their individuality to a kind of Tarot card fatalism.

For Kott, *Lear* is a play of the European avant-garde theatre of Beckett and Ionesco. It has found its time in the co-incidence of its ethical and representational modes with the existentialist procedures of mid-century modernism. For Jonathan Dollimore, however, writing in the 1980s, *King Lear* emerges as 'above all, a play about power, property and inheritance'. Dollimore dismisses questions of pity, suffering and redemption as absolutist or religious mumbo jumbo, ideological state apparatuses that repress us. In the end, Dollimore argues that the play endorses Edmund's sceptical

view that 'men / Are as the time is' (5.3.31–2) – that there are
no transcendences, only material circumstances. To focus
on King Lear himself is to buy into an individualist ideology that obscures and mystifies a more social critique. Dollimore is on the side of the sceptical Edmund, scornful of
the old (critical) order and its superstitious investment in
cosmic order ('the excellent foppery of the world' (1.2.107),
Edmund puts it, that 'we make guilty of our disasters the sun,
the moon, and stars, as if we were villains on necessity, fools
by heavenly compulsion, knaves, thieves, and treacherers by
spherical predominance, drunkards, liars, and adulterers by
an enforced obedience of planetary influence, and all that we
are evil in by a divine thrusting-on' (1.2.109–14)). His *King
Lear* decisively undermines any such comforts.

Spending some time on the critical reception of *King Lear*
shows how critics engage with the question of how bleak the
play is on their own historical, cultural and aesthetic terms.
They get the *Lear* they need, rewriting as necessary through
adaptation, criticism and also through performance. But they –
and we – are not the only ones doing the rewriting. Shakespeare
not only takes his source materials by the scruff of the neck in
order to produce this play, he also seems to have returned later
to *King Lear* to tweak, rework and revisit his concluding lines
in particular.

It's often pointed out – Dr Johnson mentioned it in his
disapproval of Cordelia's fate – that Shakespeare's historical
and other sources do not end in the way his play does. As for
most of Shakespeare's works, there is already established a
well-known story and part of what is well known about it is
that it has a happy ending: reinstating Lear to his throne, to

be succeeded by Cordelia. The play's first audiences would probably have been expecting at least Cordelia's survival and perhaps also Lear's too. The wreckage of these plots in the play's hectic final scenes must have been bewildering. Kent's 'Is this the promised end?' (5.3.237) takes on a meta-theatrical quality.

So the ending of *King Lear* is a prominent act of rewriting, and it is itself rewritten. *King Lear* exists in two early and distinct texts, printed in 1608 and in 1623. They are different in hundreds of small, and scores of larger, ways. Over the last forty years or so, *King Lear* has become the Shakespearean test case for the now widely accepted theory that Shakespeare revised his own plays. It may seem strange that scholarship has been so resistant to this completely normal aspect of writerly craft: what author doesn't work on subsequent drafts and then rework his or her writing? (Ernest Hemingway rewrote the end of *A Farewell to Arms* thirty-nine times. 'What was it that had stopped you?' an interviewer asked him. 'Getting the words right,' replied Hemingway drily.) But the adulatory reports from Shakespeare's fellow actors (which are, of course, part of a sales pitch for an expensive retrospective volume of his collected plays, the 1623 First Folio) that 'his mind and hand went together: And what he thought, he uttered with that easiness, that we have scarce received from him a blot in his papers' came to be seen as literal evidence for Shakespeare's divinely inspired genius. That Shakespeare did not revise his works was held as a tenet of Shakespearean editing until the 1970s. But the idea that the two early texts of *King Lear* represent authorial revision is now a commonplace, and most critics surmise from internal evidence that the Folio text represents Shakespeare's revision, probably undertaken in 1610. Interestingly, that means that Shakespeare reworks his play alongside other, happier versions of the ruler and his daughter story, in, for example, *The Winter's Tale* or *The Tempest*. If you look at a modern collected edition, you may well see that *King Lear* is not one play but two, often distinguished by their early titles: 'The History of King Lear' and 'The Tragedy of King Lear'.

Now, textual differences are like lampposts to canine Shakespearean critics, who can snuffle around happily for pages savouring the gamey presence or absence of a comma, or a changed pronoun (watch me). These are generally pretty arcane pleasures for most readers and theatregoers, and so I venture into this territory with some trepidation. Many of the changes between the editions are tiny – and that shows us both how small changes can have significant cumulative effects on the mood of the play, and how attentive Shakespeare was to the detail of his own work. The point here, though, is that the reworking of the 'Tragedy' might seem, on aggregate, to create a bleaker view of humanity than the 'History'. Shakespeare's revisions, that's to say, make his play sadder. One example of this might be the detail around Gloucester's torture at the end of Act 3. Gloucester is blinded on stage in a horrific scene of brutality, leaving him describing his world as 'all dark and comfortless' (3.7.85) as he is thrust out to 'smell / His way to Dover' (94–5). The 'History' has a short but telling sequence that is later cut. In this version, two servants prepare to care for the wounded Gloucester, calling for 'flax and whites of eggs / To apply to his bleeding face', and praying 'heaven help him!' (3.7.99.8–9). It's a moment of tenderness:

not everyone is indifferent to Gloucester's suffering, and servants behave with more decency than their masters. Without this, the play has no corrective to its own cruelties.

It's in the play's final lines, though, that revision really focuses our question of bleakness. There are a number of differences here between the early texts. The later version gives a stage direction indicating that Lear dies on the line 'Look there. Look there!' (5.3.287): what is he looking at, and how does this connect to the moment of his death? Perhaps this conforms to Bradley's interpretation that Lear dies in a rush of joy (but given that Cordelia is not, in fact, alive, does a misapprehension by Lear at this point make the ending of the play more, or less, sad?). The 'History' has no stage direction for Lear's death. We do not know whether he dies of his own volition: he is given the line 'Break, heart, I prithee, break' (5.3.288), in this version, which the later text reallocates to Kent, responding to his master's death. Another speech – the play's final one, in which it echoes the crisis of speech, truth and flattery with which the play began – is also transposed between speakers. The play in both versions ends:

> The weight of this sad time we must obey;
> Speak what we feel, not what we ought to say.
> The oldest hath borne most; we that are young
> Shall never see so much, nor live so long.

> (5.3.299–302)

But what difference might Shakespeare have wanted to point up by changing his mind about speakers: the Duke of Albany, Lear's son-in-law and the play's most senior survivor in the play's first version, and Edgar, the sole survivor of the wronged younger generation, in the second?

So Shakespeare is the first of the long history of literal and figurative rewriters of *King Lear*. His saddest play has prompted extraordinary spiritual, philosophical and artistic efforts to ameliorate its desolation, and the history of those interventions is a cultural history of just what it is we want from our tragic art: comfort, exhilaration or dissection.

CHAPTER 16

Macbeth

Like the English army bearing the cut boughs from Birnam Wood to Macbeth's castle, let's approach *Macbeth* by stealth, and via an intermediary: Robert Burton. Burton was a scholar and writer who wrote a couple of dull academic plays but is best known for one great encyclopaedic work, *The Anatomy of Melancholy*, first published in 1621.

At first glance, Burton's *The Anatomy of Melancholy* and Shakespeare's *Macbeth* could not be more different. Burton's epic of malaise is swollen, epic and digressive; *Macbeth* is lean and streamlined, the shortest of Shakespeare's tragedies. It seems from Burton's own vast library, donated to the Bodleian in Oxford after his death in 1640, that, while he read playwrights, including Ben Jonson, Thomas Kyd and John Webster, his preferred Shakespeare reading was narrative poetry: he owned copies of *Venus and Adonis* and *The Rape of Lucrece*. It's hard to imagine, though, that *Hamlet* and other passionate tragedies weren't on his melancholy reading list. *Macbeth*, in particular, shares with *The Anatomy of Melancholy* the distinctly Renaissance project to investigate the human mind, and a curiosity about the causes and explanations for feelings and behaviours. Burton organizes his compendious treatise in ways that can help lay out the terrain for the more oblique discussion of causation in *Macbeth*.

Burton's *Anatomy of Melancholy* is really a textbook in the modern discipline of psychology. He begins with a diagram of the structure of his book which lays out melancholy's potential causes – what medical science would call its aetiology – in a kind of rudimentary flow diagram. The first causes of melancholy are divided between supernatural and natural, and these divisions branch off into other options: supernatural causes might denote God or the devil ('or mediately, by magicians, witches'), whereas natural causes could be primary or secondary. Primary natural causes are 'as stars', as proved by horoscopes; secondary natural causes could be congenital (including heredity, old age or temperament), or contingent. Burton includes among various headings here: experiences in infancy and childhood, scoffs, calumnies and bitter jests, loss of liberty, poverty and want, and 'a heap of other accidents, death of friends, loss, etc.' Physiological causes of melancholy could be internal, including diet (top tip: keep away from melons and 'slimy fish'), or from outside: too much study, strong passions, anger or ambition. Because Burton's aim is to cover the range of possible explanations and lines of causation, he is capaciously inclusive rather than discriminating and argumentative. A single phenomenon, melancholy exists at the intersection of ancient wisdom and contemporary medical science. This is a worldview in which the influence of the stars, or of witches, coexists with a nascent understanding of hereditary factors in disease, and where diet and other forms of self-medication are alternatives to divine diktat as explanations for illness.

One way of thinking about *Macbeth* is that it asks similar organizational and causational questions. Burton's overarching headings offer three major aetiological clusters. First, melancholy can proceed from the melancholic individual him- or herself, where in some cases it will be fixed or temperamental, and in others contingent and subject to remedy (by refraining from garlic or lustful thoughts, for instance). The melancholic individual is therefore in a position of either passive impotence or of agency: in some cases, his situation can be ameliorated; and in others, nothing can be done. Second, melancholia can be caused by the negative actions of other people. Laughing or scoffing at the sufferer, or inconsiderately dying and causing him grief, or not reciprocating his love, or putting him in prison: again, the melancholic can't really do anything to affect this onslaught. And finally, there are causes that are supernatural or metaphysical in origin, a category that includes God, the devil, and their intermediaries, magicians and witches. *Macbeth* presents a similar convergence of models of causation and agency. Is this a story in which Macbeth, willingly or unwillingly, directs the action of his own play? Or is it better understood as a story in which he is acted upon by other people? Might we see him puppeted by supernatural forces beyond his control? Rather, as in Burton's *The Anatomy of Melancholy*, these possible explanations coexist in *Macbeth*, a play that is more interested in exploring its own competing aetiologies than it is in explaining them.

We could think of this question in a different context. In May 2010 the *Evening Standard* newspaper carried, under the headline 'Macbeth gets away with murder in all-star trial', an article which began excitedly: 'in a final twist that would make

Shakespeare turn in his grave Macbeth and his wife have been found not guilty of murdering King Duncan and Banquo.' The article described a mock trial at the Royal Courts of Justice, with celebrity actors playing the Shakespearean defendants, in which Macbeth's successful defence was diminished responsibility, while Lady Macbeth claimed she was coerced by her manipulative and violent husband. The question of agency, as philosophers have pointed out, is also a question of responsibility and therefore of blame and punishment.

Part of the vivid afterlife of *Macbeth* has been a genre of amateur investigations and celebrity show trials that are implicitly concerned with agency. Who is responsible for what has happened, or, more pointedly, can we get Macbeth acquitted? Often the best hope these legal-critical scenarios can propose for freeing Macbeth is to pin the blame on his wife, or otherwise to suggest that he was not in control of his actions – the grounds of diminished responsibility. A poised story by the American humorist James Thurber called 'The Macbeth Murder Mystery' also plays with this same trope, by reading *Macbeth* as a detective story, the genre in which the question of whodunnit is key. In Thurber's story, an enthusiastic detective-fiction reader encounters the play:

> 'Did you like it?' I asked. 'No, I did not,' she said, decisively. 'In the first place, I don't think for a moment that Macbeth did it.' I looked at her blankly. 'Did what?' I asked. 'I don't think for a moment that he killed the King,' she said. 'I don't think the Macbeth woman was mixed up in it, either. You suspect them the most, of course, but those are the ones that are never guilty or shouldn't be, anyway.' . . .

'Who do you suspect?' I asked, suddenly. 'Macduff,' she said, promptly.

The joke is that *Macbeth* is a story in which, contrary to the generic procedures of the whodunnit, there is no factual ambiguity about responsibility. We know how the murder of Duncan was committed and by whom: we are witnesses – perhaps even accessories – to its preparation and aftermath. Nevertheless, the play contrives, like Burton's treatise, to anatomize, and thereby to equivocate, these apparently straightforward questions of responsibility and causation.

The opening scenes of the play set out these questions in some provocative ways. Shakespeare begins with the witches, and their spooky speech rhythms and their thunder and lightning accompaniment. They seem already to know what is going to happen 'When the hurly-burly's done, / When the battle's lost and won' (1.1.3–4), and they arrange to 'meet with Macbeth' (1.1.7). Does that mean they know where to find him, or are they able to draw him to them? Is their power the power of prophecy, or of direction? Our first introduction to the imaginative world of the play is one in which supernatural agents hold some kind of sway. In the next scene we discover the aftermath of the battle: a bloodied soldier tells the king of the bravery of the valiant captains, Macbeth and Banquo, and the treachery of the Thane of Cawdor. This scene seems to establish a world of human agency: given the same situation – a battle – some men act bravely, and others are cowards, depending on individual temperament. There is further human agency in the response to the battle report. The king orders that treachery be punished (Cawdor is to be executed), and loyalty rewarded (Cawdor's title is to be given to Macbeth). Rhyming couplets attempt to rebuild an ordered world from the moral and ethical debris of war (although the emphasis of the rhyme might seem somehow ominous): 'Go pronounce his present death, / And with his former title greet Macbeth' (1.2.64–5). The first two scenes of *Macbeth*, that's to say, offer diametrically opposed views on the question of agency, as human or supernatural in original.

In Act 1 scene 3 we return to the witches. Macbeth and Banquo enter, and encounter these ambiguous creatures, 'So withered, and so wild in their attire, / That look not like th'inhabitants o'th' earth' (1.3.38–9). Does the fact that the soldiers find the witches, rather than vice versa, suggest that humans are in control, or have the witches set up the encounter as an ambush? The witches prophesy to Macbeth about his current and future greatness: Thane of Glamis, Thane of Cawdor, king hereafter. To Macbeth, the attribution Cawdor is impossible: 'The Thane of Cawdor lives, / A prosperous gentleman' (70–71). But we know, because of the scene we have just witnessed (and with it the dramatic irony so characteristic of Shakespeare), that the Thane of Cawdor has been stripped of his title and executed by the king as a traitor. So, on this point at least, the witches merely know something that we already know. Maybe that makes them seem less powerful – to the audience at least – whereas to Macbeth himself they seem creepily and immediately omnipotent, when, hard on their nomination of him as Thane of Cawdor and ultimately king, messengers from the king arrive to greet him 'Thane of Cawdor'. To Macbeth this makes the gap between prophecy and enactment frighteningly slender, but to us the gap is rather that between command – the king's words in Act 1, scene 2 – and fulfilment – the delivery of that message to Macbeth in the next scene. The witches seem to interpose in a chain of human actions, rather than to direct actions themselves. But on the other hand, we also know something else Macbeth doesn't – that they had already arranged to meet him on this heath. So maybe they are in control after all. In these three opening scenes, then, Shakespeare has set up one major facet of the dilemma of agency the play goes on to explore. Is Macbeth in control of his actions or are the witches?

As so often in Shakespeare's work, what happens to dramatic characters often echoes reflexively some aspect of the craft of writing itself. So, we could refigure Macbeth's dilemma in the early scenes as the question of who is writing this story, and as often, the story has its own prior ideas about where it wants to go. Shakespeare's source for *Macbeth* is the compendium of historical sources collected by Raphael Holinshed as his *Chronicles* (1577) – this is the same source that Shakespeare turned to for his history plays. He has his work cut out to rewrite it as a tragedy. This tragedy is not, as we might expect from his earlier plays on English historical subjects, that of the king, but rather of his usurper: it's the reverse of the story of *Richard II*. In part Shakespeare achieves this by sacralizing the sources from Scottish history. In Holinshed, Macbeth emerges from a violent, dog-eat-dog world of thanes jockeying for position and power: King Duncan had gained the throne through violence, and in turn grown weak; Macbeth's rise, supported by Banquo, is figured as inevitable in a society that has no principle of rule other than strength (Holinshed's Macbeth is also a good ruler for his term, until he, too, is superseded). A striking modern television adaptation called *Macbeth on the Estate* (directed by Penny Woolcock, 1997) began with an interpolated prologue introducing the ageing bruiser Duncan, the gangland boss of the tough estate: this version of the play is much closer to Holinshed than to the Shakespeare version, where Duncan is a holy king and Macbeth a damned regicide. In Shakespeare's play, Macbeth's own description of Duncan's 'silver skin laced with his golden blood' as 'a breach in nature' (2.3.112–13) turns the murder into a crime against natural order. For all his fascination with regime change and weak kings, and the question of what makes a good ruler, Shakespeare is here the mouthpiece for Jacobean hereditary monarchy, for his new king James, and for the Stuart dynasty safely cushioned by two young princes. The sense of moral outrage and disturbance in *Macbeth* is Shakespeare's invention, turning the brutal chaos of the sources into a story of rightful succession interrupted by the terrible ambitious agency of Macbeth.

The residue of these violent origins, though, is still visible in *Macbeth*. The vivid description of Macbeth's bravery at the beginning of the play is a telling example. Even before we have met him, the captain describes his capacity for extreme ruthlessness:

> For brave Macbeth – well he deserves that name! –
> Disdaining fortune, with his brandished steel
> Which smoked with bloody execution,
> Like valour's minion
> Carved out his passage till he faced the slave,
> Which ne'er shook hands nor bade farewell to him

Till he unseamed him from the nave to th' chops,
And fixed his head upon our battlements.

(1.2.16–23)

Quite what this signals, in terms of the rules of military engagement (would you actually expect these battle foes to shake hands or say goodbye?), is unclear, but the tone, that Macbeth is capable of breathtaking, spectacular ruthlessness, is evident. King Duncan's reply, 'O valiant cousin, worthy gentleman' (1.2.24), makes clear his approval: at this point, Shakespeare's Macbeth is, like his bloody avatar in Holinshed, a man who gains power and affirmation through extreme violence. What changes is not that he suddenly becomes violent, but that he turns that highly trained violence against his own sovereign.

We might think that the witches are not necessary to this process of redirection. There are witches in Holinshed but they play a minor role, largely related to prophecy, and an illustration in the *Chronicles* shows them as elegantly dressed courtly ladies, rather than those warty pointy-hatted hags around their cauldron that has become the play's most lasting image. Shakespeare has added to their role – and apparently their presence was so thrillingly enjoyable in stage terms that Thomas Middleton, who is believed to have added some material to the text of *Macbeth*, included more songs and an additional scene with Hecate, witch-in-chief. Perhaps these diverse influences on the presentation of the witches explain their internal contradictions. The cultural historian Diane Purkiss has written compellingly about how Shakespeare's weird sisters draw on incompatible traditions and comprise 'a low-budget, frankly exploitative collage of randomly chosen bits of witch-lore, selected not for thematic significance but for its sensation value'. It's a blow to over-solemn interpretations of the play that assume stage witches were seriously deployed: then, as now, audiences can and do enjoy in fiction things they do not believe to be true.

Even the witches themselves identify their powers as limited: punishing the husband of the 'sailor's wife' (1.3.3) who refused to share chestnuts with them is not very nice, granted, but it seems on a rather smaller scale than full-blown intervention into national government. Strikingly, although the witches are prominent at the beginning of the play, they never return at the conclusion. There's a long performance tradition that has felt that their disappearance from the play needs to be resolved – by reintroducing the witches in the final moments. Orson Welles' film of 1948, for instance, pans back to the witches looking with satisfaction on their work and intoning 'Peace, the charm's wound up'; Roman Polanski's film version of 1971 also brings them back, but with a foreboding sense that the whole violent cycle is about to begin again, as Donalbain – the younger brother of the new king – steps into the role of ambitious malcontent occupied by Macbeth at the opening. Both these film adaptations make much of the witches' agency. By contrast, their absence at the end of Shakespeare's play may suggest that there they are not in fact active agents but merely passive predictors of how things will turn out. That things do turn out in that way is conclusive enough of their roles in the play.

Perhaps we should not take the witches entirely literally either. It is often asserted that Shakespeare broke with earlier dramatic traditions. In particular, he is often credited with bringing to the stage complete and distinctively psy-chologized human beings, in place of the medieval plays in which abstracted qualities or personifications tussled with each other on a stage that represented the human psyche *in toto*. Sometimes that's true – particularly when skilful actors make us believe in the distinctive humanity of their charac-ters. But sometimes it's less applicable, when characters seem flat or instrumental or mouthpieces. In fact, Shakespeare ex-periments with different ways of creating stage characters: through dialogue, through soliloquy, through foils and dupli-cations and, perhaps, sometimes by splitting a single psy-chology between different individuals. Maybe we should think of Iago as the voice of self-destruction inside Othello's head; maybe Ophelia's madness is a projection of Hamlet's torments; maybe the witches are part of Macbeth himself. They speak out his own ambition and make it audible to us, and perhaps we should think of them less as separate un-canny agents and more as estranged but internal voices which direct his actions.

The attribution of agency in the play's opening scenes is questioned and problematized, pulled between the incom-patible but simultaneous realms of the human and the super-natural. All this Shakespeare lays out before he even introduces the character that most critical history has blamed for every-thing that happens in the play: Lady Macbeth.

The idea that the 'fiend-like queen' (5.11.35) Lady Macbeth manipulates her husband into murder has been a compel-ling one, not least because it's an argument with a long cul-tural pedigree drawing on fears about women's power. It often brings criticism into apparently willing collusion with the play's own misogyny. The outlines of the argument are so familiar that they are independent of the play itself. Lady Macbeth is the driving force behind her husband. More specifically, in calling on spirits to 'unsex me here' (1.5.40) when she reads Macbeth's letter telling her about the witches, and in using highly charged metaphorical vocabulary about killing a suckling babe, and in demeaning Macbeth's masculinity and taunting him about his manliness, and in coldly planning the murder so as to frame the grooms – in all this, Lady Macbeth is the prime culprit for the murder. She makes her conscience-stricken husband go through with a murderous act which is always against his better judgement, curdling in him that 'milk of human kindness' (1.5.16) that she herself recognizes.

Certainly, there is a cluster of activity in the first half of the play which presents Lady Macbeth's powerful agency, and it is striking the extent to which criticism has found this threatening and unnatural. If we find *Macbeth* a misogynistic play, deeply distrustful of powerful women, perhaps this is another aspect of Shakespeare's direct address to the company's new patron, King James. Like the play's Scottish setting, the whitewashed recuperation of Banquo (from whom King James traced his own family tree), who Holinshed had as Macbeth's accomplice, and the interest in witches for a king who had written a work called *Daemonologie*, misogyny is part of the play's pitch for royal approval in the newly homosocial world of James's court. In contrast to Elizabeth's court, the Jacobean power base was exclusively male, powered by male patronage and allegiances and prioritizing male lineage and authority in an overtly anti-feminist culture.

Perhaps, rather than blaming Lady Macbeth, we should recover the true synergy between the Macbeths, Shakespeare's only sustained portrait of an operative, adult marriage in process. Separating out who is responsible for what may undo what Shakespeare is trying to present – a passionate *folie à deux*, perhaps, committed by a partnership. After all, unlike other powerful women in Shakespeare's plays, Lady Macbeth never expresses personal ambition or avarice, and neither does she correspond to the standard denigration for transgressive women as sexual adulterers. She does not draw on the available theatrical shorthand for depicting wicked women. Lady Macbeth's particular characterization, and her ongoing fascination for actors and for critics, suggest her active agency – but her marginalization both from Macbeth's and from Shakespeare's plotting later in the play erases that early significance. Malcolm's judgement is of a 'dead butcher' and a 'fiend-like queen' (5.11.35), but like so many of the figures – think of Fortinbras or Octavius Caesar – who step onto the corpse-strewn stage of the end of a tragedy, his analysis is politicized, self-interested and anti-climactic. The question of Lady Macbeth's agency in the play is asked, but Shakespeare doesn't answer it. Like Macbeth himself, that's to say, and like the witches, Lady Macbeth has a claim to be the answer to the question 'Who makes the things that happen happen?' – but the fact that there are so many claimants keeps the question, rather than its answers, at the forefront.

That these questions might always have been part of the reception of the play is suggested in one intriguing and rare archival survival: a contemporary account of *Macbeth* in early modern performance. Thousands of people went to the theatre in early modern London every week, but almost no one ever wrote about what they saw there, which makes the visit of the astrologer and medicine man Simon Forman to the Globe in 1611 even more interesting. For Forman, the play's most compelling scene was the banquet at which Banquo's ghost appears. When Macbeth stood to toast Banquo, 'the ghost of Banquo came and sat down in his chair behind him. And he, turning about to sit down again, saw the ghost of Banquo, which fronted him so, that he fell into a great passion of fear and fury, uttering many words about his murder, by which, when they heard that Banquo was murdered, they suspected Macbeth.' Forman also takes a view on the question of agency. He suggests both that Macbeth is responsible for the killing of Duncan, *and* that Lady Macbeth is: 'and Macbeth contrived to kill Duncan, and through the persuasion of his wife did that night murder the King in his own castle'. The description suggests this confusion of agency was always part of the play: the murder of Duncan becomes overdetermined, in that it has too many, rather than too few, causes and agents.

Alone and barricaded in the castle of Dunsinane, Macbeth hears of his wife's death. His response is a famous speech of resignation and futility, using a striking metaphor:

> Life's but a walking shadow, a poor player
> That struts and frets his hour upon the stage,
> And then is heard no more. It is a tale
> Told by an idiot, full of sound and fury,
> Signifying nothing.

> (5.5.23–7)

Struggling for an image, Macbeth, sitting on the stage in the Globe theatre, alights on the image of the actor, strutting and fretting. It's a common enough trope in the period – the so-called 'theatrum mundi' or 'all the world's a stage', as Jaques puts it in *As You Like It* (2.7.139). But it's a useful insight into the question of agency in the period, and one of the ways in which the popular form of theatre offers itself as an epistemology, a way of knowing, for the Elizabethan and Jacobean period. Who or what makes things happen in the theatre? Is it the physical body of the actors on the stage, moving and speaking to enact narrative and character? Is it the words, penned by a playwright who may be unknown to those watching? Is it the team of theatre personnel who make sure the play gets mounted? Is it, in a more phenomenological sense, the audience, by witnessing that things are happening (a version of that old philosophical chestnut that if a tree falls in the forest and no one hears it, has it made a sound?). Even as the theatre developed compelling tragic characters, it did so within a practical and conceptual environment in which the individual can never be autonomous. And when the theatre became an image for the world, it was never entirely clear whether that suggested the amplitude of drama or the restrictions of human existence. Sir Walter Ralegh's extended analogy in his poem 'What is our life? A play of passion' saw life as a 'short comedy' after which 'we die in earnest, that's no jest'.

Macbeth does not, of course, end with this speech about futility. The script has further to go. Macbeth vows to 'die with harness on our back' (5.5.50) and agrees to fight Macduff: 'Yet I will try the last' (5.10.32). Is he now in control of his own actions in the very last moments of his life, or is he merely working out a part that has been written – by witches' prophecies, by historical chronicle, by audience expectations, by Shakespeare himself? As in Burton's *Anatomy*, it is the question and the range of possible answers that are of most interest. *Macbeth* asks why things happen: that we still can't answer is key to its unsettling hold on our imagination.

CHAPTER 17

Antony and Cleopatra

Shakespeare's plays have been translated into many different media. In the best examples, the qualities of the new medium seem particularly suited to the original: Verdi's grandiose opera *Otello*, Tchaikovsky's erotic ballet of *Romeo and Juliet*, Henry Fuseli's hallucinatory oil paintings of *Macbeth*, Joseph Mankiewicz's paranoid McCarthy-era film of *Julius Caesar*. A perfect equivalent for *Antony and Cleopatra*, the Roman tragedy of doomed love, would be a *Hello!* magazine cover article. That's the medium that best expresses the play's own preoccupations: money, sex, scandal, glamorous international locations and exotic interiors and, above all, publicity itself. *Antony and Cleopatra* is a play that disports itself in full view, a play in which privacy and interiority are overridden by celebrity and self-promotion. If we expect tragedies to take us deep into the psychology of the individual, we will be disappointed. The rival protagonists of *Antony and Cleopatra* instead show us the culture of display and consumption so intrinsic to the Jacobean theatre. And crucial to these interests is the mercurial, OTT Cleopatra herself.

Although (spoiler alert) both Antony and Cleopatra die in the play, the shape of the tragedy is organized around Cleopatra's life. Antony's death is not the end of the play, but when Cleopatra expires, it is indeed all over. This temporal gap between the deaths of the two lovers is the play's most daring structural innovation. Antony's suicide attempt and his arrival, mortally wounded, to die in Cleopatra's monument, are dramatized at the end of Act 4. Act 5 is given to Cleopatra, who prepares for her own death, in scenes cross-cut with Octavius Caesar's increasing military control over the conquered Egypt. Unlike *Romeo and Juliet*, where the gap between the deaths of the lovers is so brief as to be almost a terrible mistake, *Antony and Cleopatra* distends this gap by the length of an act: probably some thirty or forty minutes of stage time. In controlling the play's final movement, Cleopatra has the structural equivalence of Hamlet, or Macbeth, or King Lear, or Othello – the key position of the tragedy.

If this is true, that the play's true tragedian is Cleopatra, this marks a distinct change in Shakespeare's work. Women in tragedies have tended to be one-dimensional: the wicked sisters Goneril and Regan, and the saintly one Cordelia; the abused Ophelia and Desdemona. Lady Macbeth is perhaps the nearest Shakespeare has come to writing a tragic heroine, and perhaps in this context we could see her decline in the play's second half as a failure of authorial nerve, rather than a guilty breakdown. Cleopatra's dominance in the play marks a shift. One potential explanation for her enhanced role is in the acting company, the King's Men (the Lord Chamberlain's Men were so renamed in 1603 when the new king came to the English throne). Shakespeare's in-house role with a fixed and successful troupe of players enabled him to write his plays with a clear understanding of the capacities of the actors who would embody his roles. We can see how Richard

Burbage's growing status and skills are showcased and developed through substantial tragic parts such as Hamlet and Othello, and we can also see that earlier in his career Shakespeare feels that the younger male actors who play women's roles can best manage youthful, gamine parts such as Viola or Rosalind, because that's what he writes for them. But somewhere around 1606 or so, a new actor of female roles seems to have joined the company – an actor who, rather than playing off the gender ambiguity of his own epicene form, was convincing in embodying powerfully mature women, such as Lady Macbeth, Coriolanus' mother Volumnia, or here, Cleopatra. Shakespeare's writing was always collaborative because theatre is always collaborative, and it was influenced and enabled by the actors with whom he could work.

But there are generic implications of Cleopatra's dominance, too. Some years ago now, the critic Linda Bamber wrote a book on Shakespeare with a brilliant title that encapsulates its thesis: *Comic Women, Tragic Men*. In Bamber's analysis, male dominance is one of the generic traits of tragedy, and we need only look at Gertrude, or Ophelia, or Cordelia, as evidence. Women in tragedies tend to be ancillary victims of the male hero's egotistic downfall. The psyche that Shakespearean tragedy characteristically dissects is a male one, and frequently male tragic heroes' self-knowledge is inseparable from violent misogyny. Even Lady Macbeth, who might seem to be the exception, effectively exhausts herself trying to buck this stereotype and get out of the clichéd sideline role. Despite a valiant theatrical effort in her sleep-walking scene, she can't succeed in kicking against the generic pricks, and is ultimately sacrificed to Macbeth's own increasing tragic isolation. As we saw in Isabella's role in *Measure for Measure*, the woman's part becomes the play's generic battleground. Gender is, or at least contributes towards, genre.

So, to have Cleopatra as the play's central character may affirm her as Shakespeare's first true female tragic agent. But there are some contradictions too. By number of lines, Antony's is a considerably larger role: Cleopatra gets second billing. And when the play is published for the first time, its title has an unexpected piece of punctuation: 'The Tragedie of Anthonie, and Cleopatra'. The work of that comma is to split the couple, and to suggest that Antony's is the tragedy and Cleopatra the accompaniment or afterthought. In *Antony and Cleopatra* the dual protagonists compromise rather than transform the idea of Shakespearean tragedy. In some readings, the death of the two lovers gives us a double tragedy, deepening or amplifying the tragic movement through reiteration. In others, the second death either undermines the first, or is rendered bathetic by it – and this links to the ways in which the play's genre teeters between high tragedy and satirical collapse, challenging the single arc we normally associate with tragedy by its repeated structure of doubling and duplication.

First, then, let's look more closely at the deaths of the two lovers. Antony is first. After the Egyptian fleet has surrendered to Caesar's forces, Antony curses Cleopatra: 'This foul Egyptian hath betrayèd me' (4.13.10). Throughout the play Antony has failed to live up to Roman ideals of military strength and masculine self-sufficiency: here, just for a moment, he talks the talk. Calling Cleopatra a 'right gipsy' (4.13.28) sounds just like a Roman, echoing the disapproving

Philo, who opened the play by bemoaning the downfall of Antony to become the 'fan / To cool a gipsy's lust' (1.1.9–10). Antony's specific curse, though, is an interesting one:

> Let him [Caesar] take thee
> And hoist thee up to the shouting plebeians;
> Follow his chariot, like the greatest spot
> Of all thy sex; most monster-like be shown
> For poor'st diminutives
>
> (4.13.33–7)

Antony's curse to Cleopatra is that she be taken prisoner and turned into a spectacle of humiliation before the 'shouting plebeians' of Rome. Most of the interaction between Antony and Cleopatra is needy or needling in some way, designed to prompt or provoke a response, and this is no exception. Cleopatra sends her eunuch Mardian to inform Antony that she has killed herself. On hearing this news, Antony calls on his servant Eros to kill him. Eros's name – the god of love – is highly ironic in the circumstances, and Shakespeare seems to have enjoyed the irony, repeating the name almost twenty times in the dialogue over a couple of scenes. But Eros has other ideas: he will not undertake Antony's command. Rather, he kills himself to 'escape the sorrow / Of Antony's death' (4.15.94–5).

Love, then, emphatically does not kill Antony. Instead, the washed-up general attempts to kill himself with his own sword. It may be intended as a mark of his decline from that noble martial Roman remembered in the opening scenes that he cannot commit the most Roman of acts, heroic suicide. But the question of what prompts Antony's botched suicide is an interesting one. In part, the false news of Cleopatra's death has an effect – but a more immediate factor seems to be Antony's own assessment of himself. Judging that he lives in 'dishonour', he tells Eros of the fate that awaits him:

> Eros,
> Wouldst thou be windowed in great Rome and see
> Thy master thus with pleached arms, bending down
> His corrigible neck, his face subdued
> To penetrative shame, whilst the wheeled seat
> Of fortunate Caesar, drawn before him, branded
> His baseness that ensued?
>
> (4.15.71–7)

The language here is strained, and the unfamiliarity of this cluster of unusual and Latinate words somehow suggests less that Antony is struggling to understand the situation, and more that he is trying to make it sound elevated. Antony is concerned about being humiliated in public view and, referring to himself in the third person, imagines himself as the voyeuristic onlooker in a drama of physical degradation (that word 'penetrative' is a suggestive one that Shakespeare never uses elsewhere). This anticipated public shaming is closely allied to the curse Antony placed on Cleopatra.

And if we skip forward an act (like the Egyptian queen who 'hop[ped] forty paces through the public street' (2.2.236)) to Cleopatra's own preparations for death, we can see the same sentiment expressed again:

> Thou, an Egyptian puppet shall be shown
> In Rome, as well as I. Mechanic slaves

With greasy aprons, rules, and hammers shall
Uplift us to the view . . .
                    The quick comedians
Extemporally will stage us, and present
Our Alexandrian revels. Antony
Shall be brought drunken forth, and I shall see
Some squeaking Cleopatra boy my greatness
I'th' posture of a whore.

(5.2.204–17)

What Cleopatra clarifies about their shared fear of an ig-
nominious future is its theatrical – or meta-theatrical –
implications. Not only will she herself be given up to the view
of a grossly plebeian audience, but she will also be travestied
in plays and other entertainments. The ultimate degradation
will be to be performed by a young male actor, like a whore.
It's an astonishingly daring moment for that young male actor
to deliver.

When Cleopatra lifts the poisonous asp to her breast in
her own suicide, it is the defeat of Caesar that is uppermost
in her mind:

                    O, couldst thou speak,
That I might hear thee call great Caesar ass
Unpolicied!

(5.2.301–3)

What these great lovers express at their deaths is not, then,
the fear of leave-taking, nor the sentiment that they do not
want to live apart. Rather they are motivated by the horror
of public humiliation. And although *Antony and Cleopatra* is

typically categorized as a tragedy of love, to do so may be to accept the play's own compelling mythos about itself – its own *Hello!* headline – and to read it in the way it would like to be read. What Antony and Cleopatra fear is public show, or at least, public show that is not on their own terms. The prospect of a gaping, lower-class audience witnessing their degradation is insupportable – and the irony is, of course, that that is just what they, as figures on the stage, already suffer. While love, jealousy and separation are indeed part of their story, these emotions are by no means the most pressing motives. John Dryden rewrote the play in the late seventeenth century under the title *All for Love*: perhaps he should have called it 'All for Shame'.

Since the Second World War, one of the most dominant paradigms in cultural anthropology has been a distinction between cultures structured around the principle of guilt and cultures structured around shame. Popularized by Ruth Benedict in 1946 in her influential if controversial book on Japan called *The Chrysanthemum and the Sword*, guilt and shame cultures differ in how social expectations are shared and how individuals understand their own failure. Shame tends to imagine this experience in terms of negative evaluations by other people: it is externally oriented. Guilt, by contrast, is imagined as a negative evaluation by the self – it is internally oriented. Shame, wrote Benedict, 'is a reaction to other people's criticism'. 'A man is shamed either by being openly ridiculed and rejected or by fantasying to himself that he has been made ridiculous . . . But it requires an audience.' She argued that 'the primacy of shame in Japanese life means, as it does in any tribe or nation where shame is deeply felt, that any man watches the judgment of the public upon his deeds. He need only fantasy what their verdict will be, but he orients himself toward the verdict of others.'

From this thumbnail sketch of an important anthropological framework, it's possible to identify Antony and Cleopatra as shame-oriented individuals. Each anticipates their ultimate degradation in terms of a public show: being paraded through the streets of Rome in Caesar's triumph, ogled by gaping crowds, burlesqued through performance or mimicry. To be in control of a glamorous public image is one thing; to be the object of someone else's PR campaign is quite another. Cleopatra's fear of being ridiculed as 'some squeaking Cleopatra boy [her] greatness' is the obverse of her earlier publicity stunt in a barge on the River Cydnus. The gruff soldier Enobarbus, there, is moved to famous poetry: 'The barge she sat in, like a burnished throne / Burned on the water' (2.2. 198–9). He recounts how 'The city cast / Her people out upon her' (220–21), and even the very air would 'gaze on Cleopatra too, / And made a gap in nature' (224–5). This audacious management of her own imperial image is crucial to Cleopatra's power: she well understands how her Roman adversaries will use the same spectacular strategy for their own political ends.

Shame is an interesting concept in relation to Shakespearean tragedy, not least because guilt might seem to be the genre's true fellow traveller. Guilt's dependence on, in Benedict's words, 'an internalized conviction of sin' seems closer to the individualistic and interior landscape we associate with tragedy, just as it seems closer to the religion of the inner conscience associated with the sixteenth-century Protestant Reformation and its emphasis on interior reflection rather than spiritual spectacle. One common way of understanding tragic figures is via their own sense of managing their failure to meet their own standards: Macbeth, for instance, tormented by a mind 'full of scorpions' (*Macbeth* 3.2.37) or the rapist Tarquin who 'hates himself for his offence' and struggles under 'the burden of a guilty mind' (*The Rape of Lucrece* 738, 735). This emphasis on guilt as the property of the tragic character would make Antony's loyal servant Enobarbus into an alternative tragic centre. He alone in this play acts from guilt: 'I have done ill, / Of which I do accuse myself so sorely / That I will joy no more' (4.6.17–19). To 'accuse myself' is the keynote of guilt in anthropological terms; Antony's fear of being 'windowed in Rome' is the keynote of shame. But having shame as the major motivation in a tragedy reorients the locus of judgement from the individual to the lookers-on – within the play world, and in the theatre. Just as *Antony and Cleopatra* challenges the model of individual tragedy Shakespeare had been previously working in by its double protagonists, it also shifts the balance away from interior guilt to exterior shame. It turns tragedy inside out.

This same tragic reversal, the movement from interiority to exteriority, is what happens throughout *Antony and Cleopatra*. Whereas in earlier tragedies, Shakespeare develops soliloquy as one important theatrical demonstration of inner thought, in which solitude authenticates the character's words, here Shakespeare makes almost no space for soliloquy to connect us with the inner conflict of his protagonists. We never actually see the lovers alone together: as in a celebrity photo shoot, they are always surrounded by a crowd of attendants. The first time we see them, the stage direction gives an indication of the gaggle: '*Flourish. Enter Antony, Cleopatra, her ladies, the train, with eunuchs fanning her*' (1.1.10). When Antony and Cleopatra begin to banter about quantifying their love – 'tell me how much', 'There's beggary in the love that can be reckoned' (1.1.14–15) – they do this in front of, and for the benefit of, a large on stage audience. Their tragedy proceeds not by isolation and interiority but by a pervading lack of privacy and intimacy. This is a tragedy constructed for the cameras, as Caesar fastidiously describes: 'I' th' market place on a tribunal silvered, / Cleopatra and himself in chairs of gold / Were publicly enthroned' (3.6.3–5). 'This in the public eye?' asks Maecenas (11). Caesar's reply skewers the vulgarity of Alexandrine display: 'I' th' common showplace, where they exercise' (12).

When Caesar delivers his epitaph for Antony and Cleopatra at the end of the play, his adjective for them is perhaps surprising. 'No grave upon the earth shall clip in it / A pair so famous' (5.2.353–4). Final epitaphs for tragic characters – Hamlet, for example, or Brutus – always tend to the underwhelming, but this one is pure bathos. Their predominant characteristic is not passion, pride, or grandeur – certainly not passionate love – but being famous: Antony and Cleopatra are celebrities and, as with modern celebrities, this is a self-perpetuating category fuelled by carefully curated performances of themselves. Flirtation, tantrum, grandiloquence, quarrel – and perhaps love too – are all knowingly played out for the cameras / audience. The flipside of the shame culture in this context is not its anthropological opposite, guilt, but its exhibitionist best friend, celebrity performance. Celebrity, like shame, is externally oriented and needs, in Benedict's terms, an audience.

In such a culture the question of authenticity – does Cleopatra/Antony really love Antony/Cleopatra? – becomes unanswerable: how would, how could, we know? Sincerity is irrelevant to celebrity. In part, the play anticipates the difficulties of understanding the motives of public individuals, but it does more than this: it suggests that the private self is inscrutable and perhaps overrated. Previous tragedies offered us the theatrical illusion of access to the inner psyche; here we see humans constructed and displayed through dialogue and performance. Like Caesar, all we really know at the end of the play is that the pair were famous, and that our presence at the play has colluded to reinforce that very celebrity. *Antony and Cleopatra* is a tragedy of the exterior not the interior, a tragedy of shame not guilt, and this framework helps us to see that the play's apparent cultural opposites, Rome and Egypt, are closer than they first appear.

It's customary for criticism to map the play's central dichotomy, between Rome and Egypt, onto a range of related binaries: masculine and feminine, reason and emotion, head and heart, west and east. To do so is to comply with the play's own investment in these distinctions. *Antony and Cleopatra* develops the concern of all of Shakespeare's Roman plays – which is the nature of Rome itself, a civilization always understood through conflict with something else. In *Titus Andronicus* this other is racial; in *Julius Caesar* it is political; and in *Coriolanus* it is sectarian. Here the distinction is cultural and ethnic: Rome defines itself against and in opposition to

Egypt, and vice versa. The scenes alternate between the two locations as the play experiments with a radical new use of place: the successive short scenes in the long central acts of the play yearn for the invention of the cinematic cross-cut. Theatre designers have had a field day with the supposedly intrinsic differences between Rome and Egypt: Rome, all sterile hard edges, fascistic marching and harsh lighting; Egypt, an orientalist fantasia of cushions and music and sex. As often in the binary understanding of the early modern period, difference – any difference – is symbolized in the difference between two women: a version of madonna/whore which places the mercurial Egyptian Cleopatra in contrast with Antony's chillingly upright Roman wife Octavia.

Antony, of course, is caught between these two worlds, but so too are the audience. Rather as in 1 *Henry IV* we experience Prince Hal's conflict between the world of his father's court and the world of Falstaff in the taverns of Eastcheap as the theatrical difference between boring scenes and enjoyable ones, so too in *Antony and Cleopatra* we can see that Rome is less dramatically engaging than Egypt. We would rather be in the scenes with Cleopatra than in those with Caesar. The play enacts this in its opening scene. It begins with a short, disapproving prologue from two Romans talking about how Antony has been 'transformed / Into a strumpet's fool' (1.1.12–13), but they are then marginalized by a long Egyptian sequence in which Cleopatra enacts theatrically the allure she holds over Antony. The audience is also seduced. If *Antony and Cleopatra* is a Roman play, it's a Roman play that doesn't want to be Roman. Unlike those other challenges to Rome in different plays, here Rome is really on the losing side. Bookended by Egyptian scenes, Rome seems an unattractive, anti-theatrical antagonist: there will never be a sequel about the bloodless Octavius Caesar.

But while it's easy to overstate the differences between the two worlds and so to endorse the racial fatalism of the play, the framework of the shame culture also allows us to see their similarities. To be Roman or to be Egyptian is to be public, not private. Antony is a triumvir of Rome; Cleopatra an Egyptian queen: these are public figures not private lovers. Reports of Antony's previous heroism, like those of Cleopatra's charisma aboard her legendary barge, identify display, show and consumption by a watching public, as constitutive of these titanic figures' greatness. Both are in the public eye – both, in Caesar's terms, famous.

So this is a tragedy seen from the outside, and experienced on the outside, and oriented towards the outside. This is challenging to the notion of tragedy itself. A play with a central couple that works through dialogue and display is closer to a comedy than to a tragedy, just as Cleopatra's final 'Husband, I come' (5.2.282) attempts to recast death – the ending of a tragedy – as marriage – the ending of a comedy. A series of actions without interiority is closer to farce than to tragedy. And farce might, finally, be a better framework for understanding *Antony and Cleopatra*. The male Cleopatra actor, imagining her character played by a boy actor at the end of the play teeters on farcical collapse, but this same ground has been already occupied in the aftermath of Antony's suicide attempt. Brought to Cleopatra's monument, probably represented by the gallery above the stage, Antony's inert, fatally wounded body is raised to die in her arms. But rather than being presented as a moment of exquisite pathos, this action is desperately compromised by its stage awkwardness. Raising a body some fifteen feet above the stage, presumably on a rope, cannot have been easy. The physical difficulties are stressed by Cleopatra's dialogue: 'How heavy weighs my lord! / Our strength is all gone into heaviness' (4.16.33–4), but even more so by the stage direction. *'They heave Antony aloft to Cleopatra'* (38). 'Heave', applied to a human, indicates both significant physical effort on the part of the women, and a grotesquely dehumanized heaviness on the part of Antony.

One review of an all-male production at the Globe theatre in 1999 felt that 'the lifting of the dying hero up to Cleopatra's monument is inadvertently hilarious, with the captured queen of the Nile and a big, beefy Charmian hauling at the rope', and suggested that this ending to Act 4 set the final act of the play in a farcical tone: 'After that, the opening-night audience clearly found it tough to continue suspending its disbelief in a male heroine.' Perhaps the suggestion that the hilarity was inadvertent underestimates Shakespeare's satiric power to deflate his own mythos and that of his characters. At this point in his career, Shakespeare's heroes are washed-up remnants of an etiolated classical civilization. *Antony and Cleopatra* engages with classical epic in echoing Virgil's *Aeneid* and, more particularly, revisiting Virgil's account of the relation between Rome and femininity. In the *Aeneid*, Aeneas must leave his lover – another charismatically sexual foreign queen, Dido of Carthage – in order to fulfil his destiny and found Rome: Shakespeare's Antony replays Aeneas' conflict between desire and responsibility in a different, post-heroic key – akin, perhaps, to Shakespeare's sardonic rewriting of myth in *Troilus and Cressida* or the satiric anti-heroism of *Timon of Athens*.

Just as its protagonists imagine themselves pushing at the limits of their world, so too the ambition and scope of these theatrical and performative lovers pushes at tragic conventions. Shakespeare seems to be deliberately experimenting in this long, unwieldy, but grand and aspirant drama. The stage history of the play suggests it was not an entirely successful experiment, but, like the lovers themselves, it has gained the ultimate accolade. It's certainly famous.

CHAPTER 18
Coriolanus

Often it's the psychological details about Shakespeare's characters that stick in the mind. Why are we told that Lady Macbeth recognized her father in the sleeping countenance of King Duncan and so could not murder him herself? Who was it who once adored the milquetoast Sir Andrew Aguecheek in *Twelfth Night*? One detail niggles me about *Coriolanus*, Shakespeare's terrifying depiction of a hero so battle-hardened that he can scarcely operate in civilian society. Here goes. Much of the first act of the play concerns a major Roman battle offensive against the rebel Aufidius' Volscian troops. As the Roman victory under Coriolanus' leadership is announced, the consul Cominius tells the young victor that he can have anything he wants as a reward. Coriolanus recalls: 'I sometime lay here in Corioles, / And at a poor man's house. He used me kindly. / He cried to me; I saw him prisoner' (1.10.81–3). 'I request you', Coriolanus continues, 'To give my poor host freedom' (85–6). Of course, says Cominius, with an inauspicious comparison, 'Were he the butcher of my son he should / Be free as is the wind' (87–8). Who is this prisoner of war? What is his name? 'By Jupiter, forgot!', says Coriolanus. 'I am weary, yea, my memory is tired. / Have we no wine here?' (89–91). The name of the Volscian collaborator who gave his enemy sanctuary is lost. Hope of his pardon dissolves, since he cannot be identified, and nothing more is said about it. What's the purpose of this little wrinkle in the play? Why does Coriolanus forget the name of his comrade?

Of course the real agency here is not Coriolanus', but Shakespeare's. Authorial intention has been the forbidden fruit of literary criticism for over seventy years, since the American critics W. K. Wimsatt Jr. and Monroe C. Beardsley's influential essay 'The Intentional Fallacy' (1946). Wimsatt and Beardsley observe sternly that 'judging a poem is like judging a pudding or a machine': the comparison asserts that what the poet intended is both irrelevant (since what matters is how it tastes or works) and irretrievable (since the result does not obviously include the details of its own genesis). Asking what the author intended has since come to seem one of the more risibly unsophisticated manoeuvres of literary interpretation. But on the other hand, the question of intention won't go away, not least because we do care about it. As we've often seen in this book, one way to gussy up the discredited hermeneutic of intention is to turn to Shakespeare's sources. There we can glimpse Shakespeare at work as he cuts, pastes, skims and chops into pentameter. And where he adds or changes something particular – that looks like the intentionalist creative equivalent of the so-called 'God particle'.

Shakespeare's source for his Roman plays – for *Julius Caesar*, for *Antony and Cleopatra* and for *Coriolanus* – is the translation by Thomas North of Plutarch's *Lives of the Noble Grecians and Romans* published in English in 1579. The publisher of the English edition, Richard Field, was a contemporary and associate of Shakespeare's, also from Stratford-upon-Avon: perhaps it was Field who gave Shakespeare access to this important book over a period of years during which he consulted it intensively. In Plutarch, at the equivalent point after the victory at Coriole, Coriolanus also asks for pardon for a man who helped him. No name is given to this 'old friend and host of mine, an honest wealthy man', but there is no suggestion that Coriolanus has forgotten it. In Shakespeare, by contrast, the sole purpose of the dialogue about this person is to establish that Coriolanus does not know what he is called. Intentionalist junkies can get their fix: Coriolanus forgetting the name of his aider is a distinctively chosen, Shakespearean element of this play. He must have incorporated it for a reason.

The comparison with Plutarch reveals another interesting micro-shift Shakespeare has made to the source story. In the play, Coriolanus explicitly states that the man who helped him in Coriole was 'poor': 'I sometime lay here in Corioles, / And at a poor man's house.' Plutarch tells us equally explicitly that the man was 'an honest wealthy man'. In a play that is so deeply implicated in class resentment and the divide between rich and poor, this switch can't be accidental either.

Coriolanus begins with the stage direction '*Enter a company of mutinous Citizens with staves, clubs, and other weapons*' (1.1.1). These armed men have a simple aim: 'rather to die than to famish' (4–5). They are hungry and cannot afford food, so they are marching on grain stores maintained, for financial profit, by the patrician ruling class. This has its origins in Plutarch, but a more immediate prompt for Shakespeare must have been the 1607 grain riots which took place in his native Warwickshire, Northamptonshire and Leicestershire, and were known collectively as the Midland Revolt. Rural unrest was prompted by a series of poor harvests and rising food prices and shortages, some of it attributable to the spread of the new enclosure movement that was taking up arable land for profitable sheep pasture. Shakespeare may show a direct knowledge of the complaints of the rural poor in his apparent echo of their charged word 'depopulate', which is found in the petition of the 'Diggers of Warwickshire' and, for the only time in his canon, here in *Coriolanus*.

Shakespeare's own position in, and in relation to, these contemporary events is a tricky one – and here we need to ask how far biography is, or is not, an admissible element of literary criticism. One of the biographical facts we have about Shakespeare is his own speculation on barley prices, hoarding eighty bushels in his barns at New Place in Stratford. Further, we know that late in his life Shakespeare was involved in extensive negotiations around a contentious local plan in Stratford to enclose common land. Shakespeare seems to have been concerned only to protect his own rights and income as a freeholder, not with the more collective concerns about enclosure as the forcible privatization of land previously held in common. As the twentieth-century playwright Edward Bond puts it in *Bingo* (1973), an unsparing depiction of the gulf between the humanity of Shakespeare's plays and the greed and self-interest of the businessman: 'he could side either with the landowners or with the poor who would lose their land and livelihood. He sided with the landowners.' Bond's Shakespeare emerges from the archives as a capitalist more likely to be identified with the patrician grain hoarders in *Coriolanus* than with the hungry citizenry.

Where this leaves the sympathies of the antagonistic play *Coriolanus* is really hard to pin down. The history of performances shows how different ages have attempted to stabilize its ambiguous politics. Shakespeare's own text is either even-handed (if you approve of its ideological balance) or evasive (if you don't). What is clear is that Shakespeare's Coriolanus forgets the name of a poor man, within a context in which he is vocally hostile to Rome's lower classes. His first, uncompromising speech in the play makes that utterly clear:

> What's the matter, you dissentious rogues,
> That, rubbing the poor itch of your opinion,
> Make yourselves scabs?
>
> (1.1.162–4)

It doesn't get much better. When Coriolanus, pushed to seek political office on the back of his military glories, is also forced to seek the people's support, he cannot bring himself to ask for their voices. Accused by one of the citizens, 'You have not, indeed, loved the common people' (2.3.92–3), Coriolanus replies confidently and unrepentantly, 'You should account me the more virtuous that I have not been common in my love' (94–5). Baited by the tribunes, who have class conflict as their aim, Coriolanus reveals his true disdain for the people's role in the state:

> I say again,
> In soothing them we nourish 'gainst our Senate
> The cockle of rebellion, insolence, sedition,
> Which we ourselves have ploughed for, sowed, and
> scattered

By mingling them with us, the honoured number
Who lack not virtue, no, nor power, but that
Which they have given to beggars.

(3.1.72–8)

It's a clear distinction between us and them. He himself belongs to the 'honored number', the patrician class born to rule Rome; they are the 'cockle of rebellion', who fritter away the gains made by the patricians.

So, given that Coriolanus is explicitly resentful of the idle poor, what should we make of the fact that the Coriole man whose name he forgets has been changed from a wealthy man in the source to a poor man in the play? Is this a further example of his ingrained dislike of the lower orders, a sense that he simply doesn't care enough to remember? Should we interpret this mini-dialogue simply as a sign of Coriolanus' status fundamentalism: even if he is an ally, the plebeian is not really a person worthy of recall?

Perhaps. If that's the case, it would suggest that a primary way to answer the question about Coriolanus' forgetfulness is by reference to something in his character. It serves as a sign of something interior, something characterological. What William Hazlitt called Shakespeare's 'supererogation' – his sheer abundant unnecessariness, the excessiveness of all that verbal, poetic and circumstantial complexity and detail – might be usefully adduced here. The forgetting is supererogatory, and thereby a snippet of insight – one of the ways that Shakespeare gestures towards a larger and more mysterious inner life in his protagonists. These hints suggest that there is more to characters than is strictly needed by the plot and this creates the illusion of a rounded history for them even when they are out of sight. But actually Coriolanus' forgetfulness doesn't work in this way: it's already absolutely clear that he despises the poor, so we don't need another, more subtle way to reveal that, underneath, he also despises the poor.

In his great primer on forgetfulness, *The Psychopathology of Everyday Life*, Freud tells us that even the most apparently trivial of forgettings has a motive. Analysing his own inability to remember a name, Freud concludes that: 'besides the simple forgetting of proper names there is another forgetting which is motivated by repression.' What might be being repressed in the context of *Coriolanus*? 'Coriolanus' was a byword for a traitor in the early modern period: the most famous thing everybody knew about him was that he turned sides against his own people. Perhaps, then, in some way, it's himself and his own future treachery that Coriolanus is forgetting, when he can't remember the Volsci who collaborated with the enemy.

If, then, we are to understand that Coriolanus forgets the name for some deeper reason, perhaps we should read it as giving an insight into the trauma of battle. Coriolanus' mind flickers; he calls for wine: maybe this is a momentary glimpse of some humanity, barricaded within his robotic military self-presentation. If so, it's a vital moment in a play usually so thrifty with such insight into Coriolanus' psyche. Again and again the play attempts to get to know Coriolanus, and is rebuffed. Just as Coriolanus himself is not very likeable, so the critical consensus has not found the play very likeable either, as if a protagonist who treats us with contempt makes for a play that also somehow rejects us. As in other tragedies of this later period, there are only a few lines of soliloquy, those privileged moments that in earlier plays offered access into feelings the protagonist could not or would not share with the play's other characters. *Coriolanus*' nearest approach to the soliloquy is condensed and splintered into the acerbically public aside. Just as Coriolanus will not plead for the good opinion of the plebeians, so he won't give his audience a soliloquy. He won't work for the citizens' votes; he won't work for the audience's good opinion either.

This refusal throws down the gauntlet. When he is not on stage – and sometimes when he is – the main business of the scene tends to be mulling over interpretations of Coriolanus' character. Even the opening scene is an example: that *'company of mutinous Citizens'* is immediately diverted from discussion of their insurrection into an analysis of the play's central character – or 'chief enemy to the people' (1.1.7–8). The citizens argue over his conduct: he is both 'a very dog to the commonalty' (1.1.27), and also one who has done 'services' for his country (28). Opinions vary: 'though soft-conscienced men can be content to say "it was for his country", "he did it to please his mother, and to be partly proud"' (35–7). He is described as not 'covetous', but full of 'faults, with surplus' (43). 'What he cannot help in his nature you account a vice in him' (39–40). That the revolt over grain prices quickly becomes a debate about the character of the play's eponymous figure sets the tone for the tragedy. In *Coriolanus*, political events can seem merely the proxy for the anatomizing of the central character: this is a play in which inner conflict is compulsively externalized, and in which, from the very outset, the nature of Coriolanus himself remains a source and symptom of dissent. No one can get a handle on him.

There's a long scene in Act 4 when he arrives in disguise at the stronghold of his old enemy Aufidius. It turns on how difficult it is to describe him. Coriolanus' interlocutors find it increasingly hard to relay his 'singularity': 'He had, sir, a kind of face, methought – I cannot tell how to term it' (4.5.157–8); 'I thought there was more in him than I could think' (160–61). Time and again characters struggle for appropriate words. Cominius finds him 'a kind of nothing, titleless' (5.1.13), and that dehumanized word 'thing' is often used of Coriolanus: 'a thing of blood' (2.2.109); a 'noble thing' (4.5.117); 'He leads them like a thing / Made by some other deity than nature' (4.6.95–6); 'He sits in his state as a thing made for Alexander' (5.4.21–2). Coriolanus even uses the word of himself, to express his greater affinity with his enemy Aufidius than with the people of Rome: 'were I anything but what I am, / I would wish me only he' (1.1.231–2). Perhaps this repeated use registers Coriolanus' inhumanity, as a thing, rather than a man – as echoed in G. Wilson Knight's description of him as 'a blind mechanic, metallic thing of pride'.

This inhuman rigidity might suggest a traumatized Coriolanus, a man who has made himself a fighting machine at great personal cost, by the evacuation of his personality or selfhood. The vignette of his forgetting the name of the man who helped him in the terrible, unspoken and unspeakable scenes inside the sacked Coriole, then, gives us a more interior, a more accessible, a more broken hero. The American Psychiatric Association's *Diagnostic and Statistical Manual of Mental Disorders* defines post-traumatic stress disorder (PTSD) in terms that are strikingly similar to many character analyses of Coriolanus: a sense of numbness and emotional blunting, detachment from other people, unresponsiveness to surroundings, anhedonia (the inability to experience pleasure) and the avoidance of activities and situations reminiscent of the trauma. The forgetting anecdote speaks, then, of Coriolanus' unwillingness to return to the traumatic scene of Coriole.

Now, if Coriolanus were a real soldier, I'd be entirely sympathetic to this line of argument. But dramatic characters – that bundle of marks on a page or gestures on a stage – require different interpretative procedures, and ones that can acknowledge the artistry, the constructedness, and also the historical distance, of the play and its characters. For instance, the idea that identity is located within the interior private individual is a view of human character that twentieth-century psychology has completely normalized – but early modern understandings of motive and action were somewhat different: more situational, more conscious of the social context of individual formation. *Coriolanus* is a play that challenges forms of character-criticism because of its opaque, unlikeable, uncommunicative central character. But perhaps we can take up the challenge by thinking about identity verbally – that is, as denominated, as declared through naming; a matter of words rather than essences.

Forgetting the name becomes somehow overdetermined in *Coriolanus* because of the context of naming in the play. The main purpose of the first act is to unite Coriolanus with the name he is waiting to occupy: the man formerly known as 'Caius Martius' gets it as an honorific, in recognition of his bravery. Although other of Shakespeare's heroes also undergo status or name changes during the course of their plays – it's quite a common idea in history plays, for instance – none adopts that new name as the name of the play. And how the play – both its characters and its apparatus of stage directions and speech prefixes – names this character is worth examining.

The play clearly takes its name from that honorific. After Coriole, the grateful soldiers *'all cry "Martius, Martius!"'* (1.10.40), and the general Cominius declares him 'Coriolanus' (1.10.64). The Folio text – the only early edition, printed in 1623 as part of the collected dramatic works – however, continues to label the reluctant hero 'Martius' in speech prefixes throughout the remainder of the scene. It is not until his triumphant entry as Coriolanus, *'crowned with an oaken garland'* (2.1.158) in Act 2 scene 1, that the play's apparatus gives us the eponymous tragic character 'Coriol.' Coriolanus' tragic agnomen, and with it his identification as the play's tragic figure, is thus belated. But intriguingly, the new designation is further bungled by the text of the play. In the Folio text, Cominius names his general 'Marcus Caius Coriolanus', a formula repeated by 'Omnes'. From Nicholas Rowe in the early eighteenth century onwards, editors have corrected Cominius' declaration to the more usual 'Caius Martius', but the Folio's mistake seems somehow relevant to the larger questions of the play. If we look back at the source in Plutarch, there Coriolanus' new name prompts a digression, with numerous examples, to explain how Roman names work: 'the first name the Romaines have, as Caius: was our Christian name now. The second, as Martius: was the name of the house and family they came of. The third, was some addition given, either for some act or notable service, or for some mark on their face, or of some shape of their body, or else for some special virtue they had.'

Given this explanation, it is odd, but somehow brilliantly appropriate, to see the Folio commit a double mistake – both inverting the order of the names and changing 'Martius' into 'Marcus'. The effect of these muddles mean that the printed Folio text of the play inadvertently 'forgets' Coriolanus' name even in the act of bestowing it. This is a scene all about forgetting. Maybe there would be a way to extend Freud's analysis of forgetting names to treat the text itself, rather than its central character, as the patient. Maybe trauma or repression or PTSD might for some reason be the condition of the play itself, rather than a private property of its hero. The accidental or trivial printing error of Coriolanus' name is amplified into something more meaningful because it is followed within a couple of moments by that dramatic amnesia over the poor man of Coriole. Both the printed playtext, and the dramatic dialogue, that's to say, here underline the importance, and the fugitive nature, of naming.

North's detailed description of the way Roman names are allocated offers a map for different models of personal identity: the second name identifies the individual as a product of their family, while the third can be given either for deeds or for some particular intrinsic quality. These associations indicate some of the many ways in which *Coriolanus* refuses to sanction the desire for individual autonomy. The scene of Virgilia and Volumnia's embassy to the exiled Coriolanus in Antium is a good example, in which Coriolanus' vain wish that 'man were author of himself' (5.3.36) is sabotaged. It's easy to argue that this is a late, washed-up tragedy, in which Coriolanus himself resists the role of tragic hero – but another argument might also be made that this play anticipates the late romances on which Shakespeare is just about to begin. In these late plays, broken or alienated men, like Pericles, or Leontes in *The Winter's Tale*, are healed by reunion with female family members – the restored wife, the lovely daughter. Coriolanus' family is differently constituted, but the structural suggestion is the same. We think the female embassy to Antium will bring him back, make him whole, reintegrate him. In fact the success of their persuasions rather makes it inevitable that he will die. Unlike his romance successors, Coriolanus will not get a new lease of resurrected life: in this play, family is a sign of weakness – rather than, as the last plays of Shakespeare's career will recuperate, a sign of strength.

That desire 'to please his mother', which the citizens adduced as the motivation for his military success in the play's opening moments, returns here as the site of Coriolanus' greatest vulnerability. When Volumnia prevails with him not to sack Rome, he acknowledges that the peace is 'most mortal to him' (5.3.190): 'O mother, mother! / What have you done?' (5.3.183–4). She taunts him with naming: 'To his surname "Coriolanus" 'longs more pride / Than pity to our prayers' (171–2). What Coriolanus is called becomes increasingly fractious in his final interview with Aufidius, when the names 'Martius' – 'Dost thou think / I'll grace thee with that robbery, thy stol'n name, / "Coriolanus", in Corioles?' (5.6.90–92) – and 'boy' anticipate the diminution and disrespect that will end in Coriolanus' death. Shakespeare's tragedies are titled to underline the importance of the single name – as if the tragic form is somehow an exploration of what it means to be named. Many tragic heroes talk about themselves in the third person, and disputes over what a name means or the right to occupy it are often the visible sign of psychological breakdown. Here in *Coriolanus*, the proper name as a symbol of personal autonomy and individuality is held up for particular scrutiny – and the permanent forgetting of an offstage character's name gestures to that important ontological investigation.

One last point – about theatre. Some critics identify Coriolanus' particular class politics as participating in an experiment writing for a more elite audience, in the company's new indoor theatre of Blackfriars. In contrast to the open-air amphitheatre of the Globe, Blackfriars was a boutique indoor theatre, with higher ticket prices, more intimate seating and baroque stage effects made newly possible by candlelight. This new theatrical environment may have made itself felt in the reluctant dramaturgy of this prickly play. Coriolanus himself characterizes his reluctance to seek the people's voices in the language of meta-theatre. The personal political display demanded by the citizens is repeatedly understood by the costive military hero as a piece of bad drama: 'It is a part / That I shall blush in acting' (2.2.145–6). Right at the end of the play, Coriolanus again acknowledges himself as a player: 'Like a dull actor now / I have forgot my part' (5.3.40–41). Coriolanus does not want to be an actor and display himself before a hungrily consuming audience. This is, of course, a problem for a character in a play, and a particular problem for a character in a play in a new theatre with high ticket prices and seats close to the stage promising a good view. Audiences tend not to like performers who show their disdain for them. There's something suicidal about Coriolanus – not just as a military hero without any self-preservation instincts, or as an alienated Roman banished from his country and turning to his enemies, but also as a performer. The theatre audience is included in his contempt. Discussions of Shakespearean tragedy and character tend to be drawn to Hamlet, who holds out his shiny interiority to us like dramatic clickbait (Look! 'I have that within that passeth show'!). By contrast, *Coriolanus* is preoccupied with problematizing the very issue of character itself. Shakespeare's final tragedy performs that inscrutability which Hamlet aspires to, but has to forgo because he talks about it so much. At every point in Coriolanus where dramatic identity might be secured – through family, through social position, through soliloquy, through naming, through contrast with the other, through consistent action, through self-knowledge – the play instead subjects the notion of character itself to sustained, ironic analysis.

In parallel with the verbal dissection of his character with which the play began, Coriolanus is attacked physically by a mob at its conclusion. The Volscian people turn on him: 'Kill, kill, kill, kill, kill him!' (5.6.130). The penultimate stage direction in the first printed edition reads: '*Draw both the Conspirators, and kills Martius, who falls, Aufidius stands on him*'. Coriolanus is stripped of his honorific name, his dignity and his life: it's a sardonic and cheerless conclusion.

CHAPTER 19

The Winter's Tale

The most famous line in *The Winter's Tale* is actually a stage direction: '*Exit pursued by a bear*' (3.3.57). Shakespeare's not big on stage directions in general, perhaps because his printed texts often have their origins in versions of the script that didn't require them, and also because printed drama at this time hadn't yet established what readers might find useful to visualize the action. Some editors don't think that Shakespeare wrote his own stage directions and, in any case, most modern editions are uninhibited about adding more, sometimes tendentiously (there was a good example of editorial stage directions in the chapter on *The Taming of the Shrew*). Some original stage directions from the first printed texts of Shakespeare are wonderful: '*Enter Ariel, invisible*' from *The Tempest* (2.1.189) is one of my favourites, as is one discussed in the chapter on *1 Henry IV*: *Falstaff* '*riseth up*'. Many iconic stage moments, like the Dover Cliff sequence in *King Lear*, or the bloodied murderers' hands in *Macbeth*, or Desdemona dropping the fateful handkerchief, are implied by the dialogue rather than fixed in a stage direction. No stage direction, however, has captured the popular imagination in the way of this one from *The Winter's Tale*.

Partly, of course, it's that bear. Critics have been tantalized at the possibility of a real bear on stage. There were indeed numerous practical and commercial parallels in the period between theatre and bear-baiting – the sport of setting dogs onto a chained bear. Both could be enjoyed in the rowdy entertainment district of Southwark, within the same kind of amphitheatre arena (one early illustration of the south bank of the Thames, by the engraver Wenceslaus Holler, accidentally reversed the labels of the Globe and the Bear Garden, because they were so similar in design). In both venues, paying audiences wanted to see blood shed: Shakespeare's violent tragedies may have been popular more because they were the plays most proximate to the pleasures of blood sports than because they were philosophically elevated and meaningful. There would, then, have been semi-trained bears around who could have been pressed into this walk-on – or rather walk-off – part in *The Winter's Tale*. We know too that white bears were the high fashion accessories of the season after James I was presented with two polar bear cubs from a seal-hunting expedition to Svalbard, and white bears appeared in contemporaneous court entertainments and in *Mucedorus*, a crowd-pleasing romance in the King's Men repertory. A real bear is not, then, entirely out of the question. Except – would you let a bear loose in a crowded theatre? Would a bear take directorial instruction? Perhaps it might be safer to create a similar effect with an extra, wearing a bearskin and roaring?

If the historical question of the bear is part of the referential appeal of this familiar stage direction, it also has claims on us that are more closely poetic. Its specific, compressed, epigrammatic quality is key to its quotability. We have heard almost nothing before in the play about bears. There is no corresponding entrance direction for the animal. The indefinite article 'a' – 'Exit pursued by *the* bear' would be significantly different, because 'the' gives the reassuring sense that we do already know about this animal – introduces a randomness that is either joyful or terrifying or both. The stage direction itself enacts the shock of the theatrical moment. Wait . . . there's a bear? Where did that come from? But the real significance of this stage direction is the work it does as part of a cluster of dramaturgical, linguistic and structural effects in the middle of *The Winter's Tale*. These effects have one concerted purpose: to wrest the play from the path of tragedy and to pluck a comedy from its darkest reaches. It's not easy. Rerouting *The Winter's Tale* from its tragic groove is a collective effort that is going to require that bear to dig deep for his cameo performance.

The Winter's Tale comes right at the end of Shakespeare's writing career. As we have already seen, Shakespeare has experimented before with the membrane between tragedy and comedy – in the Duke's comedic commitment to multiple marriages at the end of *Measure for Measure*, for instance, or in Iago's queasy, improvisatory plotting in *Othello*. These earlier generic experiments tend to find their creative possibilities in a mismatch or unevenness of tone. In *The Winter's Tale* we get instead a radical swerving away from tragedy into comedy, which requires a rapid series of gear changes in the middle of the play. The first three acts of *The Winter's Tale* give us a condensed version of tragedy: Leontes convinces himself that his wife has been unfaithful with his dear friend Polixenes, puts her on trial and sends to Apollo's oracle for instruction. He banishes their newborn daughter as a bastard.

News of the death of his son and his wife brings about the reversal of fortune that Aristotle, in his theory of tragedy, called 'peripeteia'. Leontes' story ends with his grief-stricken recognition of his own terrible folly:

> Prithee bring me
> To the dead bodies of my queen and son.
> One grave shall be for both. Upon them shall
> The causes of their death appear, unto
> Our shame perpetual.
>
> (3.2.233–7)

So far then, so tragic. We have, at least in outline, a textbook tragedy, in which a man of high status is brought to the destruction of his own family due to his tragic flaw (Aristotle called this 'hamartia'). Leontes' hamartia is his irrational jealousy.

But this perfect tragic play is foreshortened; there is also at least an hour to go. We haven't yet heard the Shakespearean equivalent of the fat lady singing (or in this case stepping down from her statue pedestal). If the Sicilian portion of *The Winter's Tale* is a tragedy, it's too quick: rather as Leontes' jealous rage blows up from nowhere, it is all too much, too soon. 'Too hot, too hot' (1.2.110), we might say. So, unlike in those previous plays, the tragedy is not the endpoint. In refusing to fade to black on the sorrowful and bereft tragic figure, this play forces us to consider what comes next. What really happens when you've screwed up royally, and lost everything because of your own bloody-mindedness? What is it like when, rather than dying majestically (like Othello, for example, 'upon a kiss'), you are condemned to wake up every day and remember again what you have done? Shakespeare's tragedies are bleak, to be sure, but their apocalyptic conclusions actually spare us the real unbearable mundanity of grief, guilt and the consequences of our actions.

In foreshortening its tragic first movement, the play engages with suffering. It also creates space for a potentially more optimistic structure – not the inevitable and unavoidable spiral of tragedy, but a sort of philosophy of the second chance. 'Tears,' vows Leontes, 'Shall be my recreation' (3.2.238–9). The word here hovers between 'recreation' as pastime – I will spend my time now weeping – and also the stronger sense of new possibilities – I will be created anew through tears. We sometimes comfort ourselves by observing of Shakespeare's tragic characters that they have learned something from their experiences, or grown in humanity, as if tragedy were a kind of Outward Bound personal development course, helping the senior manager King Lear develop a more collaborative leadership style through harsh weather training on the heath. The ameliorative comfort is a bit hollow, though, when it is clear that the reward for these trials of mettle is – to die. What's the point, we might wonder, in learning through experience if you don't get the chance to try again and do better next time? Leontes, unlike the early flawed heroes of tragedies, does get a second chance – but he also has to wait for it. (We might be reminded of Samuel Beckett in 'Worstward Ho': 'Ever tried. Ever failed. No matter. Try again. Fail again. Fail better.')

After Leontes realizes the terrible cost of his jealousy, the play needs to regroup. For this to work out, we need to move place, tone, genre, and then time – so the middle of the play sees a number of transitional scenes. The first shifts place – from

Sicily, the hot-blooded location of the play's first half, to its pastoral counterpart, Bohemia. The nobleman Antigonus brings Hermione's banished baby in a storm to a beach and abandons her there, under Leontes' instructions. It is here that he leaves, *'pursued by a bear'*. Although admittedly it's not very funny for Antigonus, the surprise of this moment in the theatre seems most likely to provoke laughter. Modern theatrical representations, from a man in a bear suit to a shadow projection of a large claw, share this urge: these depictions are funny. The purpose of the stage direction seems to be to shift tone. Antigonus sacrifices himself to the transition between genres: as the last of the play's deaths, he completes its tragic sequence; as the victim of a slapstick stage trick, he bequeaths to *The Winter's Tale* a comic second half. Enter a shepherd, grumbling.

> I would there were no age between ten and three-and-
> twenty, or that youth would sleep out the rest; for there
> is nothing in the between but getting wenches with child,
> wronging the ancientry, stealing, fighting.
>
> (3.3.58–62)

This colourful prose registers aurally the shift away from the high tragic poetry of Sicily. In the modern theatre, we almost certainly hear rustic accents (cue more hilarity). The content of this speech is, like comedy itself, about youth, regeneration and rebirth. Addressing his son, who has reported the bear's meal of an unknown gentleman, the shepherd underlines the generic point: 'Thou metst with things dying, I with things new-born' (3.3.110–11). It's a moment from a fairy tale. The baby is saved, like Moses in the rushes, with all that that promises for the future. When the younger man describes Antigonus' death in humorous terms – 'how the poor souls roared, and the sea mocked them, and how the poor gentleman roared, and the bear mocked him' (96–8) – the transformation is complete. We have moved place, genre and tone. And in a last shift, we move time.

In shifting time, the play displays another distinctive dramaturgical experiment. Let's take *The Tempest*, the play discussed in this book's final chapter, as a parallel. Written in the same year as *The Winter's Tale*, *The Tempest* also tells a cross-generational story, in which crimes can only be expiated and recompensed in the next generation: the deposition of Prospero from Milan will take the twelve years before his enemies are brought to his island kingdom; Leontes' breach with Polixenes can only be healed by the union of their children, Perdita and Florizel. Both plays thus operate as romance stories, involving great tracts of time and space. But in *The Tempest*, Shakespeare returns to a technique he had attempted only once before, in the early play *The Comedy of Errors*. He writes a play which complies with the classical aesthetic ideal of the unities of time, place and action. *The Tempest* unfolds in the same performance time as its story time, telling the story of three decisive hours on the island. This involves Prospero in a lengthy flashback scene in Act 1, a scene that is very difficult to perform effectively because its main purpose is the undramatic one of telling, rather than showing. We hear in narrative form all that we need to know to understand the significance of the forthcoming encounter between the magus and the shipwrecked nobles: it is a reckoning for a story long past, but not forgotten. Theories of narrative call this kind of explication 'diegesis' (telling), rather than 'mimesis' (showing) (also discussed in Chapter 10 on *Julius Caesar*).

In *The Winter's Tale*, the same dramatic problem is tackled through mimesis – the scenes of the initial, traumatic event are staged for us rather than being described. Shakespeare brings in the figure of Time to explain the next chapter of the story. Straddling this 'wide gap', Time requests that the audience 'Impute it not a crime / To me or my swift passage that I slide / O'er sixteen years' (4.1.4–6). Shakespeare translates the dilated spatial and temporal coordinates of the romance genre into drama by invoking this Chorus-like character.

In the world of art appreciation, the term 'experimental' can be a euphemism for 'incomprehensible' or just 'disappointing'. That Shakespeare experiments here doesn't necessarily mean it works. But the visible effort, the play's white knuckles as it wrests its generic steering wheel, is revealing. *The Winter's Tale* completes its transformations with something like the equivalent of a film title 'Sixteen years later': it smooths over a chronological disjunction in the play. The plot is not interested in the girlhood of the baby, nor her life among her adopted family. We resume the story and turn back to this girl, Perdita, just as she is on the brink of adulthood and available for the comic Shakespearean destiny of single females: courtship.

The second half of the play introduces an entirely new cast – although they would, of course, almost certainly be the same actors doubling in new roles, which can help us make some suggestive connections between the two halves of the play. Does the same actor play Mamillius and Perdita, Leontes' two children who never appear together, for example? Or Mamillius and Florizel? Is Leontes somewhere in Bohemia, playing a different role? The scene in Bohemia is a lengthy one, whose main purpose seems to be to insulate the tragic first part – to put some distance between us and the accelerated trauma of the Sicilian scenes. The tone is festive, and the stress is on fruitfulness and comic plenty, rather than the 'sad tale' 'best for winter' (2.1.27) in Leontes' emotionally icy court. But here, too, genre is not entirely transparent. Polixenes' fury on hearing of his princely son's entanglement with an apparently unworthy woman sounds an uncomic note – or perhaps he is just unfamiliar with the genre. He obviously doesn't know that in a romance, when a prince falls in love with a shepherdess, she always turns out to be a lost or disguised princess after all; he is like those hapless suitors in *The Merchant of Venice*, who must be the only people in the world not to have got the fairy-tale memo stating that the gold and silver caskets are never what they seem.

Having turned the play towards pastoral comedy, Shakespeare still has his work cut out to deliver a happy ending. As so often, there's a disobliging source text lurking in the play's unconscious and resisting complete reinvention. Here it's a twenty-year-old prose romance by Robert Greene called *Pandosto: The Triumph of Time* (1588) which ends in a rather different way. In Greene's *Pandosto* (it's named after the Leontes equivalent, but in this description I'll stick with Shakespeare's names), when Florizel and Perdita arrive, unrecognized, at Leontes' court, the king, 'contrary to his aged years, [begins] to be somewhat tickled' with her beauty. His 'frantic affection' for her grows, despite his efforts to deny it. Perdita, however, rejects his advances summarily: 'I had rather be [Florizel's] wife and a beggar, than live in plenty and be [Leontes'] concubine.' Greene's original Leontes, 'broiling at the heat of unlawful lust', has Florizel imprisoned. Hearing of this, Polixenes commands him to kill Perdita as an unworthy bride, but before this can be enacted, the Old Shepherd, Perdita's foster father, reveals the jewels and seal found with her, and Leontes recognizes her as his lost daughter. All seems to be reconciled, but Leontes cannot enter into the rejoicing and marriage celebrations, '(calling to mind how first he betrayed his friend [Polixenes], how his jealousy was the cause of [Hermione's] death, that contrary to the law of nature he had lusted after his own daughter) moved with these desperate thoughts, he fell in a melancholy fit, and to close up the comedy with a tragical stratagem, he slew himself.'

Greene's phrasing is interesting: in his story, Leontes' death turns a comedy into a tragedy – and perhaps this gave Shakespeare the spur to reverse it, and to turn a tragedy into a comedy. By keeping Leontes alive at the end, by miraculously returning Hermione to him, and by evading the issue of a king's incestuous desire for his unrecognized daughter, Shakespeare grapples the tragedy of the opening acts into an apparently comic redemption for both generations. But we might look a little more closely at what is going on in the play, to see the faint but undeniable outline of those darker forces.

Shakespeare's late plays, including *The Winter's Tale*, are preoccupied with the relationship between fathers and adult or near-adult daughters. It's arguable that all these relationships bear the traces of incestuous paternal desire. So,

Prospero in *The Tempest* responds aggressively to any threat to Miranda's chastity, be it from the despised Caliban or the preferred Prince Ferdinand. In *Cymbeline* the wicked stepmother is jealous of the king's natural daughter Innogen, and contrives to alienate them from one another. And most prominently, *Pericles* begins with an explicit scene of father-daughter incest at Antioch. Presenting himself as a suitor to the king's daughter, Pericles has to answer her riddle in order to win her hand:

> I am no viper, yet I feed
> On mother's flesh which did me breed.
> I sought a husband, in which labour
> I found that kindness in a father.
> He's father, son, and husband mild;
> I mother, wife, and yet his child.
> How this may be and yet in two,
> As you will live resolve it you
>
> (Scene 1, 107–14)

It's not, unfortunately, rocket science. But Pericles' fear for his own life means he can neither confront the abuse nor refuse to answer the riddle. Instead he escapes, and is condemned to a long series of sea voyages, at the end of which he is reunited with his own lost daughter, Marina, who is another sexual anomaly: a chaste prostitute who has brought one of the brothel's clients, the governor of Mytilene, to repent his ways and propose marriage to her.

We know, then, that Shakespeare's long interest in father-daughter relationships – from comedies such as *As You Like It* or *The Merchant of Venice* via *King Lear* and *Othello* – reaches a particular intensity in these late plays. But we also know that, reading Greene's *Pandosto*, Shakespeare has chosen to omit this dynamic between Leontes and Perdita (as in the changes to the source discussed in the chapter on *Coriolanus*, this looks like the allure of authorial intention). Or at least, he has structured the play to suppress – or perhaps, as a more psychoanalytical vocabulary might put it, to sublimate – incestuous desire. If we read carefully, however, we might still read Leontes' first encounter with the adult Perdita as marked by this taboo. The young couple's entrance follows a discussion between Leontes and Paulina about Hermione's beauty, in which Paulina extracts from the king a promise that he will not remarry without her permission. When he sees Perdita, then, Leontes' mind is on his queen, but he is full of praise for the young bride's beauty, and tells Florizel he is 'sorry / Your choice is not so rich in worth as beauty' (5.1.212–13). When Florizel says that his father will grant Leontes anything, the king's hypothetical wish is not for the couple's marriage but for himself: 'I'd beg your precious mistress' (222), which earns from Paulina the remonstrance, 'Your eye hath too much youth in't' (224).

There is no further discussion between father and daughter. It is almost as if the play stares into the face of Pandosto's incestuous desires from Greene's source story, and is too frightened to go further. The scene in which Leontes recognizes Perdita as his daughter is recounted, not shown – in a play so structured around the visual, it is an interesting cutaway to telling. And most extraordinarily of all, and entirely without precedent in the source, Hermione is revealed to be alive. She returns to claim Leontes, to mop up that 'youth' in his eyes, to divert sexual desire back into marriage and away from incest. Perhaps Hermione is revivified at the play's conclusion precisely to interrupt Greene's incest narrative.

Lest this seem an improbable reading, let's look at the way Shakespeare structures his ending, particularly in relation to his previous plays. *The Winter's Tale* is the only play by Shakespeare which has an unforeseen twist – we do not know that Hermione will return. This is distinctly different from his usual dramaturgy – perhaps one of the reasons Shakespeare is so popular is that he makes us, the audience, feel smart: his plays are crucially dependent on dramatic irony, the technique by which audiences know more than the characters on stage. We know that both sets of twins are hurtling around Ephesus in *The Comedy of Errors*, even though it takes a while for the Antipholuses and Dromios to work it out. Much of our pleasure in the play derives from watching the comic misunderstandings proceeding from their ignorance, from the comfortable position of superior knowledge. We know that Viola in *Twelfth Night* and Rosalind in *As You Like It* are women disguised as men; we know that Iago means no good to Othello; we know that Macbeth has killed Duncan; we know that those feisty merry wives are playing a trick on their Windsor husbands. The plays are always structured to put us ahead of the game.

Given this established habit, there is no reason for us to doubt the truth of Paulina's terrible announcement in Act 3 scene 2: 'The Queen, the Queen, / The sweet'st, dear'st creature's dead' (3.2.199–200). Leontes exits the scene saying, 'Prithee bring me / to the dead bodies of my queen and son' (233–4). There is no suggestion that he cannot see these bodies (because Hermione is not really dead). Of course, Paulina could wink to the audience, or she could overplay her already histrionic lines in the scene to give us a clue that this is all a performance to punish Leontes' fatal jealousy – but this isn't scripted. Antigonus even sees the ghost of Hermione in a dream, an apparent corroboration of what has happened (people in Shakespeare's plays see ghosts of dead, not living, people, even in dreams). So dramatic irony is suspended. The play tells us Hermione is dead, so Hermione is dead.

It is only after Perdita's reappearance at court that we hear anything to prepare us for Hermione's 'revival'. One of the gentlemen discussing the reunion of father and daughter mentions that Paulina is about to reveal a statue of Hermione, and his interlocutor concurs: 'I thought she had some great matter there in hand, for she hath privately twice or thrice a day, ever since the death of Hermione, visited that removed house' (5.2.103–6). It's a rather late indication of what is to come – with what, ten minutes' notice? – patched into a narrative which has little need of Hermione, given that its terminal energies are now focused towards the next generation's recovery of what their elders have lost. Saying that the new generation will make up for the mess of the older is a bit compromised when those older ones are still so present. Two different endings seem to be jostling for narrative precedence here: one that proposes marriage between Florizel and Perdita as the future resolution to the problems of the past; the other, that the past is recuperated in the return of Hermione.

Maybe the strangeness, the unexpectedness, of Hermione's return, unlike her still-dead counterpart Bellaria in

Greene's *Pandosto*, should be seen as part of Shakespeare's wrestling with his source, and with its incestuous element which he is trying to banish from his own comic ending. The hasty way in which Hermione's survival is reintroduced as a possibility might indeed give us, as sources seem to, a glimpse of Shakespeare at work – but working rather effortfully to shape his material. Perhaps he had not always intended that Hermione would return, but he needs to quash Greene's incest story, and he does it by providing an alternative mate for Leontes – his 'dead' wife, Hermione. 'It is required / You do awake your faith' (5.3.94–5), the viewers of 'that rare Italian master' Giulio Romano's statue, are urged (5.2.96). It's a daring attempt to divert family trauma into the realm of religion, magic and the aesthetic.

CHAPTER 20

The Tempest

Shakespeare wasn't always 'Shakespeare'. That's to say, the plays (and poems) of Shakespeare were not always freighted with the cultural burden of genius we now attribute to their author. They were not always bundled up with English national identity, they were not always set as school texts, they did not always appear in editions bristling with learned footnotes and scholarly exegesis. They did not always elicit that guilty sense that Shakespeare is marvellous in theory, but in truth either too difficult or too boring, or both. These practices and assumptions have their own histories that are not identical with the life of the works themselves. Nothing much happened to Shakespeare's writings in the year 1741, but it is a watershed for the cultural icon 'Shakespeare'. On a cold January day, a statue to Shakespeare by the sculptor Peter Scheemakers was placed in Poets' Corner in Westminster Abbey, more than a century after his death in 1616: 'After an hundred and thirty years' nap', rhymed the poet and Shakespeare editor Alexander Pope, one of the project's enthusiastic champions, 'Enter Shakespear, with a loud clap.'

The fact of the statue is a landmark in Shakespeare's growing reputation, and it has since become the most familiar three-dimensional depiction of the poet. More influential still is its particular form. The statue depicts the dramatist, a compact 5′ 6″ in height, leaning his elbow on a pile of books and pointing to a scroll on which are written a variant of lines from *The Tempest*:

> The Cloud capt Tow'rs,
> The Gorgeous Palaces,
> The Solemn Temples,
> The Great Globe itself,
> Yea all which it Inherit,
> Shall Dissolve;
> And like the baseless Fabrick of a Vision
> Leave not a wreck behind.

In context in the play, these lines are delivered by the magician Prospero as he contemplates the dispersal of the magical masque he has prepared for his daughter's betrothal. As befits their redeployment in the sacred space of the Abbey, the quotation has been rearranged to downplay the words' instinctive existentialism (Shakespeare is not big on Christian visions of the afterlife), suppressing the line 'like this insubstantial pageant faded' (4.1.155) and ending the citation before its famous evocation of worldly evanescence, 'We are such stuff / As dreams are made on, and our little life / Is rounded with a sleep' (156–8).

That Prospero's lines in *The Tempest* could serve as Shakespeare's own epitaph gives marble form to a myth eliding the author and his character that began in the Restoration period and continues today. When the writers John Dryden and William Davenant began to ransack Shakespeare's plays for productions to please the newly opened playhouses, they rewrote *The Tempest* as *The Enchanted Island* (1667). There they also connected 'Shakespeare's magic' with that of Prospero. It's clear that there are suggestive parallels between the art of the playwright and the magic exercised by Prospero in his island dominion. Prospero describes his powers as 'my art', and uses magic to make things happen, just as an author uses writing. Prospero moves the shipwrecked Italians around his island stage in order to create pleasing dialogues and meaningful encounters, just as an author handles his or her characters, or a director his or her actors. Prospero controls both the present and the other characters' pasts: in a long narrative scene in the play's first act, he gives the background to the story – in the compelling account of his brother Antonio's usurpation of the dukedom, his own subsequent exile with his daughter Miranda, and of the spirit Ariel imprisoned in a tree by the witch Sycorax, mother of Caliban (discussed as diegesis, rather than mimesis, in the chapter on *The Winter's Tale*). Many of these recounted events have no independent corroboration. It is almost as if Prospero is inventing all these characters, fleshing out a backstory for them, to develop the force of his creation. In Peter Greenaway's inventively baroque film adaptation, *Prospero's Books* (1991), this idea is interpreted by having Prospero voice all the lines. He (played by John Gielgud) begins the film by writing, in exquisitely precise early modern handwriting with a sharp quill, the play's opening speeches: 'Boatswain! / Here master. What cheer'? (1.1.1–2). The play continues this meta-theatrical tone. The speech after the wedding masque is steeped in the language of theatre: 'revels', 'actors', 'pageant', and, above all, the name of Shakespeare's own company playhouse, 'the great globe itself' (4.1.148, 155, 153). For readers eager for biographical interpretations, the idea that Prospero articulates Shakespeare's own farewell to his art has been irresistible.

Key to this association is the insistent idea that *The Tempest* is Shakespeare's last play. The evidence here, as elsewhere in Shakespeare's career, is patchy. Although it definitely dates from towards the end of Shakespeare's active theatrical work in London, there is no definitive external evidence to confirm that *The Tempest*, written and performed in 1610–11, is Shakespeare's final play. We can't completely guarantee its place amid the other late plays *The Winter's Tale* and *Cymbeline*, either of which could be later. It is because we want the play's closing movement to read as Shakespeare's farewell to the stage that we place *The Tempest* at the end of Shakespeare's career, and then we use that position to affirm that the play must dramatize Shakespeare's own feelings at the end of his career. We know that Shakespeare worked with John Fletcher on *The Two Noble Kinsmen* and *All Is True* and the lost 'Cardenio', based on *Don Quixote*, afterwards, so *The Tempest* was certainly not his last writing for the stage.

Nevertheless, we have wanted to invest in Prospero's epilogue, which articulates his own freedom in terms of being liberated from his theatre-prison, as a version of what Greek theatre called 'parabasis', a digression in which the author addressed the audience directly. In fact, the epilogue does a more conventional job in scripting the bridge between role and actor, acknowledging the audience and soliciting applause:

Now my charms are all o'erthrown,
And what strength I have's mine own,
Which is most faint. Now 'tis true
I must be here confined by you
Or sent to Naples. Let me not,
Since I have my dukedom got,
And pardoned the deceiver, dwell
In this bare island by your spell;
But release me from your bands
With the help of your good hands,
Gentle breath of yours my sails
Must fill, or else my project fails,
Which was to please. Now I want
Spirits to enforce, art to enchant;
And my ending is despair
Unless I be relieved by prayer,
Which pierces so, that it assaults
Mercy itself, and frees all faults.
As you from crimes would pardoned be,
Let your indulgence set me free.

(Epilogue)

The vocabulary here – of release, despair, prayer, faults, indulgence – connects farewell with liberation, but also with death. On the one hand, this epilogue completes a comedy, but on the other, its momentum is death-driven. Prospero has already admitted that on his return to Milan, 'Every third thought shall be my grave' (5.1.315). It's a melancholic reading beautifully amplified in W. H. Auden's poetic meditation on *The Tempest*, 'The Sea and the Mirror' (1944). Part of Auden's poem, 'Prospero to Ariel', sees the magus at the end of the play addressing the newly freed spirit and admitting

> I am glad I have freed you,
> So at last I can really believe I shall die.
> For under your influence death is inconceivable.

In these readings, and others like them, Prospero's farewell is not only Shakespeare's farewell to the stage, but his dying breath, signalled by his liberation of the life-spirit Ariel.

There's a small inconvenience in this interpretation, given that Shakespeare does not die for at least another five years, but let that pass. It may seem too pedantic to observe that the last of Shakespeare's words performed on the stage were almost certainly not this valedictory epilogue from Prospero, but the rather unsonorous lines of Duke Theseus at the end of *The Two Noble Kinsmen*: 'Let's go off / And bear us like the time' (5.6.136–7: this play also has an epilogue, but most scholars attribute that to Fletcher as co-author). Further, ideas of Shakespeare's decisive retirement from the stage may have been exaggerated. In 1613 Shakespeare bought property in Blackfriars, near to the theatre. This is the first time he appears to have purchased property in London, thus giving the lie to the sentimental idea that he was withdrawing from the hurly-burly to the quiet of Stratford (and setting aside that the movement for Prospero is quite the opposite: he is supposedly returning from retirement to resume active life as Duke of Milan).

We can see here, then, that chronology and interpretation become mutually enforcing and mutually constitutive. *The*

Tempest must be Shakespeare's last play, because it depicts his own renunciation of the art of theatre in the guise of Prospero; because Prospero is Shakespeare, *The Tempest* must be Shakespeare's last play. We can extend this to notice that all authorial chronologies, including the one traced by the order of the chapters in this book, are in a sense biographical ones. *The Tempest* is not the only play to have its meaning determined by its assumed place in Shakespeare's writing career: early plays are read through the lens of youth, inexperience and experimentation, whereas later ones carry associations of summation, detachedness and philosophizing. For some reason we don't yet understand, *The Tempest* was the first play in the collected volume of the First Folio of 1623: this led earlier commentators, not unreasonably, to assume that it was Shakespeare's first, rather than his last, play, and to judge it accordingly. This critical moment offers a revealing insight into critics finding what they expect to find. When seen as an early play, *The Tempest*'s brevity became the sign of immaturity, rather than a sign of advanced refinement and compression. The fact that it deals fleetingly with issues dealt with elsewhere in his work was suggestive of a first attempt, and so too its flat characterization was seen as more akin to that of early comedies.

Readings of *The Tempest* as Shakespeare's last play, by contrast, recast these same observations within a framework of the culturally charged associations of lateness. For many critics, it has seemed a summation or retrospective on his career. Unusually for Shakespeare, there is no major source for this play – but perhaps we should see the play as cannibalistic (calibanistic?) in reusing themes and motifs from his own *oeuvre*. It's a retelling of *Hamlet* in the context of *A Midsummer Night's Dream*: a revenge quest between brothers in which forgiveness ultimately trumps violence through an encounter with the magical. Its young lovers recall Shakespeare's comedies; its magus figure recalls the patriarchs Lear and Pericles; its structure – conforming to the unities of time, place and action – recalls *The Comedy of Errors*.

These Shakespearean echoes suggest that, as in other plays of this final period, Shakespeare is revisiting the themes and influences of his early career in the 1590s – and not just his own plays. In some ways, *The Tempest*'s closest kin is the devilish *Dr Faustus*, by his brilliant contemporary Marlowe. Like Prospero, Faustus is a man of great learning who turns to magic, promising desperately to burn his books just as Prospero anticipates drowning his. Shakespeare's imitation of and rivalry with Marlowe plots the course of his early career, as he writes *Richard III* in the shadow of *The Jew of Malta*, *Richard II* to Marlowe's *Edward II*, and *Venus and Adonis* to Marlowe's *Hero and Leander*. Marlowe's violent death in 1593 gives Shakespeare the artistic space to develop his own style, but it also makes it impossible for him to supersede the now legendary young playwright who will never grow old.

One way of reading these echoes of the 1590s is to suggest that Shakespeare has run out of steam. While lateness can imply a career zenith, it also has the more negative connotations of a decline from earlier achievement or prowess. Think of Wordsworth, or Hardy, or Morrissey, or Hitchcock, or Elvis, as artists who become less rather than more, and think of those artists, like Keats or Schubert or Plath or Kurt Cobain, whose work has taken on a particular doomed brilliance because they died before they had time to get dull. The Bloomsbury writer Lytton Strachey proposed that in *The Tempest* Shakespeare was 'getting bored' with his own art, and that he couldn't really be bothered here about the characters or situation: only the poetry itself, says Strachey, now interests him. It's a view of dramatic decline echoed by Gary Taylor in a newspaper article headlined 'Shakespeare's midlife crisis'. Taylor argues that after a period of high commercial popularity in the 1590s, Shakespeare's career after 1600 was in the doldrums. 'Like many other has-beens,' Taylor continues provocatively, 'Shakespeare in his 40s tried to rescue his sinking reputation by recycling his 20s and 30s.' Collaborations with John Fletcher become, in this revisionist argument, a desperate attempt by a worn-out writer to piggyback on a younger one (rather than, as they have tended to be seen, the work created by an apprentice working under the supervision of the old master).

Taylor's argument is challenging precisely because it is so unexpected. Far more prevalent as a response to the apparently chronological phenomenon of lateness is the suggestion of summation, a high point, a culmination of wisdom and humanity. In this reading, Prospero's own wisdom leads him to forgive Antonio rather than punish him, and to renounce his magic rather than continue it. He therefore occupies an ethical high ground that we can then associate with the beneficent Shakespeare himself. Edward Dowden, writing in a hugely influential intellectual biography of Shakespeare at the end of the nineteenth century, exemplifies this association, arguing that it is because 'the grave harmony of [Prospero's] character, his self-mastery, his calm validity of will, his sensitiveness to wrong, his unfaltering justice, and, with these, a certain abandonment, a remoteness from the common joys and sorrows of the world, are characteristic of Shakspere as discovered to us in all his latest plays'. Again, Dowden's argument is beautifully circular. Prospero reminds us of Shakespeare because his character constructs our idea of what Shakespeare must have been like. The association of Prospero and Shakespeare is likewise syllogistic: 1. Prospero is a good guy. 2. Shakespeare is a good guy. 3. Therefore Prospero is Shakespeare. Syllogisms work, or rather don't, because two truthful propositions that are not causally connected are placed into a *faux* logical sequence to generate a third. But was the proposition even truthful? So far I've approached the question of the connection between Shakespeare and Prospero via Shakespeare: what about via Prospero?

The primary impulse behind early modern dramaturgy – indeed, behind early modern writing more generally – is rhetorical rather than autobiographical. The reliance on pre-existing literary sources, as we've seen in chapters on *Measure for Measure*, on *Antony and Cleopatra* and on *Hamlet*, makes playwriting an experience of crafting as much as invention (the term 'playwright', with its associations with artisanal workers like 'wheelwright' or 'cartwright', was coined during this period by the dramatist Ben Jonson). Humanist grammar-school education, such as Shakespeare's at King Edward school in Stratford-upon-Avon, as we've seen in previous chapters, stressed the techniques of arguing *in utramque partem*, on both sides of the question: it didn't matter what your personal feelings were, your task was to make a particular position or worldview compelling. No literature of this period has the revelation of the artist's own inner feelings as its legible core, and drama even less so, where the animation of different voices and different people is more important than the single narrative consciousness of, say, the traditional novel or lyric poem.

Nevertheless, in *The Tempest* Shakespeare does not quite comply with this view of the drama: here, perhaps uniquely (maybe *Hamlet* or *Richard III* might be interesting comparisons), his interest seems only really engaged by the main character, not spread more widely. There are a gallery of two-dimensional functional figures flanking him, but Prospero is the focus throughout: Ferdinand and Miranda have little of the energy and youthful verve we see in earlier romantic couples; Antonio is not a well-developed antagonist; Alonso is recessed and inaccessible. Perhaps we are to understand the play – like that prototype *Dr Faustus* – as another version of psychomachia, the medieval stage technique of showing the interior of the character through exteriorizing elements into different actors. Certainly, it has been a fruitful theory to see Caliban and Ariel as parts of Prospero that he attempts to keep in check: Caliban, appetitive, earthy and physical; Ariel, fey, spiritual and obedient, a kind of virtuous Tinker Bell. These psychic functions map so clearly onto Freudian and post-Freudian ideas about the id, ego and superego – as the locations of instinct, reality principle and conscience respectively – that it's tempting to think Shakespeare must have read Freud's *Beyond the Pleasure Principle* (of course the reality is the other way around). Together this composite character Prospero-Ariel-Caliban speaks almost half the play's lines.

And, further, there are certainly analogies between Prospero and the dramatist, if not with Shakespeare himself. Prospero's role in writing the script of his revenge against the enemies picks up a long association in the revenge tragedy genre between the avenger and the artist, which has its clearest iteration right at the beginning of the genre, in Thomas Kyd's *The Spanish Tragedy*, where Hieronimo enacts his revenge under the guise of a play he has written. The revenger as playwright is a structural and thematic topos of revenge tragedy, the genre which *The Tempest* works to rewrite by turning to 'virtue' rather than 'vengeance', under Ariel's tutelage. Identifying Prospero's role in the play as akin to that of a dramatist does not, therefore, mean he is a Shakespearean self-portrait, but it does allow us to link him with other directorial figures elsewhere in the plays. It's striking that these figures tend to be negative ones: Iago, the arch-plotter of *Othello*; the Duke who manipulates events in the guise of a friar in *Measure for Measure*; Paulina, the keeper of secrets in *The Winter's Tale*; Helen, who writes her own romantic comedy script with some decidedly unconvinced actors in *All's Well That Ends Well* – all of these controlling figures are at least ambivalent within their own plays. Relatedly, none of them has been identified as a biographical portrait of their playwright. We might also want to assess the self-reflexivity of *The Tempest* alongside that of *Hamlet* or *A Midsummer Night's Dream*, both of which perform inset plays which occasion commentary on the nature of theatre and the blurred lines between illusion and reality. Outside of Shakespeare's plays – perhaps it is in these kinds of comparison with other writers that we can best break the hold of implicitly biographical readings – we might compare the theatricality of Prospero's magic with that of the tricksters in Jonson's contemporaneous *The Alchemist*. To associate the magic in *The Tempest* with theatre, we need not inevitably place Prospero and Shakespeare together.

As we have seen from Edward Dowden, readings that associate Prospero and Shakespeare also produce very positive readings of Prospero's character. Dowden cites Prospero's 'grave harmony', 'self-mastery', 'calm validity of will', 'sensitiveness to wrong', 'unfaltering justice', which perhaps tells us something about late-nineteenth-century ideas of the admirable patriarch. More modern critics and theatre directors have seen a somewhat different Prospero: irascible, tyrannical, subjecting Caliban to slavery and Ferdinand to unnecessary physical hardship as part of his deeply felt ambivalence towards Miranda's marriage. Prospero is preoccupied with Miranda's chastity, largely because her main function for the plot is to be a virginal token. She will secure his own successful return to Milan, by buying off her new father-in-law, Antonio's erstwhile supporter. Prospero's antagonism towards Ferdinand is in part a ruse to bring the couple together (he is trying to play the traditional role of comedy's blocking paternal figure, like Egeus in *A Midsummer Night's Dream* or Shylock in *The Merchant of Venice*), but his attitude is in excess of that generic point. 'If thou dost break her virgin-knot before / All sanctimonious ceremonies may / With full and holy rite be ministered, / No sweet aspersion shall the heavens let fall / To make this contract grow; but barren hate, / Sour-eyed disdain, and discord, shall bestrew / The union of your bed' (4.1.15–21). And the marriage of daughters is a source of sorrow and loss more widely in the play: the ill-fated sea voyage which brought the noblemen dangerously close to Prospero's island was undertaken for the marriage of Alonso's daughter Claribel: 'you may thank yourself for this great loss,' Sebastian berates the king, 'That would not bless our Europe with your daughter, / But rather loose her to an African' (2.1.129–31). The absent Claribel, like her unseen counterpart Sycorax of Algiers, articulates the play's anxious, suppressed interest in international, and particularly colonial, politics.

One way, then, of seeing Prospero is as a distinctly unlikeable, manipulative control freak. The play's second scene, in which he is introduced, gives us a good example of this behaviour. Here Prospero has to give extensive background for the play to make sense, and as we've seen, he does this through a series of lengthy narrations, punctuated by Miranda's apparent disregard and eventually her falling asleep (albeit by magical intervention). These nervous tics in the narrative – 'Dost thou attend me?', 'Thou attend'st not!', 'Dost thou hear?' (1.2.78, 87, 106) – seem to betray a larger fear that this scene, heavy with narrative, might actually be quite boring. Part of the effect is to establish Prospero as a tyrant, physically, psychologically and dramaturgically. The stories of the past erode the distinction between Prospero's own supposedly benign and scholarly magic and the malign, feminized magic of Caliban's mother, the witch Sycorax. Prospero charges Ariel with remembering her cruelties to him:

> she did confine thee
> By help of her more potent ministers,
> And in her most unmitigable rage,
> Into a cloven pine; within which rift
> Imprisoned thou didst painfully remain
> A dozen years
>
> (1.2.275–80)

Prospero released him, but keeps him in servitude under threat of similar imprisonment:

> If thou more murmur'st, I will rend an oak,
> And peg thee in his knotty entrails till
> Thou hast howled away twelve winters.
>
> (1.2.295–7)

The ostensible purpose of this exchange, to establish a moral difference between Prospero and Sycorax, collapses – as their similarities become much more evident than their differences. *The Tempest* offers an early example of something that becomes a cliché in later magical literature: that good and bad magic (Gandalf / Saruman, Harry Potter / Voldemort) are troublingly similar. Our introduction to Prospero is thus more compromised than Dowden's positive construction: or, to put it another way, if this Prospero is Shakespeare, we wouldn't much like Shakespeare. More important is that the association of Prospero with Shakespeare has tended to obscure the ways Prospero is characterized in the play. And it's in this aspect that the autobiographical readings of earlier scholars have been eclipsed by geopolitical ones. The claim of *The Tempest* on modern attention rests less on Prospero as playwright, specific or not, and more on him as colonial overlord: this is Prospero less as Shakespeare, and more as slave-master.

The Tempest has long been connected with stories of exploration and, more distantly, with the early colonization of the Americas. Two sources for local aspects of the play both connect it with a discourse of exploration. One, a letter about a shipwreck in the Bermudas, provides some detail for the opening scenes. The French thinker Montaigne's essay 'Of Cannibals' provides Gonzalo with his vision of an ideal commonwealth at the beginning of Act 2, and the name Caliban may have been intended as an anagram of cannibal, then a generic term for aboriginal peoples. This reading of the play, as a parable of colonial expansion, has gained ground particularly because of significant post-colonial rewritings – among them the Martinique poet Aimé Césaire's *Une Tempête* (1969) – of its contested fable of language, domination and occupation. When the French/Madagascan psychoanalyst Octave Mannoni's book *Psychologie de la Colonalisation* was translated into English in 1956, it had the title *Prospero and Caliban*. We might sum up the shift in criticism by pointing to the difference between Frank Kermode, introducing the second Arden edition of the play in 1954 with the brisk 'it is as well to be clear that there is nothing in *The Tempest* fundamental to its structure of ideas which could not have existed had America remained undiscovered', and Virginia Mason Vaughan and Alden T. Vaughan's perspective in 1999, writing in the third edition of the Arden series: 'The extensive and varied discourses of colonialism, many critics argue, are deeply embedded in the drama's language and events' such that the play is 'a theatrical microcosm of the imperial paradigm'.

A similar shift in interpretative priorities has taken place in the theatre, where recent colonial Prosperos have tended to be so unpleasant that any association with Shakespeare would reflect very badly on the playwright himself. Like *The Taming of the Shrew* with which we began, *The Tempest*, then, offers an acute emblem of the themes of this book. We get the Shakespeare we need at different times. Shakespeare's plays generate questions rather than answers. It is for us, as readers, critics, theatregoers and theatre-makers, to take up their challenge, leverage their restless interrogation and re-imagine them for our own world.

Epilogue

The epilogue is a distinctly Shakespearean genre: a concluding moment when the play is both brought together and dis-
solved, a paradox of completion and dispersal. The typical
epilogue is delivered in a voice that shifts between character
and actor: it's a transitional threshold in the play's architec-
ture, in which the engaging fiction we've been enjoying does
a last shimmy with the consciousness that we've actually
been watching a play. This has all been a 'dream', says Robin
Goodfellow at the end of *A Midsummer Night's Dream*, and if
you're satisfied with what you've seen, he asks, 'Give me your
hands' (Epilogue 6, 15). 'My way is to conjure you', Rosalind
archly explains at the end of *As You Like It*, 'to like as much
of this play as please you' (Epilogue 10–13). The final speech
of *All's Well That Ends Well* suggests that the title's proverbial
premise will be fulfilled only by audience agreement: 'That
you express content' (Epilogue 3). Prospero asks the audience
to release him: 'Gentle breath of yours my sails / Must fill, or
else my project fails, / Which was to please' (Epilogue 11–13).
The call for approval and applause is characteristic: the epilogue is the place in Shakespeare's plays where the vitally
constitutive role of the audience is explicitly acknowledged.
Without them – without us – the play is incomplete.

This book has presented a Shakespeare whose plays are constitutionally incomplete. I've tried to show how their gappiness and their ambiguities produce creative readings. These radical uncertainties function as dramatic and intellectual cues to readers, playgoers and theatre-makers. Just as these epilogues direct audiences to make up their own minds, so Shakespeare's characters, plots and unanswered questions provide space for us to think, interrogate and experience different potential outcomes. Shakespeare's plays aren't monuments to revere, or puzzles to resolve. They are partial, shifting, unstable survivals from a very different world which have the extraordinary ability to ventriloquize and stimulate our current concerns. Sometimes these may be personal and emotional. I had never really noticed the lines in *King Lear* when, briefly reunited with Cordelia, Lear predicts their future happiness in prison together: 'we'll live, / And pray, and sing, and tell old tales, and laugh / At gilded butterflies' (5.3.11–13), until my ship-loving grandfather, momentarily lucid in the hospital bed in which he would shortly die, talked to us about the cruise which we would all go on together when he was better. Sometimes they are structural: working recently with actors preparing a new production of *Measure for Measure*, I spent time again with a scene familiar to me, that awful moment when Angelo, the deputy of Vienna, presents to Isabella an awful bargain: that she might 'give up [her] body to such sweet uncleanness' (2.4.54) and thereby save her brother Claudio. We looked at why Isabella does not seem to acknowledge Angelo's repeated insinuations, seeming even wilfully to misunderstand his language of sin and peril. One woman in the company described how she felt that, facing an encounter that has become unreciprocally sexualized, it was quite recognizable for Isabella to continue to attempt to bring the conversation back to safer ground. We saw that it isn't necessarily that Isabella is too naïve to understand Angelo's meaning, more that at first she cannot quite believe that she has indeed understood it correctly, and then that to acknowledge it would be to submit to the danger of her situation. And sometimes they are more clearly political or ethical. In a copy of Shakespeare's works smuggled into Robben Island, Nelson Mandela wrote his name next to the lines in *Julius Caesar*:

> Cowards die many times before their deaths:
> The valiant never taste of death but once.
> Of all the wonders that I yet have heard,
> It seems to me most strange that men should fear,
> Seeing that death, a necessary end,
> Will come when it will come.

$$(2.2.32-7)$$

All these examples show how Shakespeare can resonate in particular circumstances, and how we bring to the plays our own emotional, political, ideological and creative energies.

I write this at the end of a long, dry summer in the UK, marked by the re-emergence in the landscape of long forgotten outlines of past buildings and settlements and field systems, visible against the parched ground. It strikes me that there are other outlines just visible in this book too. One might have been a literary biography, structured around Shakespeare the writer: his ongoing engagement with his early rivals, Christopher Marlowe and Thomas Kyd, and with collaborators, including Thomas Middleton and John Fletcher, his reading and his influences, his writing changing genre and tone through topical histories and escapist comedies into more existential and then satiric plays in the early years of the seventeenth century, and then into those fairy-tale romances of his final years. Another might have been a more theatrical study, drawing first on the personnel of the Chamberlain's and King's Men and the influence of this specific resource on Shakespeare's writing, and then on later adaptations from John Dryden in Restoration London to Aimé Césaire in postcolonial Martinique, and using more recent performance history to illustrate the changing meanings of Shakespeare's plays. A third might have been more historical: I'm fascinated by what these plays might have meant to their first audiences and readers, and my interpretations often refer to contemporary cultural issues, about Elizabethan succession politics, religion, social organization and city life. All of these alternative books are just present in the archaeology of this one, but the Shakespeare I have ultimately tried to bring forward is more varied, and more available to different approaches and different reading priorities.

So, this is Shakespeare.

Permissive, modern, challenging, gappy, frustrating, moving, attenuated, beautiful, ambiguous, resourceful, provoking, necessary.

Yours.

I hope you enjoy it as much as I do.

References and Further Reading

Except for the chapter on *King Lear*, my references to
Shakespeare's works cite the second edition of *The Oxford
Shakespeare: The Complete Works*, edited by Stanley Wells, Gary
Taylor, John Jowett and William Montgomery (Oxford University
Press, 2005), though, because editors have to leave things out
and make things consistent, I sometimes quote – particularly
stage directions – from the early printed texts of Shakespeare's
plays. You can look at individual plays published before 1623 via
the British Library: <https://www.bl.uk/treasures/shakespeare/>,
and at the collected First Folio edition of 1623 from the Bodleian
Library: <https://firstfolio.bodleian.ox.ac.uk>.

CHAPTER 1: THE TAMING OF THE SHREW

The John Fletcher play *The Woman's Prize, or, The Tamer Tam'd*,
is available in printed editions, including my *Women on the Early
Modern Stage* (Bloomsbury/Methuen Drama, 2014), and online
from the Folger Shakespeare Library *Digital Anthology of Early
Modern English Drama*: <https://emed.folger.edu/featured-plays>.
The same anthology includes *The Taming of a Shrew*. I've quoted
Germaine Greer from the 1971 edition of *The Female Eunuch*. On
companionate marriage and conduct literature, I've found the
contemporary extracts edited by Kate Aughterson in *The English
Renaissance: An Anthology of Sources and Documents* (Routledge,
1998) really useful. Elizabeth Schafer's *Shakespeare in Production:
The Taming of the Shrew* (Cambridge University Press, 2002) is
invaluable on the stage history.

CHAPTER 2: RICHARD III

John Manningham's anecdote is quoted from Lois Potter's *The Life of William Shakespeare: A Critical Biography* (Wiley-Blackwell, 2012), which I like among all the many biographies of Shakespeare because it is so rooted in the theatre industry. E. M. W. Tillyard's *Shakespeare's History Plays* was first published in 1944. Trevor Nunn's nice phrase about the histories as a box set comes from his article in *The Guardian* of 12 September 2015.

CHAPTER 3: THE COMEDY OF ERRORS

The New Oxford Shakespeare *The Complete Works*, edited by Gary Taylor, Terri Bourus, John Jowett and Gabriel Egan (Oxford University Press, 2016), has a bricolage of critical quotations instead of introductions to the plays and these directed me to George Steevens's observation on *The Comedy of Errors*. T. S. Eliot's famous observation about poets borrowing or stealing comes from an essay on another early modern playwright, Philip Massinger, in his collection *The Sacred Wood*, first published in 1920. You can access a digital facsimile of the First Folio to look at the confusions of the play before editors get hold of it, via the Bodleian Library: <http://firstfolio.bodleian.ox.ac.uk>. Carol Ann Duffy wrote a wonderful adaptation of the medieval play *Everyman*, published by Faber in 2015. Coleridge's view of *The Comedy of Errors* can be found in Jonathan Bate (ed.), *The Romantics on Shakespeare* (Penguin, 1992); John Mortimer and Michael Frayn on farce are both from interviews with the *New York Times*, on 26 January 1992 and 8 December 1985, respectively. Philip Sidney's *The Defence of Poesy* is available in an edition by Gavin Alexander (Penguin Classics, 2004); Henri Bergson's work on laughter is much reprinted, or in digital form from Project Gutenberg: <https://www.gutenberg.org/files/4352/4352-h/ 4352-h.htm>.

CHAPTER 4: RICHARD II

The official Elizabethan homilies are available online via the Internet Shakespeare project: <http://internetshakespeare.uvic.ca/Library/SLT/ideas/religion/homilies.html>. Shakespeare's great historical source Raphael Holinshed has been digitized at the Holinshed Project: <http://www.cems.ox.ac.uk/holinshed/texts.shtml>. Ernst Kantorowicz developed his ideas in a book called *The King's Two Bodies: A Study in Mediaeval Political Theology*, first published in 1957. There's more on the stage history of the play, including John Barton's production, in Margaret Shewring's *Shakespeare in Performance: King Richard II* (Manchester University Press, 1996). Simon Palfrey's *Doing Shakespeare* (Bloomsbury Arden Shakespeare, 2011) has a dazzling section on rhyme in *Richard II*. Ireland, Essex and Elizabeth feature prominently in James Shapiro's excellent *A Year in the Life of William Shakespeare: 1599* (Faber, 2005).

CHAPTER 5: ROMEO AND JULIET

I've quoted Jean Anouilh's *Antigone* from the English translation by Barbara Bray, published in *Anouilh: Five Plays* (Methuen, 1987). Susan Snyder's term 'evitability' comes from her book *The Comic Matrix of Shakespeare's Tragedies* (Princeton University Press, 1979). Arthur Brooke's poem is printed in Geoffrey Bullough's *Narrative and Dramatic Sources of Shakespeare* (1957) (Routledge and Kegan Paul, 1973). George Puttenham's work is reprinted by Gavin Alexander in his Penguin Classics edition of *Sidney's 'The Defence of Poesy' and Selected Renaissance Literary Criticism* (2004). Narrative theories, including those likening reading to sexual pleasure, are discussed in Paul Cobley's *Narrative* (Routledge, 2001). The comic Restoration version of *Romeo and Juliet* was by James Howard and performed in tandem with its tragic sibling at Lincoln's Inn Fields in 1663–4. You can read the play as printed without its Prologue in the First Folio via the Bodleian Library: <http://firstfolio.bodleian.ox.ac.uk>.

CHAPTER 6: A MIDSUMMER NIGHT'S DREAM

The unfortunate school party shocked by the Royal Shakespeare Company performance was reported by the BBC in 1999: <http://news.bbc.co.uk/1/hi/talking_point/321208.stm>. There are lots of Victorian illustrations of scenes from the play available from the Folger Shakespeare Library's digital collection: <http://luna.folger.edu>. Thomas Nashe's *The Terrors of the Night* is included in the Penguin Classics edition of *The Unfortunate Traveller and Other Works* (1978). I've quoted from one of my favourite works of Shakespeare criticism, Jan Kott's *Shakespeare Our Contemporary* (Methuen, 1964).

CHAPTER 7: THE MERCHANT OF VENICE

Documentary information about Shakespeare, including digital facsimiles of the fascinating and often informative title pages of his work, is collected at <http://shakespearedocumented .folger.edu>. Freud's essay 'The Theme of the Three Caskets' was published in 1913 and is included in volume 14 of the Penguin Freud Library, *Art and Literature* (1985). Karl Marx writes on *Timon of Athens* in *The Paris Manuscripts* and in *Capital*.

CHAPTER 8: 1 HENRY IV

Title-page information on early printed texts of Shakespeare can be found at <https://shakespearedocumented.folger.edu>. Harold Bloom's book *Shakespeare: The Invention of the Human* (Fourth Estate, 1999) is a compelling read: some useful critiques of its approach are by Geoffrey O'Brien in *The New York Review of Books* (18 February 1999) and A. C. Grayling in *Prospect* (April 1999); the quotation 'Falstaff is life! Falstaff is the blessing' comes from an interview Bloom gave to John Heilpern in *Vanity Fair* (20 April 2011). Maurice Morgann's essay on Falstaff is digitized at <https://archive.org/details/essayondramaticc00morgiala>; H. R. Woudhuysen's Penguin Classics collection *Samuel Johnson on Shakespeare* (1990) is recommended. I'm indebted

to Wikisimpsons (<https://simpsonswiki.com>) for information
on Matt Groening's animated sitcom. Anti-theatrical writing,
including Philip Stubbes's phrase 'Satan's synagogue', along with
lots of other contemporary documentation about theatre practice,
audiences and the place of the stage, is excerpted in Tanya
Pollard (ed.), *Shakespeare's Theater: A Sourcebook* (Blackwell
Publishing, 2004).

CHAPTER 9: MUCH ADO ABOUT NOTHING

Geoffrey Bullough's *Narrative and Dramatic Sources of Shakespeare*
is the go-to on Shakespeare's influences and source material.
George Bernard Shaw's comment on Don John is included in
Edwin Wilson's *Shaw on Shakespeare* (Penguin, 1961). The 1600
Quarto of *Much Ado* is available from the British Library: <https://
www.bl.uk/treasures/shakespeare/>. There's more on the actors
of the Chamberlain's Men and their impact on Shakespeare's
plays in Bart van Es, *Shakespeare in Company* (Oxford University
Press, 2013).

CHAPTER 10: JULIUS CAESAR

Critics worrying about whether 'The Tragedy of Brutus' would be
more appropriate include Ernest Schanzer in the journal *English
Literary History* 22 (1955) and Horst Zander in *Julius Caesar: New
Critical Essays* (Routledge, 2005). Jean Baudrillard's provocative
ideas about the Gulf War were published as three short essays
in *Liberation* (in French) and *The Guardian* (in English) in
January–March 1991, and then as a book, *The Gulf War Did Not
Take Place* (Indiana University Press, 1995). Marx's insight about
tragedy and farce comes from his essay *The Eighteenth Brumaire
of Louis Bonaparte*, first published in German in 1852. Thomas
North's translation of Plutarch's *Lives of the Noble Grecians and
Romans* is included in Geoffrey Bullough's *Narrative and Dramatic
Sources of Shakespeare*. There's a good Penguin Classics edition
of Arthur Golding's version of Ovid, *Metamorphoses*, edited by

Madeleine Forey (2002). The first plays to be published with Shakespeare's name on the title page date from 1598: see <https://shakespearedocumented.folger.edu>. Richard McCabe's essay is the best account of the Bishops' Ban, 'Elizabethan Satire and the Bishops' Ban of 1599', in *The Yearbook of English Studies* 11 (1981); Thomas Platter's travelogue was translated by Clare Williams and published as *Thomas Platter's Travels in England 1599* (Jonathan Cape, 1937).

CHAPTER 11: HAMLET

I've quoted Joyce's *Ulysses* from the Oxford World's Classics text edited by Jeri Johnson (1993). Freud writes on *Hamlet* in *The Interpretation of Dreams* (1900; first English translation, 1913), volume 4 in the Penguin Freud Library (1991); Marx uses *Hamlet* in his discussion of revolution in *The Eighteenth Brumaire of Louis Bonaparte* (1852); twentieth-century philosophers' responses to the play are explored in *The Hamlet Doctrine* (Verso, 2013) by Simon Critchley and Jamieson Webster. T. S. Eliot's 'The Love Song of J. Alfred Prufrock' was first published in 1915 in *Poetry* magazine. Jan Kott's book *Shakespeare Our Contemporary* (Methuen, 1964) is always suggestive. On the stage history of the play, see David Bevington, *Murder Most Foul: Hamlet Through the Ages* (Oxford University Press, 2011). The description of Jonathan Pryce's performance is taken from a review in the *Listener* (4 April 1980). On Protestantism and the wider historical context, Peter Marshall's *Heretics and Believers: A History of the English Reformation* (Yale University Press, 2017) is highly recommended, as is Stephen Greenblatt's *Hamlet in Purgatory* (expanded edition, Princeton University Press, 2013). Thomas Kyd's brilliant *The Spanish Tragedy* is available in lots of print editions, including my *Five Revenge Tragedies* (Penguin Classics, 2012), and online at <https://emed.folger.edu/featured-plays>, the Folger Shakespeare Library's *Digital Anthology of Early Modern Drama*. Hamnet Shakespeare is discussed by Graham Holderness in the group biography of Shakespeare and his associates, *The Shakespeare Circle*, edited by Paul Edmondson and Stanley Wells (Cambridge University Press, 2015).

CHAPTER 12: TWELFTH NIGHT

Stephen Orgel's *Impersonations: The Performance of Gender in Shakespeare's England* (Cambridge University Press, 1996) and Will Tosh's *Male Friendship and Testimonies of Love in Shakespeare's England* (Palgrave Macmillan, 2016) flesh out some of the issues around sexuality in the period. Montaigne's essays are available in a modern English translation by M. A. Screech (Penguin Classics, 2003): for the early modern translation by John Florio with which Shakespeare was familiar, see Stephen Greenblatt and Peter Platt (eds), *Shakespeare's Montaigne* (NYRB Classics, 2014). Thomas Heywood's description of genres comes from his *An Apology for Actors* (1612), reprinted in Tanya Pollard's *Shakespeare's Theater: A Sourcebook* (Blackwell Publishing, 2004). I've quoted the definition of 'great' from the *Oxford English Dictionary* at <http://www.oed.com>. The exhilarating Northrop Frye can be sampled in the book *Northrop Frye on Shakespeare*, edited by Robert Sandler (Yale University Press, 1986), but I particularly recommend his book on comedies which takes its title from *Twelfth Night*, *A Natural Perspective: The Development of Shakespearean Comedy and Romance* (Harcourt, Brace and World, 1965). Thanks to the work of Phil Gyford, you can read *The Diary of Samuel Pepys* online: <https://www.pepysdiary.com>.

CHAPTER 13: MEASURE FOR MEASURE

Charlotte Lennox's pioneering scholarship on Shakespeare's sources is available online at <https://archive.org/details/shakespearillusoounkngoog>; the more modern version of this material is Geoffrey Bullough's *Narrative and Dramatic Sources of Shakespeare*, which includes Cinthio and Whetstone. The catalogue page to the First Folio is viewable in the preliminaries

to the digitized text from the Bodleian Library: <http://firstfolio
.bodleian.ox.ac.uk>. Liz Lochhead delivers 'Men Talk' in a
recording available on YouTube: <https://www.youtube.com/
watch?v=SUhlskKe6BY>. Lots of online texts can generate
proportions of lines spoken by different characters: I've used the
figures from my *The Cambridge Shakespeare Guide* (Cambridge
University Press, 2012). I discuss William Johnstoune (the
probable early reader and annotator of a copy of Shakespeare's
First Folio) in my *Shakespeare's First Folio: Four Centuries of an
Iconic Book* (Oxford University Press, 2016): the annotations,
from a copy now in Meisei University, Japan, are also available
online: <http://shakes.meisei-u.ac.jp/e-index.html>. I discuss,
with great and I hope evident enjoyment, Middleton's *A Chaste
Maid in Cheapside* in the 'Not Shakespeare' audio lecture series
available from Apple Podcasts or <http://www.podcasts.ox.ac
.uk>. Comparisons between the Duke and James I have been made
by numerous scholars, including Leah S. Marcus in her *Puzzling
Shakespeare: Local Reading and Its Discontents* (University of
California Press, 1988).

CHAPTER 14: OTHELLO

John Kani recalled the Suzman production of *Othello* in an
essay published by the British Council, 'Apartheid and *Othello*'
(2016): <https://literature.britishcouncil.org/assets/Uploads/06
.-shakespeare-lives-south-africa-john-kani-digital-download.
pdf>. Other landmark productions of the play are discussed in
Lois Potter, *Othello: Shakespeare in Performance* (Manchester
University Press, 2002). Burbage's skills and the response to
his death are discussed by Bart van Es in his study *Shakespeare
in Company* (Oxford University Press, 2013), from where these
quotations are taken. *Othello*'s critical history is surveyed in
Othello: A Critical Reader, edited by Robert C. Evans (Bloomsbury
Arden Shakespeare, 2015), and in Ayanna Thompson's
introduction to the Arden edition of the play (2016). Jonathan

Bate wrote about the contemporary echoes in the *Times Literary Supplement* of 21 October 2001. Intersectionality is a concept initially outlined by Kimberlé Crenshaw in the *University of Chicago Legal Forum* (1989) and developed by many social theorists and activists, as explained in Patricia Hill Collins and Sirma Bilge's *Intersectionality: Key Concepts* (Polity Press, 2016). W. H. Auden's 'The Joker in the Pack' was published in *The Dyer's Hand and Other Essays* (Faber, 1963); Thomas Rymer's scornful analysis of *Othello* comes from his *A Short View of Tragedy* (1692); Thomas Heywood's defence of the stage, *An Apology for Actors* (1612), is included in Tanya Pollard's *Shakespeare's Theater: A Sourcebook* (Blackwell Publishing, 2004).

CHAPTER 15: KING LEAR

Because of the issues around the texts of *King Lear* with which this chapter concludes, *The Oxford Shakespeare*, which prints the Quarto and Folio as separate plays, is awkward to cite here: I've shifted for this chapter only to *The Norton Shakespeare* (W. W. Norton, 2016), edited by Stephen Greenblatt, Walter Cohen, Suzanne Gossett, Jean E. Howard, Katharine Eisaman Maus and Gordon McMullan. The two texts of *King Lear* are available as digital facsimiles: the 1608 Quarto from the British Library: <https://www.bl.uk/treasures/shakespeare/>; the 1623 First Folio from the Bodleian Library: <https://firstfolio.bodleian.ox.ac.uk>. Terry Eagleton's summary account of tragic theory forms the first chapter of his book *Sweet Violence: The Idea of the Tragic* (Wiley-Blackwell, 2002); the insight about changing meanings of 'uncomfortable' comes from A. D. Nuttall's book *Why Does Tragedy Give Pleasure?* (Oxford University Press, 1996). Nahum Tate's Restoration rewrite of *King Lear*, *The History of King Lear* (1681), is available from the Internet Shakespeare: <http://internetshakespeare.uvic.ca/doc/Tate-Lr_M/complete/>; Samuel Johnson on *Lear* is included in H. R. Woudhuysen's Penguin Classics collection *Samuel Johnson on Shakespeare* (1990).

Jonathan Bate's Penguin anthology *The Romantics on Shakespeare* (Penguin, 1992) is the source of quotations from Schlegel, Hazlitt and Coleridge. A. C. Bradley's 1904 *Shakespearean Tragedy* is much reprinted (Penguin Classics, 1991); G. Wilson Knight's account of the play is in his whirlingly brilliant *The Wheel of Fire* (first published in 1930 by Oxford University Press; Routledge Classics, 2001); Jan Kott's *Shakespeare Our Contemporary* (Methuen, 1964) is, I hope you're seeing, required reading. Jonathan Dollimore's *Radical Tragedy: Religion, Ideology and Power in the Drama of Shakespeare and His Contemporaries*, 3rd edition (Palgrave Macmillan, 2010) reviews some of the play's critical history, as does Kiernan Ryan in his introduction to the *New Casebook* of essays on *King Lear* (Palgrave, 1992). The argument about Shakespeare revising *King Lear* was first developed in the book *The Division of the Kingdoms: Shakespeare's Two Versions of King Lear,* edited by Gary Taylor and Michael Warren (Oxford University Press, 1983). Taylor gives a great account of this critical bromide in his entertaining *Reinventing Shakespeare: A Cultural History from the Restoration to the Present* (Oxford University Press, 1991). It's still a contentious issue: look up responses to Brian Vickers's *The One King Lear* (Harvard University Press, 2016) to get a sense of the debate. Ernest Hemingway talked about the ending of *A Farewell to Arms* in an interview with *The Paris Review* in 1958, reprinted in *The Paris Review Interviews, 1* (2006).

CHAPTER 16: MACBETH

Robert Burton's *The Anatomy of Melancholy* is widely available, including in a Penguin edition edited by Angus Gowland (forthcoming, 2019). Burton's library of over 1,700 books is catalogued by Nicolas K. Kiessling in *The Library of Robert Burton* (Oxford Bibliographical Society, 1988). The mock trial was reported in the *Evening Standard* (17 May 2010). James Thurber's 'The Macbeth Murder Mystery' was first published in *The New Yorker* in 1937, and is printed in *The Thurber Carnival* (Penguin

Classics, 2014). Diane Purkiss's book *The Witch in History: Early Modern and Twentieth-Century Representations* (Routledge, 1996) is highly recommended. Forman's account of *Macbeth* is recorded on the Shakespeare Documented site: <https://shakespearedocumented.folger.edu/>. Ralegh's poem is printed in the edition of his *Selected Writings*, edited by Gerald Hammond (Penguin Classics, 1986).

CHAPTER 17: ANTONY AND CLEOPATRA

Van Es's book *Shakespeare in Company* (Oxford University Press, 2013) is recommended for the impact Shakespeare's actors had on his writing. Linda Bamber's book *Comic Women, Tragic Men: A Study of Gender and Genre in Shakespeare* was published in 1982 (Stanford University Press). The unconvinced review of the Globe performance is by Benedict Nightingale from the *New York Times* of 29 August 1999.

CHAPTER 18: CORIOLANUS

I've quoted Wimsatt and Beardsley's essay 'The Intentional Fallacy' from *The Norton Anthology of Theory and Criticism*, edited by Vincent B. Leitch, 3rd edn. (W. W. Norton, 2018). Shakespeare's sources are reprinted in Geoffrey Bullough's *Narrative and Dramatic Sources of Shakespeare*; the historian Steve Hindle has written brilliantly on food riots and the play in his article in *History Workshop Journal*, Vol. 66, Issue 1 (October 2008), 'Imagining Insurrection in Seventeenth-Century England: Representations of the Midland Rising of 1607'. Amid admirable Shakespeare biographies by Katherine Duncan-Jones, Lois Potter, Stephen Greenblatt and Park Honan, Samuel Schoenbaum's *William Shakespeare: A Documentary Life* (Oxford University Press, 1975) presents a balanced account based on evidence rather than creative speculation. Creative speculation is very much the territory of Edward Bond's unsympathetic play *Bingo* (1973): I've quoted here from Bond's introduction to the play as published by Methuen in *Bond Plays: 3* (2007). Hazlitt's insight about Shakespeare's characteristic excessiveness or supererogation comes from his *Characters of Shakespeare's Plays*, first published in 1817 and excerpted in Jonathan Bate (ed.), *The Romantics on Shakespeare* (Penguin, 1992). I've quoted Freud's *The Psychopathology of Everyday Life*, first published in 1901, from the edition translated by Anthea Bell with an introduction by Paul Keegan (Penguin Classics, 2002). G. Wilson Knight writes about *Coriolanus* in *The Imperial Theme: Further Interpretations of Shakespeare's Tragedies*, 3rd edn. (Methuen, 1954). I've used the terms associated with PTSD from the fifth edition of the *Diagnostic and Statistical Manual of Mental Disorders* (American Psychiatric Publishing, 2013). My argument about speech prefixes and stage directions will probably be easier to follow if you look at the pages of the First Folio (digitized by the Bodleian Library at <https://firstfolio.bodleian.ox.ac.uk>), rather than at a modern edition, which will have smoothed out these interesting and revealing textual niggles. There's more about the new theatre of Blackfriars in Sarah Dustagheer's *Shakespeare's Two Playhouses: Repertory and Theatre Space and the Globe and the Blackfriars, 1599–1613* (Cambridge University Press, 2017).

CHAPTER 19: THE WINTER'S TALE

Samuel Beckett's prose work 'Worstward Ho' (1983) was published in *Nohow On* (John Calder Publishing, 1992). Greene's *Pandosto* is reprinted in Geoffrey Bullough's *Narrative and Dramatic Sources of Shakespeare*.

CHAPTER 20: THE TEMPEST

Michael Dobson's book *The Making of the National Poet: Shakespeare Adaptation and Authorship, 1660–1769* (Clarendon Press, 1992) is excellent on the establishment of 'Shakespeare', and the quotation from Pope is taken from it. *The Enchanted Island* is reprinted in Sandra Clark's anthology *Shakespeare*

Made Fit: Restoration Adaptations of Shakespeare (J. M. Dent, 1997). Auden's poetic sequence 'The Sea and the Mirror' was published in *For the Time Being* (Faber, 1945). Gordon McMullan's book *Shakespeare and the Idea of Late Writing* (Cambridge University Press, 2007) discusses the connotations of 'lateness' in stimulating and learned ways. Lytton Strachey's comment on *The Tempest* comes from his 1904 essay 'Shakespeare's Final Period' and was published in his *Books and Characters* (Chatto and Windus, 1922); Edward Dowden's *Shakespeare: A Critical Study of this Mind and Art* was first published in 1875 and is much reprinted. Gary Taylor's caustic commentary was published in *The Guardian* on 3 May 2004, the anniversary of Shakespeare's fortieth birthday (given calendrical differences). Freud's *Beyond the Pleasure Principle* was first published in 1920 and included in volume 18 of the *Standard Edition of the Complete Psychological Works of Sigmund Freud*, edited by James Strachey. Thomas Kyd's *The Spanish Tragedy* is widely available in print, including in my *Five Revenge Tragedies* (Penguin Classics, 2012), and online at <https://emed.folger.edu/featured-plays>, the Folger Shakespeare Library's *Digital Anthology of Early Modern Drama*; Jonson's *The Alchemist* is printed in *Volpone and Other Plays* (Penguin Classics, 2004). On *The Tempest* and colonialism, the essays in the Norton critical edition, edited by Peter Hulme and William H. Sherman, are recommended (W. W. Norton, 2004). Aimé Césaire's *Une Tempête*, translated into English by Richard Miller, was published in 2002 (Theatre Communications Group). The two Arden editions, almost half a century apart, are Kermode's Arden second edition (Methuen, 1954) and the Vaughans' Arden third edition (Bloomsbury Arden Shakespeare, 1999; revised in 2011).

Acknowledgements

This Is Shakespeare has its genesis in wide discussions about Shakespeare in lots of different academic, theatrical and literary contexts, and I am thankful for all those conversations. More specifically, I would like to acknowledge the audiences at the Faculty of English, University of Oxford, and beyond, who have listened to these ideas in an earlier form via the lecture series podcast 'Approaching Shakespeare' (available from Apple Podcasts), and especially those who have been willing to discuss them with me. In preparing the lectures for publication, I am indebted to Esther Osorio Whewell, and also to Rose Brougham, Catherine Clarke, Chloe Currens, David Dwan, Polly Findlay, Kate Harvey, Laurie Maguire, Moses Mathias, Alex Preston, Peter Robinson, Josie Rourke and Viv Smith for their feedback, dialogue and support. I am grateful to the many other Shakespeareans in the theatre and in academia whose work has deeply influenced my thinking and my approach over many years, and to all the Hertford students with whom I've had the privilege of puzzling over Shakespeare together. This book is for Elizabeth Macfarlane, with love.

Index